CLASSIC MYSTERY WRITERS

Writers of English: Lives and Works

CLASSIC
MYSTERY
WRITERS

Edited and with an Introduction by

Harold Bloom

CHELSEA HOUSE PUBLISHERS
New York   Philadelphia

Jacket illustration: Augustus Egg, *Past and Present, Number 1* (1858) (courtesy of the Tate Gallery, London/Art Resource).

CHELSEA HOUSE PUBLISHERS

Editorial Director Richard Rennert
Executive Managing Editor Karyn Gullen Browne
Picture Editor Adrian G. Allen
Copy Chief Robin James
Art Director Robert Mitchell
Manufacturing Director Gerald Levine

Writers of English: Lives and Works

Senior Editor S. T. Joshi
Senior Designer Rae Grant

Staff for CLASSIC MYSTERY WRITERS

Assistant Editor Mary Sisson
Research Peter Cannon, Stefan Dziemianowicz, Richard Fumosa, Robert Green
Picture Researcher Patricia Burns

First Printing

1 3 5 7 9 8 6 4 2

Classic mystery writers / edited and with an introduction by Harold Bloom.
        p.   cm.—(Writers of English)
    Includes bibliographical references.
    ISBN 0-7910-2210-2.—ISBN 0-7910-2235-8 (pbk.)
    1. Detective and mystery stories, English—History and criticism. 2. Detective and mystery stories, American—History and criticism. 3. Detective and mystery stories, American—Bio-bibliography. 4. Detective and mystery stories, English—Bio-bibliography.
I. Bloom, Harold. II. Series.
PR830.D4C58 1994   94-5882
823'.087209—dc20   CIP

▣ Contents

◨ User's Guide

THIS VOLUME PROVIDES biographical, critical, and bibliographical information on the thirteen most significant writers of mystery and detective fiction through the 1920s. Each chapter consists of three parts: a biography of the author; a selection of brief critical extracts about the author; and a bibliography of the author's published books.

The biography supplies a detailed outline of the important events in the author's life, including his or her major writings. The critical extracts are taken from a wide array of books and periodicals, from the author's lifetime to the present, and range in content from biographical to critical to historical. The extracts are arranged in chronological order by date of writing or publication, and a full bibliographical citation is provided at the end of each extract. Editorial additions or deletions are indicated within carets.

The author bibliographies list every separate publication—including books, pamphlets, broadsides, collaborations, and works edited or translated by the author—for works published in the author's lifetime; selected important posthumous publications are also listed. Titles are those of the first edition; if a work has subsequently come to be known under a variant title, this title is supplied within carets. In selected instances dates of revised editions are given where these are significant. Pseudonymous works are listed, but the pseudonyms under which these works were published are not. Periodicals edited by the author are listed only when the author has written most or all of the contents. Titles enclosed in square brackets are of doubtful authenticity. All works by the author, whether in English or in other languages, have been listed; English translations of foreign-language works are not listed unless the author has done the translation.

❖ The Life of the Author

Harold Bloom

NIETZSCHE, WITH EXULTANT ANGUISH, famously proclaimed that God was dead. Whatever the consequences of this for the ethical life, its ultimate literary effect certainly would have surprised the author Nietzsche. His French disciples, Foucault most prominent among them, developed the Nietzschean proclamation into the dogma that all authors, God included, were dead. The death of the author, which is no more than a Parisian trope, another metaphor for fashion's setting of skirt-lengths, is now accepted as literal truth by most of our current apostles of what should be called French Nietzsche, to distinguish it from the merely original Nietzsche. We also have French Freud or Lacan, which has little to do with the actual thought of Sigmund Freud, and even French Joyce, which interprets *Finnegans Wake* as the major work of Jacques Derrida. But all this is as nothing compared to the final triumph of the doctrine of the death of the author: French Shakespeare. That delicious absurdity is given us by the New Historicism, which blends Foucault and California fruit juice to give us the Word that Renaissance "social energies," and not William Shakespeare, composed *Hamlet* and *King Lear*. It seems a proper moment to murmur "enough" and to return to a study of the life of the author.

Sometimes it troubles me that there are so few masterpieces in the vast ocean of literary biography that stretches between James Boswell's great *Life* of Dr. Samuel Johnson and the late Richard Ellmann's wonderful *Oscar Wilde*. Literary biography is a crucial genre, and clearly a difficult one in which to excel. The actual nature of the lives of the poets seems to have little effect upon the quality of their biographies. Everything happened to Lord Byron and nothing at all to Wallace Stevens, and yet their biographers seem equally daunted by them. But even inadequate biographies of strong writers, or of weak ones, are of immense use. I have never read a literary biography from which I have not profited, a statement I cannot make about any other genre whatsoever. And when it comes to figures who are central to us—Dante, Shakespeare, Cervantes, Montaigne, Goethe, Whitman, Tolstoi, Freud, Joyce, Kafka among them—we reach out eagerly for every scrap that the biographers have gleaned. Concerning Dante and Shakespeare we know much too little, yet when we come to Goethe and Freud, where we seem to know more than everything, we still want to know more. The death of the author, despite our current resentniks, clearly was only a momentary fad. Something vital in every authentic lover of literature responds to Emerson's battle-cry sentence: "There is no history, only biography." Beyond that there is a deeper truth, difficult to come at and requiring a lifetime to understand, which is that there is no literature, only autobiography, however mediated, however veiled, however transformed. The events of Shakespeare's life included the composition of *Hamlet*, and that act of writing was itself a crucial act of living, though we do not yet know altogether how to read so doubled an act. When an author takes up a more overtly autobiograph-ical stance, as so many do in their youth, again we still do not know precisely how to accommodate the vexed relation between life and work. T. S. Eliot, meditating upon James Joyce, made a classic statement as to such accommodation:

> We want to know who are the originals of his characters, and what were the origins of his episodes, so that we may unravel the web of memory and invention and discover how far and in what ways the crude material has been transformed.

When a writer is not even covertly autobiographical, the web of memory and invention is still there, but so subtly woven that we may never unravel it. And yet we want deeply never to stop trying, and not merely because we are curious, but because each of us is caught in her own network of memory and invention. We do not always recall our inventions, and long before we age we cease to be certain of the extent to which we have invented our memories. Perhaps one motive for reading is our need to unravel our own webs. If our masters could make, from their lives, what we read, then we can be moved by them to ask: What have we made or lived in relation to what we have read? The answers may be sad, or confused, but the question is likely, implicitly, to go on being asked as long as we read. In Freudian terms, we are asking: What is it that we have repressed? What have we forgotten, unconsciously but purposively: What is it that we flee? Art, literature necessarily included, is regression in the service of the ego, according to a famous Freudian formula. I doubt the Freudian wisdom here, but indubitably it is profoundly suggestive. When we read, something in us keeps asking the equivalent of the Freudian questions: From what or whom is the author in flight, and to what earlier stages in her life is she returning, and why?

Reading, whether as an art or a pastime, has been damaged by the visual media, television in particular, and might be in some danger of extinction in the age of the computer, except that the psychic need for it continues to endure, presumably because it alone can assuage a central loneliness in elitist society. Despite all sophisticated or resentful denials, the reading of imaginative literature remains a quest to overcome the isolation of the individual consciousness. We can read for information, or entertainment, or for love of the language, but in the end we seek, in the author, the person whom we have not found, whether in ourselves or in others. In that quest, there always are elements at once aggressive and defensive, so that reading, even in childhood, is rarely free of hidden anxieties. And yet it remains one of the few activities not contaminated by an entropy of spirit. We read in hope, because we lack companionship, and the author can become the object of the most idealistic elements in our search for the wit and inventiveness we so desperately require. We read biography, not as a supplement to reading the author, but as a second, fresh attempt to understand what always seems to evade us in the work, our drive towards a kind of identity with the author.

This will-to-identity, though recently much deprecated, is a prime basis for the experience of sublimity in reading. *Hamlet* retains its unique position in the Western canon not because most readers and playgoers identify themselves with the prince, who clearly is beyond them, but rather because they find themselves again in the power of the language that represents him with such immediacy and force. Yet we know that neither language nor social energy created Hamlet. Our curiosity about Shakespeare is endless, and never will be appeased. That curiosity itself is a value, and cannot be separated from the value of *Hamlet* the tragedy, or Hamlet the literary character. It provokes us that Shakespeare the man seems so unknowable, at once everyone and no one as Borges shrewdly observes. Critics keep telling us otherwise, yet something valid in us keeps believing that we would know Hamlet better if Shakespeare's life were as fully known as the lives of Goethe and Freud, Byron and Oscar Wilde, or best of all, Dr. Samuel Johnson. Shakespeare never will have his Boswell, and Dante never will have his Richard Ellmann. How much one would give for a detailed and candid *Life of Dante* by Petrarch, or an outspoken memoir of Shakespeare by Ben Jonson! Or, in the age just past, how superb would be rival studies of one another by Hemingway and Scott Fitzgerald! But the list is endless: think of *Oscar Wilde* by Lord Alfred Douglas, or a joint biography of Shelley by Mary Godwin, Emilia Viviani, and Jane Williams. More than our insatiable desire for scandal would be satisfied. The literary rivals and the lovers of the great writers possessed perspectives we will never enjoy, and without those perspectives we dwell in some poverty in regard to the writers with whom we ourselves never can be done.

There is a sense in which imaginative literature *is* perspectivism, so that the reader is likely to be overwhelmed by the work's difficulty unless its multiple perspectives are mastered. Literary biography matters most because it is a storehouse of perspectives, frequently far surpassing any that are grasped by the particular biographer. There are relations between authors' lives and their works of kinds we have yet to discover, because our analytical instruments are not yet advanced enough to perform the necessary labor. Perhaps a novel, poem, or play is not so much a regression in the service of the ego, as it is an amalgam of *all* the Freudian mechanisms of defense, all working together for the apotheosis of the ego. Freud valued art highly, but thought that the aesthetic enterprise was no rival for psycho-analysis, unlike religion and philosophy. Clearly Freud was mistaken; his own anxieties about his indebtedness to Shakespeare helped produce the weirdness of his joining in the lunacy that argued for the Earl of Oxford as the author of Shakespeare's plays. It was Shakespeare, and not "the poets," who was there before Freud arrived at his depth psychology, and it is Shakespeare who is there still, well out ahead of psychoanalysis. We see what Freud would not see, that psychoanalysis is Shakespeare prosified and systematized. Freud is part of literature, not of "science," and the biography of Freud has the same relations to psychoanalysis as the biography of Shakespeare has to *Hamlet* and *King Lear,* if only we knew more of the life of Shakespeare.

Western literature, particularly since Shakespeare, is marked by the representa-tion of internalized change in its characters. A literature of the ever-growing inner self is in itself a large form of biography, even though this is the biography of imaginary beings, from Hamlet to the sometimes nameless protagonists of Kafka and Beckett. Skeptics might want to argue that all literary biography concerns imaginary beings, since authors make themselves up, and every biographer gives us a creation curiously different from the same author as seen by the writer of a rival *Life.* Boswell's Johnson is not quite anyone else's Johnson, though it is now very difficult for us to disentangle the great Doctor from his gifted Scottish friend and follower. The life of the author is not merely a metaphor or a fiction, as is "the Death of the Author," but it always does contain metaphorical or fictive elements. Those elements are a part of the value of literary biography, but not the largest or the crucial part, which is the separation of the mask from the man or woman who hid behind it. James Joyce and Samuel Beckett, master and sometime disciple, were both of them enigmatic personalities, and their biographers have not, as yet, fully expounded the mystery of these contrasting natures. Beckett seems very nearly to have been a secular saint: personally disinterested, heroic in the French Resistance, as humane a person ever to have composed major fictions and dramas. Joyce, self-obsessed even as Beckett was preternaturally selfless, was the Milton of the twentieth century. Beckett was perhaps the least egoistic post-Joycean, post-Proustian, post-Kafkan of writers. Does that illuminate the problematical nature of his work, or does it simply constitute another problem? Whatever the cause, the question matters. The only death of the author that is other than literal, and that matters, is the fate only of weak writers. The strong, who become canonical, never die, which is what the canon truly is about. To be read forever is the Life of the Author.

◈ Introduction

IT COULD BE ARGUED that the best of the classic mystery writers is neither Poe nor Conan Doyle but G. K. Chesterton, whose Father Brown eclipses Dupin and even Holmes. Certainly Borges, the most astute theorist of the mystery genre, would have awarded the palm to Chesterton:

> Edgar Allan Poe wrote stories of pure fantastic horror or pure *bizarrerie;* he invented the detective story. That is no less certain than the fact that he did not combine the two genres. He did not inflict on C. Auguste Dupin the task of solving the ancient crime of the Man of the Crowd or of explaining the image that terrified the masked Prince Prospero in the chamber of black and scarlet. On the other hand, Chesterton lavished such *tours de force* with passion and joy. Each story in the Father Brown Saga presents a mystery, proposes explanations of a demonical or magical sort, and then replaces them at the end with solutions of this world.

Borges located in Chesterton one of the prime precursors of the fantastic mode we now call Borgesian. Meditating on "Chesterton and the Labyrinth of the Detective Story," Borges came up with a code for the ideal story of mystery and detection:

A. A discretional maximum of six characters.
B. Resolution of all the loose ends to the mystery.
C. Avaricious economy of means.
D. Priority of how over who.
E. Necessity and wonder of the solution.

Whether or not that code is universal, Chesterton observes it with classical rigor, and Conan Doyle does not. And yet Borges is also accurate as to the extraordinary emblems of the Father Brown stories: topless towers, mirrors, labyrinths, secret gardens, weirdly assorted footsteps, purple wigs, wicked shapes manifesting nearly everywhere. Again and again, in the midst of the Father Brown saga, comes the uncanny sense that the Gnostic Argentine, and not the English Catholic, is the tale-teller. When Father Brown tells us his "secret" is that he identifies the murderer by *identifying with* the murderer, we recall the dark principle of Borges: all men are one man, or the "universal history of infamy." Chesterton's normative theology is absorbed into the grotesque sublimity that Chesterton shared with Dickens and with Browning, upon both of whom he had written permanently valuable commentaries. From Dickens, Chesterton had learned to naturalize every coincidence, however outrageous. From Browning, the creator of Father Brown derived the hallucinatory perspectivism of the great dramatic monologues: every murderer in Chesterton is another Childe Roland who quests against the grain, and is fit only to fail. Borges memorably found in Browning a precursor for Kafka and then taught us to read Chesterton rather as we are compelled to read Kafka, as a demonic allegorist. "The Oracle of the Dog," a Borgesian favorite, is the archetypal Father Brown story because it concludes in the priestly detective's working principle: "Anything that anybody talks about, and says there's a good deal in, extends itself indefinitely, like a vista in a nightmare." Vistas in a nightmare: Chesterton's passionate apprehensions always are phantasmagorias, and as such delighted Borges. They are likely to go on delighting many among us because their fantasy restores mystery to the mystery story, without which it collapses into abysses of the commonplace. The triumph of Father Brown is that the sober explanations do not dismiss the aura of wonder that rarely abandons Chesterton.

—H. B.

Anthony Berkeley/Francis Iles
1893–1971

ANTHONY BERKELEY COX was born on July 5, 1893, in Watford, Hertfordshire. Cox was an extremely private person and avoided publicity where possible; consequently, little is known about many phases and periods of his life. He attended Sherborne College and then University College, Oxford, and served in France for the first three years of World War I; in 1917 he was invalided out of the army with his health permanently impaired, although the precise nature of his malady is not known.

Around 1920 Cox began writing humorous sketches for *Punch*, many of which were collected in his first book, *Jugged Journalism* (1925). After publishing a volume of short stories and a mainstream novel, Cox wrote his first detective story, *The Layton Court Mystery* (1925), which introduced Roger Sheringham, his most popular detective. Cox admitted that Sheringham had initially been created as a self-parody, being based on an "offensive person" of his acquaintance; but he was later forced to modify his detective's behavior when readers began taking him seriously. His first detective story had been published anonymously, but the next one—*The Wychford Poisoning Case* (1926)—appeared under the Anthony Berkeley pseudonym, as did most of its successors.

In 1928 Cox founded the Detection Club, becoming its first honorary secretary. This club, whose members included most of the prominent British mystery writers of the day, published a number of volumes, including the round-robin novels *The Floating Admiral* (1931) and *Six against the Yard* (1936), in which each chapter was written by a different member. Cox's *The Poisoned Chocolates Case* (1929) is a tart parody of the Detection Club.

In 1931 Cox published *Malice Aforethought* under the pseudonym Francis Iles. This novel is a radical departure from conventional detective fiction: based partly on a true crime, it dispenses with the mystery element altogether by showing an unscrupulous doctor planning and committing the murder of his wife. The next year *Before the Fact* appeared, also as by Francis Iles; this work, one of the greatest suspense novels ever written, presents another

1

ruthless murderer as seen from the point of view of his wife, who is to be his next victim. The novel—dedicated to Cox's own wife, Helen Macgregor, whom he married in 1932—was filmed by Alfred Hitchcock as *Suspicion* (1941), although the ending was altered because it was believed that audiences would not stand for the portrayal of Cary Grant as a murderer. For many years Cox refused to acknowledge that he had written the Francis Iles novels (a third, *As for the Woman*, appeared in 1939), and there was widespread speculation that they were collaborations or the work of some prominent mainstream writer.

Two years after publishing his most celebrated Anthony Berkeley novel, *Trial and Error* (1937), Cox gave up mystery writing, for reasons not entirely clear: ill health, discouragement at the reception of his last novel, and resentment at the high taxes he had to pay as a writer in England might have been contributory factors. He continued, however, to review mystery novels in the *Daily Telegraph*, the London Sunday *Times*, and the *Manchester Guardian*, mostly as Francis Iles. Cox was one of the directors of a company named A. B. Cox, Ltd., although the nature of its business is not known. Cox and his wife, who had no children, lived for many years in a home in St. John's Wood, London, where he died on March 9, 1971, after a long illness.

▧ *Critical Extracts*

UNSIGNED   *Malice Aforethought* is put forward as being "The Story of a Commonplace Crime" and the work of "a famous novelist," who elects to call himself Francis Iles. One may accept the sub-title to this extent— that the crime is one of poisoning committed by a person who understands poisons, but with the qualification that in the technical details of the poisoning there is contrivance that is not commonplace, and that nevertheless not the crime but the criminal is the object of chief interest. One would guess, too, that the author is not at his first novel from his skill in the art of narrative. His ending is a triumph of stage management. It is more than that; through it Francis Iles is enabled to administer deserved chastisement while pulling the leg of Justice, so that he scores off of everybody at once!

In the world as it presents itself to his acrid temperament it is an ideal ending.

But the world which he is presumably presenting to his readers is a world they know as well as he does, and in making it recognizable to them this acrid temperament and the desire to administer chastisement that goes with it is a handicap. His people belong to the upper middle class and live in a small provincial town. Almost without exception they at once excite dislike. The objection to this general condemnation is not the sentimentalist's objection that it is unkind, but the statistician's that it is wrong. Moreover, where these people have but small parts to play emphasis on their defects is distracting. Throughout the book Francis Iles uses more force than is needed for producing the results at which he aims.

Unsigned, [Review of *Malice Aforethought*], *Times Literary Supplement*, 19 March 1931, p. 225

BEN RAY REDMAN ⟨. . .⟩ Francis Iles has written a thriller ⟨*Before the Fact*⟩ which makes me wish that I commanded five-score housetops, or newspaper columns, that I might proclaim its extraordinary merits from each and all of them. And the word "thriller," as it is used here, is meant to convey no suggestion of clutching hands, murderous simians, self-opening doors, mysterious gusts of chilling air, flitting ghosts, Indian blow-pipes, screams in the dark, disappearing bodies, international conspiracies, or master minds. *Before the Fact* is a thriller of so high an order that one may be proud to acknowledge being thrilled by it; there is no more reason to apologize for the emotions that it evokes than there is to be shamefaced over one's reactions to *The Turn of the Screw*. Indeed, I have already involved myself in several more or less acrimonious arguments by insisting that the tale of Johnnie, the ever-smiling, and of Lina, more patient than any Griselda, makes James's much praised masterpiece seem like a bedtime story in comparison. But I shall not insist here. ⟨. . .⟩

There is a theory current among the more hard-boiled devotees of horror-murder-mystery-detective fiction that good writing has little or no place in their beloved type of literature, that it too frequently trips up the yarn, and dilutes the groggy mixture. Give us the raw meat, they say, and away with condiments, sauces, and fancy carving. *Before the Fact* is enough to disprove this barbaric theory, enough to prove that the better a murder or mystery yarn is written, the better a murder or mystery yarn it will be. For here we have good writing, remarkable characterization, perfect construction, climax instead of anti-climax, sophistication instead of naiveté, sardonic wit, and genial humour; in short, almost all the elements that are usually absent from fiction of this kind. And at the same time we have the best study of a murderer that has appeared in our day, and, so far as I know, the most extraordinary study of a born murderer that is anywhere discoverable. *Before the Fact* is a high mark at which other workers in the genre will do well to shoot.

Ben Ray Redman, "Murder Will Out," *Saturday Review of Literature*, 10 December 1932, p. 306

ISAAC ANDERSON   From the opening sentence, "The sanctity of human life has been much exaggerated," this novel ⟨*Trial and Error*⟩ goes on to tell a completely unconventional story of murder. The central character is Mr. Todhunter, who has been told by his own physician and by two eminent specialists that he has at most only a few months to live. He wishes to round out his life with some meritorious deed, and after due consideration he decides that he can best serve humanity by committing a murder. The person to be removed must, of course, be one whose continued existence is a menace to the happiness and well-being of others. Having selected his victim, Mr. Todhunter lays his plans carefully, for it is important that neither he nor any one else shall be suspected. But something goes wrong, and another man is charged with the murder.

Since it is no part of Mr. Todhunter's plan that another shall suffer for his crime, he goes to Scotland Yard and gives himself up. To his surprise, the police refuse to take his confession seriously. They ask for proof, and Mr. Todhunter has none that is at all convincing. The rest of the book, and by far the best part of it, deals with Mr. Todhunter's frantic efforts to prove himself a murderer, with what success the reader must learn for himself, for it would be unfair to divulge any more of the plot of this ingenious and highly entertaining novel.

Isaac Anderson, "New Mystery Stories," *New York Times Book Review*, 14 November 1937, p. 26

HOWARD HAYCRAFT   Asked by the present writer to tell something of his literary backgrounds and ideas (since his reluctance to talk about his more personal life is known to be unassailable) he has replied from London with characteristic good nature: "I began by writing sketches for *Punch*, a (so-called) humorous periodical peculiar to this country, but found that detective stories paid better. When I find something that pays better than detective stories I shall write that. . . . Roger Sheringham is an offensive person, founded on an offensive person I once knew, because in my original innocence I thought it would be amusing to have an offensive detective. Since he has been taken in all seriousness, I have had to tone his offensiveness down and pretend he never was." ⟨. . .⟩

⟨. . .⟩ *The Poisoned Chocolates Case* (1929), a notable tour de force with no less than six separate solutions, and a veritable textbook of the literature, must in the present writer's estimation be accorded top place among the Berkeley products. But *The Second Shot* (1930) needs also be given special mention if only for the author's often-quoted and prophetic prefatory remarks, which will bear repetition once more:

> . . . I am personally convinced [Berkeley wrote] that the days of
> the old crime-puzzle pure and simple, relying entirely upon plot
> and without any added attractions of character, style, or even
> humor, are in the hands of the auditor; and that the detective
> story is in the process of developing into the novel with a
> detective or crime interest, holding its readers less by
> mathematical than by psychological ties. The puzzle element will
> no doubt remain, but it will become a puzzle of character rather
> than a puzzle of time, place, motive, and opportunity.

This is the Berkeley credo, to which the author has stuck admirably. ⟨. . .⟩

Few authors have had a more salutary or vitalizing effect on the detective story than this same A. B. Cox, with his acute perceptiveness, urbanity, humor, literacy, and unfailing taste, whether he is writing as Anthony Berkeley or as Francis Iles. Perhaps because his contributions are usually disguised under a light-hearted style and wear the motley of entertainment— which should be a cause for rejoicing than otherwise—his importance in shaping the contemporary crime novel has not been adequately recognized by historians of the genre. More, almost, than any other single writer of his time he has constituted the necessary evolutionary link between the naturalism of E. C. Bentley and its logical result—the "character" detective novel of the 1930's. He perpetuated and elaborated the one form, and introduced the other.

Howard Haycraft, *Murder for Pleasure: The Life and Times of the Detective Story* (New York: D. Appleton-Century Co., 1941), pp. 145–47, 149

COLIN WATSON   Another writer who obeyed the convention of having an aristocratic detective—or at least one who was supposedly at home with wealthy and distinguished people—and then felt uncomfortable about it afterwards was Anthony Berkeley Cox. It was in 1925 that Cox, writing as Anthony Berkeley, introduced Roger Sheringham in *The Layton Court Mystery*. 'An offensive person' was how Cox once frankly described his hero. Sheringham was certainly a little on the loud side, and he associated with characters who made up in volubility what they so patently lacked in social usefulness. But by 1934, when *Panic Party* was published, Sheringham had acquired a more self-effacing manner and a skill—perhaps associated with his success as a bestselling novelist—in provoking his companions to let down their guard of class attitudinizing and reveal human fears and weaknesses. It was only to be expected from an author of considerable insight (Anthony Berkeley Cox was also 'Francis Iles') that he would hasten to produce the kind of detective story which in the words of his dedication to Milward Kennedy, 'breaks every rule of the austere Club to which we both belong'. He had written in 1930 that the detective story was in the process of developing into the novel with a crime theme, 'holding its readers less by mathematical than by psychological ties'. Perhaps it was, but public approval of the change did not show for several more years. Cox's pioneering, his rejection of the stock pasteboard figures of detective fiction in favour of real characters, carefully observed, was not what the commercial whodunnit purveyors wanted to sponsor. A leading popular magazine rejected a slightly shortened version of *Panic Party* on the grounds that it was 'lacking sufficient human interest'. 'Life,' commented Cox patiently, 'is very, very difficult' and he went on to write more crime novels that bore a disconcerting resemblance to literature.

Colin Watson, *Snobbery with Violence: Crime Stories and Their Audience* (New York: St. Martin's Press, 1971), p. 191

JOHN DICKSON CARR   Of well-to-do family, with an independent income, he had no need to struggle in the marketplace. Turning to detective stories because he so much enjoyed them, in 1924 he wrote *The Layton Court Mystery* as Anthony Berkeley.

Then came a distinguished series, his sleuths Roger Sheringham and milquetoast Ambrose Chitterwick: each novel of dazzling ingenuity, each with a twist or double-twist to yank the rug from under us at the end. As the world's best practitioner Anthony Berkeley (Great Britain) shared equal honors, as he still shares them, with the editor-in-chief of this magazine (U.S.A.).

As early as '31 he had opened a new door. In *Malice Aforethought*, calling himself Francis Iles, he studied the mind of a homicidal country doctor. "Murder without mystery," his publisher rather triumphantly cried. With *Before the Fact*, which followed, we met a young man of such charm and callousness as to be the death of any person who got in Johnnie Aysgarth's way.

Among aesthetes, who shudder at detective fiction, it has become the fashion to praise these "psychological" studies for superior characterization, and to exalt Francis Iles as though Anthony Berkeley had never existed. The true reason they say this lies deeper. Having no ingenuity of their own, they resent ingenuity in others and bitterly decry it as they decry the element of surprise.

Much though I admire Tony's work as Iles, give me Berkeley every time! Give me murder *with* mystery, characters no less vivid for wearing masks; give me the sensational case, the fair but cryptic evidence building towards some thunderbolt disclosure.

John Dickson Carr, "The Jury Box," *Ellery Queen's Mystery Magazine* 60, No. 1 (July 1972): 87–88

LeROY PANEK   While the Iles books seem substantially different from Cox's other detective novels because of their new approach to the subject of crime, they grow from a number of elements implicit and explicit in the earlier books about Sheringham and Chitterwick. Perhaps the most prominent of these is Cox's fascination with puny, little people. Priestley and Chitterwick in the earlier novels are meek, little men into whom Cox pours several romantic themes: the worm turning to show its intelligence and resources is the most prominent of these. As Cox moved from Priestley to Chitterwick he became less romantic in his treatment of this type, and in the Iles novels this movement continues. They are loaded with meek, prissy, petty individuals. In *Malice Aforethought* we see Dr. Bickleigh—as downtrodden a little twirp as Ambrose Chitterwick. Bickleigh is deferential, insecure, and secretly idiosyncratic. The difference in the Iles character lies in the fact that Bickleigh dreams of getting out of his trap—he dreams of power and love—but when he takes steps to achieve his dreams he simply becomes more petty, insignificant, and pathetic; he becomes wicked (evil is too grandiose for him) and more repellent than he was originally. Virtually the same thing happens to Alan Littlewood in *As for the Woman*. Littlewood (again, notice the name) is a young man of modest competence who nurses a sense of inferiority in the company of his more talented family. He is seduced by a married woman and builds their grubby, little affair into a grand passion. But Alan is so petty that he does not even rate a serious recognition of his illusions. He attempts murder in a heated moment only to fail at this too and he is punished in a particularly humiliating way by Dr. Pawle, the cuckolded husband. The third Iles character is somewhat different, partly because she is a woman, and partly because she is the victim of a crime instead of its perpetrator. Lina Aysgarth in *Before the Fact*, however, is like Bickleigh and Littlewood because she is so insecure and mentally limited. Any reasonable reader who experiences *Before the Fact* wants to strangle her for her abysmal stupidity even before she is murdered at the end of the book.

Cox's rendition of these petty, insecure, limited individuals is the hallmark of the Iles novels. Instead of turning out to be heroes, these people never rise above themselves. Part of Cox's motive in these novels was to give a psychological portrait of this type of person which was ruthlessly honest. The books, for this reason, make for very oppressive reading; it may be useful and interesting to know about this kind of people, but reading repeated incidents grounded on stupidity, inflated egotism, and ludicrous fantasies is certainly not the sort of escape which many seek in popular fiction. And this is also part of what Cox aims at. If in the Anthony Berkeley books Cox dances through human affairs giving a jovial, horatian quip to a personality defect here and a social institution there, in the Francis Iles books he wields a juvenalian lash which cuts again and again into the nasty perversity of human behavior.

LeRoy Panek, "Anthony Berkeley Cox," *Watteau's Shepherds: The Detective Novel in Britain 1914–1940* (Bowling Green, OH: Bowling Green University Popular Press, 1979), pp. 120–21

PATRICIA CRAIG and MARY CADOGAN   In *Dead Mrs Stratton*, the author's flair for showmanship is well to the fore. The events of the story are presented in a splendidly theatrical and frivolous way. We have, to begin with, a fancy-dress party, with all the guests got up as murderers and victims. Just to get things going in a suitable spirit, the host has erected a triple gallows, complete with dangling figures stuffed with straw, on the flat roof of his Jacobean house. This gruesome prop is mentioned in the first line, and it's easy to infer from this that a real hanged body will shortly take the place of one of the fakes. Sure enough, everybody's favourite victim is presently discovered in the appropriate position.

From this point on, the author engagingly proffers a view of murder as an altruistic gesture. His 'great detective' Roger Sheringham, a friend of the host, makes it his business to see that things are hushed up, instead of being brought to light in the usual manner—but Sheringham, in fact, is barking up the wrong gallows tree. He comes up with several explanations which fit the facts—and incidentally provides an outlet for Anthony Berkeley's humorous exasperation with the old-fashioned type of detective story, in which 'one deduction only was drawn from each fact, and it was invariably the right deduction . . . In real life one can draw a hundred plausible deductions from one fact, and they're all equally wrong . . .' ⟨. . .⟩

⟨. . .⟩ A series of sparkling complications ensues, with half the cast at cross-purposes with someone or other in the matter of concocting a suitable scenario to take in the investigating officers. Here we have conventional plot-making overturned with a vengeance.

> Patricia Craig and Mary Cadogan, "Introduction," *Dead Mrs Stratton* by Anthony Berkeley (London: Hogarth Press, 1984), n.p.

GENE D. FRENCH   Hitchcock had initially hoped that he could be more faithful to the novel by Francis Iles on which the film ⟨*Suspicion*⟩ was based than an earlier draft of the screenplay co-authored by Nathanael West had been, by having Johnny actually murder Lina for her money. To head off objections from the industry's censor, who would certainly not permit Johnny to get away with killing off his wife any more than he would allow Max de Winter to do so in *Rebecca*, the director came up with what he thought to be an ideal solution. He proposed that in the final scene of *Suspicion*, after Johnny has slain Lina, he would unwittingly seal his own doom by mailing an incriminating letter to his dead spouse's mother, in which Lina expresses her conviction that her husband was planning to poison her. But this time it was the front office, not the censor, that persisted in giving Hitchcock trouble. The RKO officials categorically refused to sanction Cary Grant's playing a murderer, just as years before Hitchcock's bosses at Gainsborough spurned the notion of Ivor Novello enacting the role of a killer in *The Lodger*. In any event, it is just possible that Hitchcock's signature appearance in *Suspicion,* which shows him posting a letter in a mailbox, may be a playful private reference to his favored ending for the film, which he was never even allowed to shoot. As Hitchcock later wrote, he was pressured into making the wife's misgivings about her husband "a figment of her imagination," because the official consensus at the studio was that "audiences would not want to be told in the last few frames of a film that so popular a personality as Cary Grant was a murderer doomed to exposure."

Another ending, in which Johnny, desperately despondent over his mounting personal debts, tries to kill himself instead of Lina, was actually shot, but previewed badly. It was replaced by the compromise ending with which the film was finally released. In it Johnny is totally exonerated of Lina's doubts about him, and a passing reference to his contemplating suicide (salvaged from the first of the endings that were shot) is even tossed in for good measure to explain away the manual of poison he had been surreptitiously studying. But this studio-engineered denouement is not the cop-out it might at first appear to be. It does nudge the reflective viewer to consider how Lina's paranoid fears about Johnny had come close to poisoning their marriage as surely as the deadly draught with which Lina suspected Johnny had laced her bedtime milk.

Hitchcock's own suspicions that the last-minute tinkering with the film's conclusion might have done the film permanent damage were quickly dispelled when *Suspicion* quickly became, like *Rebecca,* a big box-office favorite.

Gene D. French, *Alfred Hitchcock* (Boston: Twayne, 1984), pp. 96–98

WILLIAM BRADLEY STRICKLAND   Writing both as Francis Iles and Anthony Berkeley, Cox provides us with a bridge from the formal puzzle stories of the British Golden Age to the post-war realistic studies in crime and criminal psychology. As a constructor of formal puzzles, Berkeley was adept, though never the equal of Agatha Christie. As a satirical and often sardonic observer of the London literary scene, Cox was an incisive and often delightful writer. As a pioneer of the psychological method, Cox is both deserving of praise and a bit of a problem.

The fact that Iles' use of psychology wears thin at times or appears superficial at others is not, perhaps, so much his own fault as the result of his living in his particular era. Psychological theory has changed greatly since the thirties, and Cox's labored explication of outdated ideas has caused portions of his books to age poorly. Then, too, Iles (to a greater extent than Berkeley) apparently felt no call to create engaging and sympathetic characters. As a result, his books often lack focus. *Malice Aforethought* is indeed a landmark work, one deserving of praise for what it attempts, and yet one cannot help feeling that its protagonist is at least as deserving of being murdered as his repellent wife. Since the book lacks a clear center, its humor and social commentary seem scattered. In this respect, *Before the Fact* is the most successful work, for the reader finds Lina Aysgarth a more sympathetic character.

Still, the novel that manages to break out of all molds by cheerfully turning conventions upside-down is more effective than either of the two Iles works. With its engaging but absurd hero, its mad murder trial in reverse, and its free-swinging high-spirited assault on the British legal system, *Trial and Error* stands as the most successful of all Cox's works. It is a pity that he ceased to write shortly after completing this work. The final Iles work, *As for the Woman*, is frankly dull, centering on adultery and not murder. Had Cox continued to mine the vein of *Trial and Error*, he might easily have established his own peculiar niche rivaling, in his own way, Christie and Sayers.

But these observations may be too harsh. Cox was about something new and different, and explorers often take risks that later travelers easily avoid. Anthony Berkeley/Francis Iles is an unjustly neglected figure today, one whose works richly repay one's time. That he has worn not quite as well as some of his contemporaries is surely not his own fault; and the historical interest of his novels, not to mention their undeniable delights as detective and crime stories, commends them to the attention of any fancier of mystery fiction.

William Bradley Strickland, "Anthony Berkeley Cox," *Twelve Englishmen of Mystery*, ed. Earl F. Bargainnier (Bowling Green, OH: Bowling Green University Popular Press, 1984), pp. 139–40

JULIAN SYMONS   The promise of 'a novel with a detective or crime interest' made by Anthony Berkeley (Cox) was fulfilled by his alter ego, Francis Iles. In *Malice Aforethought* (1931) and its successor *Before the Fact* (1932) there is no puzzle of the classical kind. From the start the villain is plain to us, and his intentions are known. The problem is whether he will be able to carry them out successfully. What was new about the books may be expressed in the first sentences of *Malice Aforethought*: 'It was not until several weeks after he had decided to murder his wife that Dr Bickleigh took any active steps in the matter. Murder is a serious business.'

Everything is laid out, the doctor's plans, their fulfilment, the police investigation. Some critics have said that a similar approach was made earlier, by Mrs Belloc Lowndes and by Austin Freeman in his 'inverted' stories, but Iles's method is so much more subtle that his work is really not comparable. The fascination of these two books lies in the interplay of character, the gaps between plot and execution, and the air of suburban or small-town normality with which Iles invests the whole thing. The slow revelation of the villain's character in *Before the Fact* is beautifully done, and the books show very clearly that the naming of the criminal in the last chapter is not the only way of surprising the reader. Iles was a very clever writer, and the only criticism that might be made of these outstandingly original books is that they have just occasionally an air of contrivance out of keeping with their generally realistic tone.

Julian Symons, *Bloody Murder: From the Detective Story to the Crime Novel: A History* (1972; rev. ed. Harmondsworth, UK: Penguin, 1985), p. 121

▨ *Bibliography*

Brenda Entertains. 1925.

Jugged Journalism. 1925.

The Family Witch: An Essay in Absurdity. 1925.

The Layton Court Mystery. 1925.

The Wychford Poisoning Case: An Essay in Criminology. 1926.

The Professor on Paws. 1926.

Roger Sheringham and the Vane Mystery ⟨The Mystery at Lovers' Cave⟩. 1927.

Cicely Disappears. 1927.

Mr. Priestley's Problem ⟨The Amateur Crime⟩. 1927.

The Silk Stocking Murders. 1928.

The Piccadilly Murder. 1929.

The Poisoned Chocolates Case: An Academic Detective Story. 1929.

The Second Shot. 1930.

Top Storey Murder. 1931.

Malice Aforethought: The Story of a Commonplace Crime. 1931.

Murder in the Basement. 1932.

Before the Fact: A Murder Story for Ladies. 1932.

Jumping Jenny 〈*Dead Mrs. Stratton*〉. 1933.

Panic Party 〈*Mr. Pidgeon's Island*〉. 1934.

O England! 1934.

Trial and Error. 1937.

Not to Be Taken 〈*A Puzzle in Poison*〉. 1938.

Death in the House. 1939.

As for the Woman: A Love Story. 1939.

A Pocketful of One Hundred New Limericks. 1960.

⊞ ⊞ ⊞

G. K. Chesterton
1874–1936

GILBERT KEITH CHESTERTON was born on May 29, 1874, in London. He attended St. Paul's School (where he, along with the future detective writer E. C. Bentley, formed the Junior Debating Society), the Slade School of Art, and the University of London. In 1896 he took the first of several publishing jobs and began the prolific spate of writing that continued until his death. He was also a voluminous journalist, writing weekly columns for the London *Daily News* and, for thirty-one years, the *Illustrated London News* (1905–36). Along with his younger brother Cecil and his colleague Hilaire Belloc, Chesterton founded the journal *Eye Witness* in 1911; Chesterton edited it (as the *New Witness*) from 1916 to 1923 and (as *G.K.'s Weekly*) from 1925 to 1936. He married Frances Alice Blogg in 1901; they had no children.

Chesterton's work was deeply informed by moral and religious sentiment, although he did not convert to Catholicism until 1922. In much of his work he exhibited a hostility toward the advance of modern science (he attacked both Darwin's theory of evolution and the psychoanalysis of Freud), embodying his views in such works as *Heretics* (1905), *Orthodoxy* (1908) and *The Everlasting Man* (1925). He and Belloc engaged in vicious polemics on philosophical, religious, and social issues with George Bernard Shaw, H. G. Wells, Sir Arthur Conan Doyle, and others; Shaw satirized both of them by branding them "the Chesterbelloc."

Although Chesterton gained some renown as a poet (*Greybeards at Play*, 1900; *The Ballad of the White Horse*, 1911; "Lepanto," 1915) and playwright (*Magic: A Fantastic Comedy*, 1913, *The Judgement of Dr. Johnson*, 1927), his current reputation rests on his literary criticism and his fiction. He was one of the acutest critics of nineteenth-century literature, and his *The Victorian Age in Literature* (1913) is a landmark. He also wrote critical studies of Dickens, Browning, Tennyson, Blake, and many others, and such collections of critical essays as *Twelve Types* (1902) and *All I Survey* (1933) contain penetrating evaluations of many writers.

The detective story held an abiding interest for Chesterton. In 1901 he published the essay "A Defence of Detective Stories" (in *The Defendant*), and several years later he began writing stories about the Catholic priest Father Brown, who was based on an actual priest, Father John O'Connor, with whom Chesterton was acquainted. The stories fill five volumes: *The Innocence of Father Brown* (1911), *The Wisdom of Father Brown* (1914), *The Incredulity of Father Brown* (1926), *The Secret of Father Brown* (1927), and *The Scandal of Father Brown* (1935). These tales adhere even more rigidly than do Conan Doyle's Sherlock Holmes stories to the tradition of "fair play"—the presentation of all the relevant clues to the reader. Moreover, they add a moral and spiritual dimension to the detective story, something largely lacking in the Sherlock Holmes adventures and in many subsequent works in the field.

Chesterton's interest in crime, guilt, and detection extends far beyond the Father Brown stories. Nearly all his fiction—the short story collections *The Club of Queer Trades* (1905), *Tales of the Long Bow* (1925), *Four Faultless Felons* (1930), and *The Paradoxes of Mr. Pond* (1937); the novels *The Man Who Was Thursday* (1908), *Manalive* (1912), and *The Poet and the Lunatics* (1929)—features criminals or detectives. One of the strangest of his novels is the eschatological fantasy *The Napoleon of Notting Hill* (1904).

In 1934, after a long and distinguished career as a writer, Chesterton was named Knight Commander with Star of the Order of St. Gregory; he also became a fellow of the Royal Society of Literature. His autobiography was published just after his death on June 14, 1936. A multivolume edition of his *Collected Works* began publication in 1986.

◈ *Critical Extracts*

WINIFRED HOLTBY   Most writers of detective stories isolate their robberies and murders into a specialized world where the drama might as well consist of snakes and ladders as of human beings with nerves, souls and hearts. The crime and its discovery are everything. Mr. G. K. Chesterton is too good a Catholic and humanitarian for that. To him the souls and hearts and consciences of men are so important that he prefers, if possible, to leave the crime out altogether, or to prove that, whatever its appearance, it was in truth no crime. Thus in these eight short stories of the moon-faced priest with the bulky umbrella, who has become one of our institutional literary detectives, four are concerned not with the existence of the criminal but with the non-existence of the crime.

This is good fun, and as legitimate a pursuit as any other. There are few wittier and more inventive sleuths than Mr. Chesterton, and he is never happier than when he can prove that a corpse which was apparently poisoned, stabbed and hanged, really died happily and peacefully in bed from natural causes. But all tricks become a little tedious in time—those of the soft as well as those of the hard heart. Erudition, dexterity and ingenuity prevent Mr. Chesterton's tales from the sin of monotony, and it is only sometimes that one wishes he would take a page out of his great contemporary's *Ruthless Rhymes for Heartless Homes*. Perhaps, however, it would not do. The creator of Father Brown must be true to his particular type of temperament, and it is only fair to say that the most impressive story in the volume (to mention its title would be to give the show away) is based upon nothing more substantial than a practical joke.

Winifred Holtby, [Review of *The Scandal of Father Brown*], *London Mercury* No. 186 (April 1935): 605–6

G. K. CHESTERTON   When a writer invents a character for the purposes of fiction, especially of light or fanciful fiction, he fits him out with all sorts of features meant to be effective in that setting and against that background. He may have taken, and probably has taken, a hint from a human being. But he will not hesitate to alter the human being, especially in externals, because he is not thinking of a portrait but of a picture. In Father Brown, it was the chief feature to be featureless. The point of him was to appear pointless; and one might say that his conspicuous quality was not being conspicuous. His commonplace exterior was meant to contrast with his unsuspected vigilance and intelligence; and that being so, of course I made his appearance shabby and shapeless, his face round and expressionless, his manners clumsy, and so on. At the same time, I did take some of his inner intellectual qualities from my friend, Father John O'Connor of Bradford, who has not, as a matter of fact, any of these external qualities. He is not shabby, but rather neat; he is not clumsy, but very delicate and dexterous; he not only is but looks amusing and amused. He is a sensitive and quick-witted Irishman, with the profound irony and some of the potential irritability of his race. My Father Brown was deliberately described as a Suffolk dumpling from East Anglia. That, and the rest of his description, was a deliberate disguise for the purpose of detective fiction. ⟨. . .⟩

And there sprang up in my mind the vague idea of ⟨. . .⟩ constructing a comedy in which a priest should appear to know nothing and in fact know more about crime than the criminals. I afterwards summed up the special idea in the story called "The Blue Cross", otherwise very slight and improbable, and continued it through the interminable series of tales with which I have afflicted the world. In short, I permitted myself the grave liberty of taking my friend and knocking him about; beating his hat and umbrella shapeless, untidying his clothes, punching his intelligent countenance into a condition of pudding-faced fatuity, and generally disguising Father O'Connor as Father Brown. The disguise, as I have said, was a deliberate piece of fiction, meant to bring out or accentuate the contrast that was the point of the comedy. There is also in the conception, as in nearly everything I have ever written, a good deal of inconsistency and inaccuracy on minor points; not the least of such flaws being the general suggestion of Father Brown as having nothing in particular to do, except to hang about in any household where there was likely to be a murder. A very charming Catholic lady I know once paid my detective priest the appropriate compliment of saying, "I am very fond of that officious little loafer."

> G. K. Chesterton, *The Autobiography of G. K. Chesterton* (New York: Sheed & Ward, 1936), pp. 333–34, 339–40

JORGE LUIS BORGES   Edgar Allan Poe wrote stories of pure fantastic horror or pure *bizarrerie*; he invented the detective story. That is no less certain than the fact that he did not combine the two genres. He did not inflict on C. Auguste Dupin the task of solving the ancient crime of the Man of the Crowd or of explaining the image that terrified the masked Prince Prospero in the chamber of black and scarlet. On the other hand, Chesterton lavished such *tours de force* with passion and joy. Each story in the Father Brown Saga presents a mystery, proposes explanations of a demoniacal or magical sort, and then replaces them at the end with solutions of this world. Skill is not the only virtue of those brief bits of fiction; I believe I can perceive in them an abbreviation of Chesterton's

life, a symbol or reflection of Chesterton. The repetition of his formula
through the years and through the books (*The Man Who Knew Too Much*,
The Poet and the Lunatics, *The Paradoxes of Mr. Pond*) seems to confirm that
this is an essential form, not a rhetorical artifice.

Jorge Luis Borges, "On Chesterton" (1952), *Other Inquisitions 1937–1952*, tr. Ruth
L. C. Simms (Austin: University of Texas Press, 1964), p. 82

RONALD KNOX   The real secret of Father Brown is that there is
nothing of the mystic about him. When he falls into a reverie—I had almost
said, a brown study—the other people in the story think that he must be
having an ecstasy, because he is a Catholic priest, and will proceed to solve
the mystery by some kind of heaven-sent intuition. And the reader, if he
is not careful, will get carried away by the same miscalculation; here, surely,
is Chesterton preparing to show the Protestants where they get off. Unconsciously, this adds to the feeling of suspense; you never imagine that Poirot
will have an ecstasy, or that Albert Campion will receive enlightenment
from the supernatural world. And all the time, Father Brown is doing just
what Poirot does; he is using his little grey cells. He is noticing something
which the reader hasn't noticed, and will kick himself later for not having
noticed. The lawyer who asks 'Where was the body found?' when he is told
about the Admiral's drowning has given himself away as knowing too much,
already, about the duck-pond; if he had been an honest man, he would
have assumed that the Admiral was drowned at sea. The prophet who goes
on chanting his litany from the balcony, when the crowd beneath is rushing
to the aid of the murdered woman, gives himself away as the murderer; he
was expecting it. We had all the data to go upon, only Father Brown saw
the point and we didn't. ⟨. . .⟩

For Chesterton (as for Father Brown) the characters were the really
important thing. The little priest could see not as a psychologist, but as a
moralist, into the dark places of the human heart; could guess, therefore,
at what point envy, or fear, or resentment would pass the bounds of the
normal, and the cords of convention would snap, so that a man was hurried
into crime. Into crime, not necessarily into murder: the Father Brown stories
are not bloodthirsty, as detective stories go; a full third of them deal neither
with murder nor with attempted murder, which is an unusual average nowadays; most readers demand a corpse. The motives which made it necessary

for Hypatia Hard to elope with her husband, the motives which induced the Master of the Mountain to pretend that he had stolen the ruby when he hadn't—the reader may find them unimpressive, because there is no black cap and no drop at the end of them. But, unless he is a man of unusual perspicacity, he will have to admit that he also found them unexpected.

The truth is that what we demand of a detective story is neither sensations, nor horrors, but ingenuity. And Chesterton was a man of limitless ingenuity. What really contents us is when we see at last, and kick ourselves for not having seen before, that the man who was murdered in the Turkish bath without any trace of a weapon was stabbed with an icicle; that the poisoner did drink the tea which accounted for her victim, but took a stiff emetic immediately afterwards; that the time of a particular incident was given wrongly, not because the witness was in bad faith, but because she saw, not the clock, but the reflection of the clock in a looking-glass. All those brilliant twists which a Mason and an Agatha Christie give to their stories, Chesterton, when he was in the mood for it, could give to his.

Ronald Knox, "Chesterton's Father Brown" (1954), G. K. Chesterton: A Half Century of Views, ed. D. J. Conlon (Oxford: Oxford University Press, 1987), pp. 135, 137

GARRY WILLS   The first Father Brown story—"The Blue Cross"— is like the event which gave rise to it; it only concerns the knowledge the priest has gained in the confessional. But the later stories revolve around the doctrine of *Heretics* and *Orthodoxy*, the idea that humility is the root of knowledge. This is a common-sense argument, not strictly theological, and the fact that Father Brown is a priest did not mean much in the stories written between 1910 and 1914. Father Brown wore a collar for the same reason that he wore rumpled clothes and a blank expression—because one does not expect shrewd knowledge of the world from a priest, just as one does not expect it from a moon-faced dumpling of a man. The first series was interrupted by the war, and Father Brown did not reappear until 1923, after Chesterton's entry into the Church; this second series, comprising the last three of the five volumes written, gave deeper meaning to Father Brown's innocence ⟨. . .⟩

The success of the stories was merited. For one thing, their brevity was an advantage. Chesterton's technique of juxtaposing vivid symbols was always rapid, and he had obvious difficulty keeping a long story in motion.

Even in the Father Brown tales he symbolically tells the story several times. One is not supposed to follow clues so much as to read an heraldic device which foreshadows the story's point—the French cartoon which gives away the fury of the guillotine; the set of mirrors that presents beforehand the mystery of self-knowledge through self-ignorance; the dummies which suggest the real men we treat as automata. Social satire, comedy, and debate give the complication necessary to detective stories; but the secret at the core is simple, as it must be in all such mysteries. The priest is only a marionette, but the puppets act out entertaining and deeply significant parables. By giving a moral significance to the action, Chesterton avoided the anti-climax and mere dispersal of interest which is the danger of the detective novel's concluding pages.

> Garry Wills, *Chesterton: Man and Mask* (New York: Sheed & Ward, 1961), pp. 124–25

V. S. PRITCHETT   Whether they are very good or only workman-like, the Father Brown stories owe their attraction to things outside pure puzzle. They insinuate themselves in the mind by being seen, most often, as journeys. People move from street to street, from valley to hill, from cold weather to snow, and, if we except '(The Honour of) Israel Gow', the journeys are set in a low key out of loving respect for the commonplace. The London scene is always beautifully done, intimately, sharply, with eloquence or sentiment. The lights in a small shop in Camden Town will shine from a distance, like the butt end of a cigar. Chesterton's journeys are always small—the every day ones. Another advantage is that his narrative is a series of criticisms. One thoughtful quarter of an hour is demolished by what happens in the one that follows it. Chesterton's eye for the normal and commonplace was, of course, quite abnormal. He sees that one of the characteristics of the commonplace is that it is a surface, therefore a disguise. It is so normal to pass a coat stand that one cannot be blamed for not noticing a body is hanging on it. Father Brown has a sharp clerical brain, a feeling for the turn of the screw and an unastounded sense of the human drama. Who more likely to commit a crime of jealous passion than the postman who is compelled by his job to deliver his rival's letters? In the Father Brown stories Chesterton made paradox work for him. Elsewhere it became a nuisance, but here it had the theatrical value of the trap-door.

> V. S. Pritchett, "Pugnacious Paradoxes," *New Statesman*, 19 January 1973, p. 95

W. W. ROBSON   Again and again in these stories Chesterton shows how much the common dislike of Catholicism is (or was) due to dislike of 'religious externals'. But the deeper religious meaning of these stories is to do with something more important than cultural considerations. The abundance of quacks, mystagogues, sorcerers in them is not only due to the desire to point a contrast with Father Brown. It is to illustrate, in terms proper to the genre in which Chesterton is writing, his belief that what Christianity has shown is that the age-old effort of man to grasp the Divine is bankrupt. Man cannot come to God. Christianity says that God came to man. This was what Chesterton was saying over and over again, in different tones and with varying degrees of humour and earnestness. Orwell claimed that writers like Chesterton seem to have only one subject: that they are Catholics. One might as well retort that Orwell's only subject seems to be that he was not one. Either the Catholic faith is relevant to the whole of life, or it is relevant to none of it. That, at any rate, was Chesterton's position.

In the end, then, the priest's 'steady humble gaze' owes its power to more than observation. When he realized that the doctor did the murder, he 'looked him gravely and steadily in the face'; and the doctor went away and wrote his confession. He is an atheist, and he begins his confession: 'Vicisti, Galilaee!' But he goes on at once 'In other words, damn your eyes, which are very remarkable and penetrating ones.'

W. W. Robson, "Father Brown and Others," G. K. Chesterton: A Centenary Appraisal, ed. John Sullivan (New York: Harper & Row, 1974), pp. 67–68.

LYNETTE HUNTER   The first collection of detective stories that Chesterton published is *The Club of Queer Trades*. The stories, while all centred on an event, are really concerned with how the mind of the detective, Basil Grant, works. The main plan of the short stories is similar to the Sherlock Holmes story. We have a Watson in the narrator. The action takes place out of a comfortable bachelor apartment in central London, and is nearly always initiated by a sudden arrival on the step of a mystery that needs to be solved. However, the whole intent is to reverse the Sherlock Holmes method of thought. The book is not a parody but a demonstration of a different kind of thinking. The rational is not satirised but merely shown to be ineffective. The author speaks of the 'fantasies of detective deduction' that are worthless in the face of a moral problem.

The first story sets up the lines along which the remainder will run. The narrator is familiar and friendly and appears trustworthy because he seems to expect us to know things about the situation. But once inside the story he is merely matter for Basil Grant to work upon. He provides the 'normal' response, carrying the reader into the event with ordinary eyes. When Basil Grant reveals the truth to him, we also experience it as a revelation. Grant himself is described as a poet, a man who needs people but who can do without them. We are also told that he was a judge who went mad on the bench. In the first case he forms an impression about a story and combines it with common sense and impartial observation. It is impossible for him to explain how he feels, for he has no logic to his actions. He judges the 'spiritual atmosphere' of the case. For him 'facts obscure the truth' so he follows his intuition until he discovers the solution. In contrast is Basil's brother Rupert who is a professional detective. He is rational in the Sherlock Holmes style and insists that 'It's a matter of fact'. Similarly his client, at the centre of the mystery, is 'incurably sane', rational, 'perfectly clear and intellectual'. But neither Rupert nor his client can solve the mystery. The rational approach limits one's understanding to oneself. Basil Grant succeeds because he combines personal intuition with objective views of the characteristics of the event itself.

Lynette Hunter, G. K. Chesterton: Explorations in Allegory (New York: St. Martin's Press, 1979), pp. 139–40

MARIE SMITH   In Mr. Pond and Gabriel Gale we have two more of Chesterton's serial detectives, both of whose adventures appeared in magazines before they were collected into books. Mr. Pond is another of Chesterton's 'political' detectives, a mild-mannered Civil Servant not unlike Edgar Wallace's Mr. J. G. Reeder, given to dropping into his conversation some seemingly outrageous remark ("Naturally, having no legs, he won the walking race easily"). It is a characteristic of Chesterton's detectives that they are often considered mad until the rightness of their remarks is ultimately revealed, and both Mr. Pond and Gabriel Gale suffer this annoyance repeatedly. Some of these 'paradoxes' have passed into legend, for example

Mr. Pond's "They say travel broadens the mind, but you must have the mind."

Jorge Luis Borges, that acute critic and admirer of Chesterton, wrote: "One must anticipate an era in which Poe's invention, the detective story, will vanish. It is the most artificial of all literary *genres*, the one most like a game. Chesterton himself wrote that if the novel is a game of faces, then the detective story is a game of masks. But in spite of this I am sure that Chesterton's stories will always be read, since a mystery that so imaginatively suggests an impossible, fantastic occurrence is interesting for more than the logical explanation contained in the last few lines." Borges considered 'The Three Horsemen of the Apocalypse', one of the Mr. Pond stories ⟨. . .⟩, to be the best of all Chesterton's tales, with its "long white road, white hussars and white horses, and a fascinating struggle of wills".

Gabriel Gale, the poet in *The Poet and the Lunatics*, has been described as an older version of Gabriel Syme, the poet in *The Man Who Was Thursday*, and he anticipates R. D. Laing's proposition that the apparent madman may be the only truly sane person. Gale represents the common people against the ruling elite, solving crimes through his poetic sensibility and his sensitivity to atmospheres and personalities. That said, it must be added that the stories are wonderful set-pieces, with highly ingenious crimes— although 'The Finger of Stone' contains one of the most outrageous explanations in the entire history of detective fiction; within its own framework it is 'fair', but it requires a cheerful abandonment of disbelief on the part of the reader.

Marie Smith, "Introduction," *Thirteen Detectives* by G. K. Chesterton, ed. Marie Smith (London: Xanadu, 1987), pp. 10–11

WILLIAM DAVID SPENCER   Ultimately ⟨. . .⟩ all the complexities that confront and baffle the detective, as we are confronted and baffled in life, reduce to a simple truth. Every clever crime, like every great enigma, is founded on some simple fact. In "The Queer Feet" the simple fact is that a gentleman's evening dress is the same as a waiter's. The truth in "The Eye of Apollo" is the cruelty of nature, of the worship that deludes one into thinking all is quite well, as "The Three Tools of Death" portrays the cruelty of humorless cheerfulness as a religion in a world that is not cheerful, where only a fool sings songs to a heavy heart (Proverbs 25:30). In "The

Sign of the Broken Sword" the truth is the misunderstood fallacy of false piety, "that it is useless for a man to read his Bible unless he also reads everybody else's Bible." The heart of true piety is not "me and God" but "God and we." The central truth is always simple, but true humility, perceiving one's place in relation to God, is required to see it. And this truth for Chesterton unlocks the secrets of the universe:

> The modern mind always mixes up two different ideas: mystery in the sense of what is marvellous, and mystery in the sense of what is complicated. That is half its difficulty about miracles. A miracle is startling; but it is simple. It is simple because it *is* a miracle. It is power coming directly from God (or the devil) instead of directly through nature or human wills.

So the task for Father Brown is to cut through the complex manner to the simple truth, which is also unique and discoverable. As he demonstrates in the perplexing case of Israel Gow, when he easily comes up with creative but invalid theories that will connect all the clues, "Ten false philosophies will fit the universe; ten false theories will fit Gengyle Castle. But we want the real explanation of the castle and the universe."

Thus Father Brown relaxes in the paradoxes and employs them, along with his own paradoxical character of having chosen good from a heart that could easily have chosen evil, to bring murderers before the bar of God's justice, rather than simply delivering them up to human authority. Why does he let murderers go? Murderers belong to God and God's justice, and in the revelation of the true tapestry each will see that a fitting place in the pattern has been assigned to all. So he can warn, "No; let him pass. . . . Let Cain pass by, for he belongs to God." For Father Brown, experiencing salvation begins with the knowledge that leads to repentance, and his task is to encourage that knowledge in the fish he catches with his holy hook. So he exacts a confession from the doctor in "The Wrong Shape" and counsels for hours with the culprit in "The Invisible Man": "But Father Brown walked those snow-covered hills under the stars for many hours with a murderer, and what they said to each other will never be known." It will never be known because for Father Brown it is God's business.

William David Spencer, "Father Brown: Chesterton's Paradoxical, Prototypical Priest," *Mysterium and Mystery: The Clerical Crime Novel* (Carbondale: Southern Illinois University Press, 1992), pp. 86–87

⬛ *Bibliography*

Greybeards at Play. 1900.

The Wild Knight and Other Poems. 1900.

The Defendant. 1901.

Twelve Types. 1902, 1908 (as *Varied Types*).

Thomas Carlyle (with J. E. Hodder Williams). 1902.

Robert Louis Stevenson (with W. Robertson Nicoll). 1903.

Leo Tolstoy (with G. H. Perris and Edward Garnett). 1903.

Charles Dickens (with F. G. Kitton). 1903.

Robert Browning. 1903.

Tennyson (with Richard Garnett). 1903.

Thackeray (with Lewis Melville). 1903.

The Tremendous Adventures of Major Brown. 1903.

G. F. Watts. 1904.

The Napoleon of Notting Hill. 1904.

Mr. Crowley and the Creeds and The Creed of Mr. Chesterton (with Aleister
  Crowley). 1904.

The Club of Queer Trades. 1905.

Heretics. 1905.

Charles Dickens. 1906.

The Man Who Was Thursday. 1908.

All Things Considered. 1908.

Orthodoxy. 1908.

George Bernard Shaw. 1909.

Tremendous Trifles. 1909.

Thackery (editor). 1909.

The Ball and the Cross. 1909.

What's Wrong with the World. 1910.

The Glory of Grey. 1910.

Alarms and Discussions. 1910.

William Blake. 1910.

The Ultimate Lie. 1910.

A Chesterton Character. 1911.

Appreciations and Criticisms of the Works of Charles Dickens. 1911.

A Defence of Nonsense and Other Essays. 1911.

Samuel Johnson (editor; with Alice Meynell). 1911.

The Innocence of Father Brown. 1911.

The Ballad of the White Horse. 1911.

The Future of Religion: Mr. G. K. Chesterton's Reply to Mr. Bernard Shaw.
    1911.

The Conversion of an Anarchist. 1912.

Manalive. 1912.

A Miscellany of Men. 1912.

The Victorian Age in Literature. 1913.

Thoughts from Chesterton. Ed. Elsie E. Morton. 1913.

Magic: A Fantastic Comedy. 1913.

Do Miracles Happen? (with others). 1914.

The Flying Inn. 1914.

The Wisdom of Father Brown. 1914.

The Barbarism of Berlin. 1914.

London. 1914.

Prussian versus Belgian Culture. 1914.

The Perishing of the Pendragons. 1914.

Letters to an Old Garibaldian. 1915.

Poems. 1915.

Wine, Water and Song. 1915.

The So-Called Belgian Bargain. 1915.

A Poem. 1915.

The Crimes of England. 1915.

Divorce versus Democracy. 1916.

Temperance and the Great Alliance. 1916.

The G. K. Chesterton Calendar. Ed. H. Cecil Palmer. 1916.

A Shilling for My Thoughts. Ed. E. V. Lucas. 1916.

Lord Kitchener. 1917.

A Short History of England. 1917.

Utopia of Usurers and Other Essays. 1917.

How to Help Annexation. 1918.

Irish Impressions. 1919.

The Superstition of Divorce. 1920.

Charles Dickens Fifty Years After. 1920.

Old King Cole. 1920.

The Uses of Diversity: A Book of Essays. 1920.

The New Jerusalem. 1920.

Eugenics and Other Evils. 1922.

What I Saw in America. 1922.

The Ballad of St. Barbara and Other Verses. 1922.

The Man Who Knew Too Much and Other Stories. 1922.

Fancies versus Fads. 1923.

St. Francis of Assisi. 1923.

The End of the Roman Road: A Pageant of Wayfarers. 1924.

The Superstitions of the Sceptic. 1925.

Tales of the Long Bow. 1925.

The Everlasting Man. 1925.

William Cobbett. 1925.

G. K. Chesterton (Augustan Books of Modern Poetry). 1925.

The Incredulity of Father Brown. 1926.

The Outline of Sanity. 1926.

The Queen of Seven Swords. 1926.

Essays by Divers Hands (editor). 1926.

A Gleaming Cohort: Being Selections from the Works of G. K. Chesterton. Ed.
     E. V. Lucas. 1926.

Works. 1926. 9 vols.

The Catholic Church and Conversion. 1927.

Social Reform versus Birth Control. 1927.

The Return of Don Quixote. 1927.

Collected Poems. 1927.

Gloria in Profundis. 1927.

The Secret of Father Brown. 1927.

Culture and the Coming Peril. 1927.

The Judgement of Dr. Johnson. 1927.

Robert Louis Stevenson. 1927.

Generally Speaking: A Book of Essays. 1928.

G. K. Chesterton (Short Stories of To-day and Yesterday). 1928.

G. K. Chesterton (Essays of To-day and Yesterday). 1928.

Do We Agree? (with George Bernard Shaw). 1928.

A Chesterton Catholic Anthology. Ed. Patrick Braybrooke. 1928.

The Sword of Wood. 1928.

The Poet and the Lunatics: Episodes in the Life of Gabriel Gale. 1929.

Ubi Ecclesia. 1929.

The Father Brown Stories. 1929, 1947, 1953.

Christmas Poems. 1929.

The Thing. 1929.

G.K.C. as M.C.: Being a Collection of Thirty-seven Introductions. Ed. J. P. de Fonseka. 1929.

Thomas Carlyle 1795–1881. 1929.

Robert Browning 1812–1889. 1929.

The Moderate Murderer and The Honest Quack. 1929.

The Ecstatic Thief. 1930.

Four Faultless Felons. 1930.

The Grave of Arthur. 1930.

The Resurrection of Rome. 1930.

Come to Think of It . . .: A Book of Essays. 1930.

The Turkey and the Turk. 1930.

At the Sign of the World's End. 1930.

Is There a Return to Religion? (with E. Haldeman-Julius). 1931.

All Is Grist: A Book of Essays. 1931.

Chaucer. 1932.

Sidelights on New London and Newer York and Other Essays. 1932.

Christendom in Dublin. 1932.

"All I Survey": A Book of Essays. 1933.

St. Thomas Aquinas. 1933.

G. K. Chesterton (Methuen's Library of Humour). Ed. Ronald Knox. 1933.

Avowals and Denials. 1934.

G.K.'s: A Miscellany of the First 500 Issues of G.K.'s Weekly (editor). 1934.

The Scandal of Father Brown. 1935.

The Well and the Shallows. 1935.

The Way of the Cross (with Frank Brangwyn). 1935.

G. K. Chesterton Explains the English. 1935.

Stories, Essays and Poems. 1935.

As I Was Saying: A Book of Essays. 1936.

Autobiography. 1936.

G. K. Chesterton Omnibus. 1936.

The Legend of the Sword. 1936.

A Beaconsfield Ballad. c. 1936.

The Paradoxes of Mr. Pond. 1937.

The Man Who Was Chesterton. Ed. Raymond T. Bond. 1937.

The Coloured Lands. 1938.

Essays. Ed. John Guest. 1939.

Pocket Book of Father Brown. 1939.

The End of the Armistice. Ed. F. J. Sheed. 1940.

"I Say a Democracy Means . . ." 1941.

Selected Essays. Ed. Dorothy Collins. 1949.

The Common Man. 1950.

The Surprise. 1952.

Essays. Ed. K. E. Whitehorn. 1953.

A Handful of Authors: Essays on Books and Writers. Ed. Dorothy Collins. 1953.

The Amazing Adventures of Father Brown. 1954.

The Glass Walking-Stick and Other Essays from the Illustrated London News *1905–1936.* Ed. Dorothy Collins. 1955.

Father Brown: Selected Stories. Ed. Ronald Knox. 1955.

G. K. Chesterton: An Anthology. Ed. D. B. Wyndham Lewis. 1957.

Books of Father Brown. Ed. Andrew Scotland. 1958. 4 vols.

Essays and Poems. Ed. Wilfred Sheed. 1958.

Lunacy and Letters. Ed. Dorothy Collins. 1958.

Father Brown Stories. 1959.

Where All Roads Lead. 1961.

The Man Who Was Orthodox: A Selection from the Uncollected Writings of G. K. Chesterton. Ed. A. L. Maycock. 1964.

The Spice of Life and Other Essays. Ed. Dorothy Collins. 1964.

G. K. Chesterton: A Selection from His Non-fictional Prose. Ed. W. H. Auden. 1970.

Chesterton on Shakespeare. Ed. Dorothy Collins. 1971.

Selected Stories. Ed. Kingsley Amis. 1972.

Greybeards at Play and Other Comic Verse. Ed. John Sullivan. 1974.

The Apostle and the Wild Ducks and Other Essays. Ed. Dorothy Collins. 1975.

Father Brown Detective Stories. 1975.

The Penguin Complete Father Brown. 1981.

The Bodley Head G. K. Chesterton. Ed. P. J. Kavanagh. 1985.

Collected Works. 1986– .

Daylight and Nightmare: Uncollected Stories and Fables. Ed. Marie Smith. 1986.

The Annotated Innocence of Father Brown. Ed. Martin Gardner. 1987.

Thirteen Detectives. Ed. Marie Smith. 1987.

Collected Nonsense and Light Verse. Ed. Marie Smith. 1987.

More Quotable Chesterton. Ed. George L. Marlin, Richard P. Rabatin, and John L. Swan. 1988.

Agatha Christie
1890–1976

AGATHA MARY CLARISSA MILLER was born on September 15, 1890, in Torquay, Devon. She was an isolated, lonely child, raised largely by her mother after the death of her father in 1901. At sixteen she attended a finishing school in Paris, specializing in music. In 1914 she married Archibald Christie, who soon rose to the rank of colonel in the Royal Air Corps. They had one child, Rosalind. During World War I Christie worked as a Red Cross nurse in Torquay, and after the war she accepted a dare from her sister to write a mystery novel. The result was *The Mysterious Affair at Styles,* published in 1920, which introduced the fussy Belgian detective Hercule Poirot.

After writing several espionage thrillers, Christie wrote another Poirot novel, *The Murder of Roger Ackroyd* (1926), one of the most daring mystery novels ever published. The controversy aroused by the book made Christie famous, as did her "disappearance" in December 1926, caused by the stress of her mother's death and of her husband's wish to divorce her. The divorce was finalized in 1928, and in 1930 Christie married archaeologist Max Mallowan. Their expeditions to the Middle East inspired some of Christie's most famous novels, including *Murder in Mesopotamia* (1936), *Death on the Nile* (1937), and the nonfiction account *Come, Tell Me How You Live* (1946).

Christie, having settled in a lavish home in Devon, Greenway House, became a mainstay of the bestseller lists from the 1930s onward with such successes as *Murder on the Orient Express* (1934), *The A.B.C. Murders* (1936), and *The Body in the Library* (1942). These works established the "cozy" British mystery, which usually takes place in a village or the countryside. By the 1930s this convention was already being condemned as frivolous and unrealistic by such "hard-boiled" writers as Dashiell Hammett and Raymond Chandler, but Christie persisted in it to the end.

By World War II Agatha Christie had become an institution. Not only Poirot but Miss Jane Marple, Parker Pyne, and several other detectives solved her intricate puzzles, which were presented not only in print but on stage and screen as well. *Witness for the Prosecution* and *Ten Little Niggers* (titled *And Then There Were None* in the United States) appeared in all three media. *The Mousetrap* was a stage original that has run continuously since 1952, becoming the longest-running play in history.

Christie's later novels were not as highly regarded as her earlier ones, and readers and critics alike detected an increasing repetition of conventional formulas in her works; but her popularity continued unabated, and she became perhaps the most translated author in literary history. Christie also wrote several volumes of short stories as well as poems (collected in 1973), romances (published under the pseudonym Mary Westmacott), and an auto-biography, written between 1950 and 1965 and published posthumously in 1977. She killed off Hercule Poirot in *Curtain* (1975) and Miss Marple in *Sleeping Murder* (1976).

Christie received the Grand Master Award of the Mystery Writers of America in 1954 and an LL.D. from the University of Exeter in 1961; she became a Commander of the British Empire in 1956 and a Dame of the British Empire in 1971. Agatha Christie died in Wallingford on January 12, 1976.

◆ *Critical Extracts*

WILLIAM ROSE BENÉT   To us at least *The Murder of Roger Ackroyd* really turns a new trick in detective fiction, surely a difficult enough achievement "with the competition so strong." Most writers of detective stories develop their own special detectives, following the lead of the famous. Agatha Christie's pet detective is Hercule Poirot, a Frenchman. She has cherished him and his exploits through other tales. No, he did not disappear from a cliff finally, to necessitate perpetual resurrection! But in this her seventh book he has retired from "active practice." Nevertheless from such retirement springs his greatest achievement—and hers. ⟨. . .⟩

For those who prefer certain backgrounds to others for their mystery tales we may say that Miss Christie's are always English in setting. To those who hate "loose ends" we may remark that this author ties all her knots neatly and bites off the thread. Her characterization is sharp in outline, her motivation is sound, complications of the plot never "get away from her." Everything in the puzzle falls neatly into place, and the complete picture leaves upon us an ineradicable impression. There are no inexplicable and glozed-over details. It is all an almost mathematical demonstration so far as the fundamental brainwork goes. Yet that it is no mere clever intellectual exercise, witness the fact that the reader is left with the strongest emotions of pity and wonder over the disastrous coil the weak and erring weave. There are indications, in fact, of an even deeper psychological insight than can be actively exercised in a book of this kind. For a detective story must move. The author cannot pause to philosophize. But one is rather closer in touch, in this tale, with the mad logic of actual criminality, with the criminal as a mainly average human being with one tragic twist, than is at all usual.

We do not overpraise this story, we believe, when we say that it should go on the shelf with the books of first rank in the field. The detective story pure and simple has as definite limitations of form as the sonnet in poetry. Within these limitations, with admirable structural art, Miss Christie has genuinely achieved.

William Rose Benét, "Out of the Usual," *Saturday Review of Literature*, 24 July 1926, p. 951

EDMUND WILSON   I have read ⟨. . .⟩ the new Agatha Christie, *Death Comes as the End,* and I confess that I have been had by Mrs. Christie. I did not guess who the murderer was, I was incited to keep on and find out, and when I did finally find out, I was surprised. Yet I did not care for Agatha Christie and I hope never to read another of her books. I ought, perhaps, to discount the fact that *Death Comes as the End* is supposed to take place in Egypt two thousand years before Christ, so that the book has a flavor of Lloyd C. Douglas not, I understand, quite typical of the author. ("No more Khay in this world to sail on the Nile and catch fish and laugh up into the sun whilst she, stretched out in the boat with little Teti on her lap, laughed back at him"); but her writing is of a mawkishness and banality which seem to me literally impossible to read. You cannot *read* such a book, you run through it to see the problem worked out; and you cannot become interested in the characters, because they can never be allowed an existence of their own even in a flat two dimensions but have always to be contrived so that they can seem either reliable or sinister, depending on which quarter, at the moment, is to be baited for the reader's suspicion. This I had found also a source of annoyance in the case of Mr. ⟨Rex⟩ Stout, who, however, has created, after a fashion, Nero Wolfe and Archie Goodwin and has made some attempt at characterization of the people that figure in the crimes; but Mrs. Christie, in proportion as she is more expert and concentrates more narrowly on the puzzle, has to eliminate human interest completely, or, rather, fill in the picture with what seems to me a distasteful parody of it. In this new novel, she has to provide herself with puppets who will be good for three stages of suspense: you must first wonder who is going to be murdered, you must then wonder who is committing the murders, and you must finally be unable to foresee which of two men the heroine will marry. It is all like a sleight-of-hand trick, in which the magician diverts your attention from the awkward or irrelevant movements that conceal the manipulation of the cards, and it may mildly entertain and astonish you, as such a sleight-of-hand performance may. But in a performance like *Death Comes as the End*, the patter is a constant bore and the properties lack the elegance of playing cards.

Edmund Wilson, "Why Do People Read Detective Stories?" (1944), *Classics and Commercials: A Literary Chronicle of the Forties* (New York: Farrar, Straus, 1950), pp. 234–35

ANTHONY BURGESS   What makes all Agatha Christie's work commendable, on stage or between covers, is its total incapacity for offending, despite its burden of rage, hate and offensive weapons. Characters murder and are murdered, and not in jest either, but everything is cleansed and purified and raised to a level of calm speculation and cool logic. There's no gratuitous poring over horror: the camera-eye doesn't dwell on flies drinking the blood of the victim. The corpse is an item in an argument. We end up admiring the shape of this argument, not shuddering at the distortions of the criminal mind.

Agatha is Greek for "good." Paradoxically, it's a sense of the fundamental goodness or wholesomeness of the world that emerges from all these studies of crime and detection. And there's something Greek about the Christie concern with form: more than anything else, her artifacts are well-shaped. Certainly, it's the shape and wholesomeness of *The Mousetrap*, added to devilish ingenuity and a sense of fun, that are making it outlive such vagaries as the Theatre of Cruelty. One of the jobs of art is to persuade us that life has a pattern, and Mrs. Christie's art has done that ever since it began.

It began a long time ago. *The Mysterious Affair at Styles* appeared in 1920, and it still finds new readers. Perhaps her first real masterpiece was *The Murder of Roger Ackroyd*, though there are some critics who say that, as with P. G. Wodehouse, Shakespeare and Faulkner, we should think rather of the building of a world than the production of a series of separate items. With each book (at least one new one every year since she started, 72 in all; Mrs. Christie is 76), we re-enter Christie country, but we always find fresh additions, imports from the world outside: murder and detection are eternal, but their modes and motives must change with the times.

Anthony Burgess, "Murder Most Fair by Agatha the Good," *Life*, 1 December 1967, p. 8

COLIN WATSON   Agatha Christie maintained, after her very earliest books, an air of slightly sardonic detachment from the events of which she wrote. One feels it to be an attitude characteristic of an astute professional author. The sellers' market in crime fiction which lasted throughout the 1920s and 1930s permitted the publication of many books that not only lacked literary merit but, by being gauchely imitative, brought into ridicule a number of contrivances that had been used with discretion and therefore effectively by more capable writers. By 1926 when *The Murder of Roger Ackroyd* consolidated Mrs. Christie's reputation, already it was inadvisable to postulate crimes committed by hypnotists, men armed with South American blowpipes, purveyors of untraceable poisons, and butlers. Murders of, or by, identical twins and long lost brothers were also questionable propositions. The last chapter gathering of suspects calculated to encompass the dramatic self-betrayal of the guilty party was not yet discredited, but a few sophisticated readers were beginning to wince at each recurrence of the device.

A less shrewd practitioner than Mrs. Christie would have been tempted to bar all those elements of crime fiction that had become absurdities in the eyes of intelligent people. But she seems to have been well aware that intelligence and readership-potential are quite unrelated. So she hedged her bets. While preserving the essential artificialities, unlikelihoods and clichés of the bestselling whodunnit, she evolved a style of narration that hinted, just delicately enough not to offend British sensitivity to 'sarcasm', at self-parody.

> Colin Watson, *Snobbery with Violence: Crime Stories and Their Audience* (New York: St. Martin's Press, 1971), pp. 173–74

THOMAS LASK   Hercule Poirot, a Belgian detective who became internationally famous, has died in England. His age was unknown.

Mr. Poirot achieved fame as a private investigator after he retired as a member of the Belgian police force in 1904. His career, as chronicled in the novels of Dame Agatha Christie, was one of the most illustrious in fiction.

At the end of his life, he was arthritic and had a bad heart. He was in a wheelchair often, and was carried from his bedroom to the public lounge at Styles Court, a nursing home in Essex, wearing a wig and false moustaches to mask signs of age that offended his vanity. In his active days, he was always impeccably dressed.

The news of his death, given by Dame Agatha, was not unsuspected. Word that he was near death reached here last May.

Dame Agatha reports in *Curtain* that he managed, in one final gesture, to perform one more act of cerebration that saved an innocent bystander from disaster. "Nothing in his life became him like the leaving it," to quote Shakespeare, whom Poirot frequently misquoted.

> Thomas Lask, "Hercule Poirot Is Dead; Famed Belgian Detective," *New York Times*, 6 August 1975, pp. 1, 16

AGATHA CHRISTIE   Economy of wording, I think, is particularly necessary in detective stories. You don't want to hear the same thing rehashed three or four times over. But it is tempting when one is speaking into a dictaphone to say the same thing over and over again in slightly different words. Of course, one can cut it out later, but that is irritating, and destroys the smooth flow which one gets otherwise. It is important to profit by the fact that a human being is naturally lazy and so won't write more than is absolutely necessary to convey his meaning.

Of course, there is a right length for everything. I think myself that the *right* length for a detective story is fifty-thousand words. I know this is considered by publishers as too short. Possibly readers feel themselves cheated if they pay their money and only get fifty-thousand words—so sixty thousand or seventy thousand are more acceptable. If your book runs to more than that I think that you will usually find that it would have been better if it had been shorter. Twenty thousand words for a long short story is an excellent length for a thriller. Unfortunately there is less and less market for stories of that size, and the authors tend not to be particularly well paid. One feels therefore that one would do better to continue the story and expand it to a full-length novel. The short-story technique, I think, is not really suited to the detective story at all. A thriller, possibly—but a detective story, no. The Mr. Fortune stories of H. C. Bailey were good in that line, because they were longer than the average magazine story.

By now Hugh Massie has settled me with a new publisher, William Collins, with whom I still remain as I am writing this book.

My first book for them, *The Murder of Roger Ackroyd*, was far and away my most successful to date; in fact it is still remembered and quoted. I got hold of a good formula there—and I owe it in part to my brother-in-law, James, who some years previously had said somewhat fretfully as he put down a detective story, "Almost everybody turns out to be a criminal nowadays in detective stories—even the detective. What *I* would like to see is a Watson who turned out to be the criminal." It was a remarkably original thought and I mulled over it lengthily. Then, as it happened, very much the same idea was also suggested to me by Lord Louis Mountbatten, as he then was, who wrote to suggest that a story should be narrated in the first person by someone who later turned out to be the murderer.

I thought it was a good idea, and considered it for a long time. It had enormous difficulties, of course. My mind boggled at the thought of Hastings murdering anybody, and it was anyway going to be difficult to do it in such a way that it would not be cheating. Of course, a lot of people say that *The Murder of Roger Ackroyd* is cheating; but if they read it carefully they will see that they are wrong.

Agatha Christie, *An Autobiography* (New York: Dodd, Mead, 1977), pp. 329–30

EARL F. BARGAINNIER   Christie's brilliance in plotting can most clearly be seen in her ability to dramatize the investigation of a crime.

She rarely resorts to just a series of interviews of suspects. Rather she employs various plot strategems to enliven the often tedious parade of witnesses, while also deceiving the reader by misdirection so that her detective does not seem stupid for not having the answers at once. Since, as said, the investigation may be three-fourths or more of the novel, such dramatization is required to prevent a dully repetitive pattern. Among her methods are seven prevalent enough to merit comment here ⟨. . .⟩. First is her typically large number of suspects, usually eight to twelve, the prefatory lists lining them up for the reader. Such a number allows for continual shifting of suspicion from one to another: any one of them *might* have done it. A suspects B, who is shielding C, who is unaware that D is deeply jealous of C's attraction to E; meanwhile, F is attempting to frame G, who hated the victim H, but is being foiled by an alibi provided by I. Christie's ability to spread effectively the possibilities throughout such a group is perhaps her most important means of avoiding tedium during an investigation. It is so common that when she chose to limit the suspects in *Cards on the Table*, she felt the need to include a "Foreword by the Author": "There are only *four* starters and any one of them, *given the right circumstances*, might have committed the crime. That knocks out forcibly the element of surprise. Nevertheless there should be, I think, an equal interest attached to four persons, each of whom has committed murder and is capable of committing further murders." A second method, the most obvious, is the later murder, which, as Hastings declares, "cheers things up" in a book. Related to it is the faked attempt by the murderer on himself to throw off suspicion. Though avid readers of the genre may have become wary of any character who survives an attempt on his life, the device can if not cheer at least confuse. The addition of thriller elements is a fourth method. Christie does not use it to a great degree, but occasionally there is what might be called a *coup de chapitre*, such as ending a chapter of *Easy to Kill* with the murderer's hands around the heroine's throat and then not returning to the scene until the end of the next chapter. Such *coups* are artificial but legitimate. Fifth is the murder-suicide-accident gambit. Very often what looks like suicide or accident is murder, but also what looks like murder may be suicide or accident. Christie's most intricate plot for a novel joins all three; in *There Is a Tide* each type of death occurs, and all three are thought to be murder until Poirot untangles the complexity. A sixth method involves the conceal-ment of the murderer's identity. The first suspect, apparently exonerated, may prove eventually to be the actual murderer or the person thought guilty throughout the novel may prove to be innocent—or, indeed, guilty. The least likely person, not even suspected, as with a person not in the group of suspects of *Hercule Poirot's Christmas* and *What Mrs. McGillicuddy Saw!*, may have committed the crime. Needless to say, Christie's tricks with her murderers are many. Finally, though the reader may guess the identity of the murderer, he may not be able to explain how the murder was done. Can anyone, without reading the "Epilogue," fully explain *And Then There Were None?* This talent of Christie for complicating a "simple" murder and going beyond just the *who* of *what really happened* is one of her principal strengths as a writer of detective fiction.

Earl F. Bargainnier, The Gentle Art of Murder: The Detective Fiction of Agatha Christie (Bowling Green, OH: Bowling Green University Popular Press, 1980), pp. 145–46

ROBERT BARNARD   Of the eleven titles which Agatha Christie published in the 'twenties, only five or six are works of detection. The rest are what, for want of a better title, we must call "thrillers." They are in fact extravaganzas of international espionage and worldwide conspiracy. The villains are not just murderers; they are monomaniacs whose aim— like that of the Big Four in the book of that title—is "world domination." We are closer, then, to the world of James Bond than to that of St. Mary Mead, though it seems to us, with the hindsight of a post-Bond generation, to be a world of rather amateur investigators and unmechanized villains. Not only Fleming but the daily newspapers as well have accustomed us to viewing espionage in terms of fantastic gadgetry and hideous professional experience.

These thrillers, we can now see, represent something of a false start for Agatha Christie: she was not yet quite sure where her real talent lay. In the first part of this period she was a young and apparently carefree married woman writing for pocket money; in the later part she was a deeply unhappy and disturbed woman with a breakdown and a ruined marriage in her past, hardly able to settle down to concentrated writing. These thrillers were easier to do than the brand of detective story she was beginning to perfect. In *An Autobiography* she defined them as "the light-hearted thriller which is particularly pleasant to do," and distinguished them from "the intricate detective story with an involved plot which is technically interesting and requires a great deal of work." It was a form she returned to from time to time throughout her long career—for example, in N or M (1941), *Destination Unknown* (1954) [U.S. *So Many Steps to Death*] and *Passenger to Frankfurt* (1970).

Almost always with disastrous results. The ease with which these stories could be cobbled together shows all too clearly. Though they are admired in America, where (incredibly) *Passenger to Frankfurt* set the final seal on her best-seller status, in Britain these are the Christies that are usually shrugged off as an obvious embarrassment: even the *Times Literary Supplement*, in a generous and enthusiastic tribute on her eightieth birthday, could only manage to give that particular thriller a passing "alas." What makes them intermittently interesting is the fact that *because* she was relaxing, writing lighthearted nonsense, her guard was down. In the detective stories ⟨. . .⟩ there is little or nothing that can be pinned down as a Christie opinion or a Christie taste. She is infinitely more circumspect than Dorothy L. Sayers. In the thrillers, on the other hand, she sometimes gives herself away.

Robert Barnard, *A Talent to Deceive: An Appreciation of Agatha Christie* (New York: Dodd, Mead, 1980), pp. 11–12

STEPHEN KNIGHT   Presentation of character ⟨in *The Murder of Roger Ackroyd*⟩ is shallow and naturalised. A few details are given, and a general summary of the person's nature suffices. In the description of Ralph Paton in Chapter Three he is said to be selfish, both indulging himself and respecting no-one else. But at the same time, and with no explanation, he is loved and admired by his friends. That presentation at once admits and forgives the weakness of individualism; but it is also curiously, and crucially, non-individual in its flat simplicity. This sort of cursory but confident assessment is given to all the characters. No depth is sought and no change occurs to them in the story. If discoveries are made they resolve enigmas in the original presentation—as with Flora, Ralph, Ursula, Miss Russell and Parker. Just as character is flat and single-faceted so when all the details are collected motive is uniform and simple. People do not undergo changes of mind, are not in dialectic with others or themselves. Ralph's concealed marriage is explained by his 'weakness', not by any perceived tension between personal desires and family pressures. The individual is conceived as a unit, guided by his or her own intentions and responding to, not controlled by, external forces. The relevance to the bourgeois idea of self is obvious; both

the forces beyond the individual and the fissures in the private personality
are concealed. We wait for each character to be given its brief notation—
charming, efficient, nervous, servile and so on. Bizarre secrets and humble
characteristics are narrated in an undifferentiating, and so antiseptic way.
Marionettes are provided to play out the extraordinarily complicated action,
the puzzle plot is made possible, suspicion of all can be created without
probing the real roots or mechanisms of unsocial behaviour.

> Stephen Knight, " '. . . Done from Within'—Agatha Christie's World," *Form and
> Ideology in Crime Fiction* (London: Macmillan Press, 1980), p. 124

GILLIAN GILL   Painstakingly, reliably, year after year, Agatha
Christie built up a fictional world which three generations of men and
women have turned to in search of that apparently simple commodity,
"mere" entertainment. The progress of the writer herself through fifty-five
years of writing and some eighty-six completed volumes indicates an authorial compulsiveness that goes beyond the simply financial motivations Christie avows. Had Christie really written her books for the practical and
contingent reasons she admits to in her autobiography, had writing been
as tiresome and nerve-wracking a job as she likes to tell us, she would surely
not have continued writing until the very end of her life. After 1938, for
example, when Max's career had taken off, Rosalind was grown up, Greenway
was bought, and royalties from some thirty successful titles were rolling in,
Christie had no practical need to keep writing. Dorthy L. Sayers at essentially
this stage in her life did decide to write no more detective stories. Sayers
felt she would be happier doing something else and had already published
enough to keep her in comfort for the rest of her days. And just as Christie
compulsively produced book after book, in good times and bad, whether
she needed the money or not, so the public has responded to Christie's
books, buying them in larger and larger numbers, regardless of "quality,"
apparently insatiable for plays and films based on her writing. Such compulsiveness in an international public over many decades demands more complex explanations than that people like a good yarn, or a neat puzzle.

Agatha Christie was herself a devoted reader of detective fiction. She
remembers in her autobiography how fascinated she was at age eight when
Madge read her *The Leavenworth Case,* and she refers to herself and Madge
as connoisseurs of the detective story. Thus, when she came to write mystery

fiction, Christie had not only expert knowledge but also a fan's intuitive understanding of the genre and the hold it had over the public. However, this empathy between Christie and her potential audience was built upon a rare and much more fundamental correlation between writer and target reader.

The public for the various subgenres of popular literature divides sharply into subgroups that find pleasure in subtle variations on an established formula. The detective-story readers, in contrast with devotees of romance or adventure, see themselves as intelligent realists, not romantic escapists, and they have a strong preference that message and meaning be presented implicitly through clues laid by an authorial voice that is trustworthy but never intrusive. This readership preference coincided to an almost unique extent with the psychic requirements of Agatha Christie. Agatha Miller had, from childhood, a quite extraordinary problem in speaking her inner world or giving even trivial information about what she thought and knew. This intense reserve was reinforced by the failure of her first marriage. In later life, Christie's exceptional success and happiness depended upon her rare freedom to structure a private and public realm in which she was not required to explain herself, even to friends, or to make speeches for the public. Consciously, her novels are an attempt not to reveal but to mask the self, yet even as she succeeds in eliminating personal opinions and autobiographical information, Christie thereby gives free rein to her unconscious. Hers is a fictional world in which the author is hidden, and which fixes readers' minds upon the analysis of emotionally neutral elements, such as cigarette butts and railway timetables, while sweeping their fantasies along on an effortless, unthinking race to the denouement.

Gillian Gill, *Agatha Christie: The Woman and Her Mysteries* (New York: Free Press, 1990), pp. 206–7

MARION SHAW and SABINE VANACKER   The abilities old ladies possess—knowing what, how, and why something happened, and what ought to have happened—amount to the essential qualities of the detective: a strong moral sense, a knowledge of human nature, and a capacity for deduction based on carefully observed evidence. It is the 'trivial' lives of old ladies, who have plenty of leisure, the wisdom of experience, long memories, little personal drama in their own lives, and a huge capacity for vicarious living through observation of and gossip about the lives of others, that makes them into potentially excellent detectives. In *Gyn/Ecology* Mary Daly notes that the term *trivia* was one of the names of the ancient triple goddess from whom Christian notions of the Trinity sprang; its modern meaning has been devalued into that which is slight, unimportant, commonplace, but its earlier meaning had to do with omnipresence, commonplace in the sense of being everywhere and facing in all directions. In the figure of Miss Marple Christie takes the patriarchal notion of the trivial and transforms it into something approaching its old meaning. The ordinary, gossipy, unsung life of an old lady is shown as a powerful force for good, and the full exercise of the womanly, highly personalized approach to society is portrayed in Miss Marple as necessary and life-saving. Agatha Christie was no obvious feminist, as she testifies in her *Autobiography*, and in her novels she shows a deep dislike of career women, but she did give a high value to conventionally womanly attributes and habits and showed them, in the figure of Miss Marple, as the vehicles of logic, morality, and justice. In this respect Christie differs from many of her more obviously progressive contemporaries, for within her separate sphere Miss Marple is not only moral and caring—the traditional attributes of the good woman within patriarchy—but she is also an intellectual force, invading the male territories of logic and rationality. This makes her, as Inspector Craddock realizes, as 'dangerous as a rattlesnake'. Much of the pleasure of reading about Miss Marple, and watching her in the televised versions, stems from the contradiction involved in seeing a little old lady, a figure whom society in its ageism condemns as, at best, charmingly quaint and, at worst, as a tiresome nuisance, prove more inexorably logical than the most skilful policemen, and more depraved than the most ambitious evil-doer in the sense that, as Mrs. Dane Calthrop says, she 'knows more about the different kinds of human wickedness than anyone I've ever known' (*The Moving Finger*, ch. 14). 〈. . .〉

Because she is an old woman, Miss Marple's detecting is largely sedentary and a typical Marple plot involves little travelling or activity of a physical kind. It is armchair detection in a multiple sense of the term; Miss Marple conducts the investigation from her armchair and we not only read about it from ours but also can make parallels between that investigation and our own lifestyle with its familiar terrain of sitting-room, garden, local shops, visitors to tea, and all the usual homely paraphernalia of ordinary (though middle-class) life. What Miss Marple helps us do is not only discover the murderer in the novel but also 'read' our own world in the novel, or something sufficiently resembling it to stand in its place. The Marple novels are the folktales of twentieth-century suburban life, and Miss Marple herself is the presiding genius, the good fairy, and guide, in these narratives. The typical plot of one of her novels is, therefore, an adventure story for the middle-class, middle-aged or elderly, householding and fairly housebound British reader.

Marion Shaw and Sabine Vanacker, *Reflecting on Miss Marple* (New York: Routledge, 1991), pp. 63–64, 84–85

▣ *Bibliography*

The Mysterious Affair at Styles. 1920.

The Secret Adversary. 1922.

The Murder on the Links. 1923.

The Man in the Brown Suit. 1924.

Poirot Investigates. 1924.

The Secret of Chimneys. 1925.

The Road of Dreams. 1925.

The Murder of Roger Ackroyd. 1926.

The Big Four. 1927.

The Mystery of the Blue Train. 1928.

The Seven Dials Mystery. 1929.

Partners in Crime. 1929.

The Under Dog. 1929.

The Murder at the Vicarage. 1930.

The Mysterious Mr. Quin. 1930.

Giants' Bread. 1930.

The Sittaford Mystery ⟨The Murder at Hazelmoor⟩. 1931.

Peril at End House. 1932.

The Thirteen Problems ⟨The Tuesday Club Murders⟩. 1932.

Lord Edgware Dies ⟨Thirteen at Dinner⟩. 1933.

The Hound of Death and Other Stories. 1933.

Why Didn't They Ask Evans? ⟨The Boomerang Clue⟩. 1934.

Parker Pyne Investigates. 1934.

The Listerdale Mystery and Other Stories. 1934.

Unfinished Portrait. 1934.

Black Coffee. 1934.

Murder on the Orient Express ⟨*Murder in the Calais Coach*⟩. 1934.

Murder in Three Acts ⟨*Three Act Tragedy*⟩. 1934.

Death in the Clouds ⟨*Death in the Air*⟩. 1935.

The A.B.C. Murders. 1936.

Cards on the Table. 1936.

Murder in Mesopotamia. 1936.

Death on the Nile. 1937.

Dumb Witness ⟨*Poirot Loses a Client*⟩. 1937.

Murder in the Mews and Other Stories ⟨*Dead Man's Mirror and Other Stories*⟩.
      1937.

Appointment with Death. 1938.

Hercule Poirot's Christmas ⟨*Murder for Christmas* or *A Holiday for Murder*⟩.
      1938.

Murder Is Easy ⟨*Easy to Kill*⟩. 1939.

Ten Little Niggers ⟨*Ten Little Indians; And Then There Were None*⟩. 1939.

The Regatta Mystery and Other Stories. 1939.

One, Two, Buckle My Shoe ⟨*The Patriotic Murders*⟩. 1940.

Sad Cypress. 1940.

Evil under the Sun. 1941.

N or M? 1941.

The Body in the Library. 1942.

The Moving Finger. 1942.

Five Little Pigs ⟨*Murder in Retrospect*⟩. 1942.

The Mystery of the Baghdad Chest. 1943.

The Mystery of the Crime in Cabin 66. 1943.

Poirot and the Regatta Mystery. 1943.

Poirot on Holiday. 1943.

Problem at Pollensa Bay and Christmas Adventure. 1943.

Death Comes as the End. 1944.

Towards Zero. 1944.

The Veiled Lady and The Mystery of the Baghdad Chest. 1944.

Absent in the Spring. 1944.

Ten Little Niggers (drama). 1944.

Sparkling Cyanide ⟨*Remembered Death*⟩. 1945.

The Hollow. 1946.

Poirot Knows the Murderer. 1946.

Come, Tell Me How You Live. 1946, 1975.

Poirot Lends a Hand. 1946.

The Labours of Hercules. 1947.

Taken at the Flood ⟨*There Is a Tide . . .*⟩. 1948.

The Witness for the Prosecution and Other Stories. 1948.

Murder on the Nile. 1948.

The Rose and the Yew Tree. 1948.

Crooked House. 1949.

The Mousetrap and Other Stories ⟨*Three Blind Mice and Other Stories*⟩. 1949.

A Murder Is Announced. 1950.

They Came to Baghdad. 1951.

The Under Dog and Other Stories. 1951.

They Do It with Mirrors ⟨*Murder with Mirrors*⟩. 1952.

Mrs. McGinty's Dead. 1952.

The Hollow (drama). 1952.

A Daughter's a Daughter. 1952.

After the Funeral ⟨*Funerals Are Fatal*⟩. 1953.

A Pocket Full of Rye. 1953.

Destination Unknown ⟨*So Many Steps to Death*⟩. 1954.

The Mousetrap. 1954.

Witness for the Prosecution. 1954.

Hickory, Dickory, Dock ⟨*Hickory, Dickory, Death*⟩. 1955.

Dead Man's Folly. 1956.

Appointment with Death (drama). 1956.

The Burden. 1956.

The 4.50 from Paddington ⟨*What Mrs. McGillicuddy Saw!*⟩. 1957.

Spider's Web. 1957.

Towards Zero (drama; with Gerald Verner). 1957.

Ordeal by Innocence. 1958.

Verdict. 1958.

The Unexpected Guest. 1958.

Cat among the Pigeons. 1959.

The Adventure of the Christmas Pudding and Selection of Entrées. 1960.

Go Back for Murder. 1960.

The Pale Horse. 1961.

Double Sin and Other Stories. 1961.

13 for Luck! A Selection of Mystery Stories for Young Readers. 1961.

The Mirror Crack'd from Side to Side. 1962.

The Clocks. 1963.

Rule of Three: Afternoon at the Seaside, The Patient, The Rats. 1963. 3 vols.

A Caribbean Mystery. 1964.

At Bertram's Hotel. 1965.

Star over Bethlehem and Other Stories. 1965.

Surprise! Surprise! A Collection of Mystery Stories with Unexpected Endings. Ed.
        Raymond T. Bond. 1965.

Third Girl. 1966.

13 Clues for Miss Marple. 1966.

Endless Night. 1967.

By the Pricking of My Thumbs. 1968.

Hallowe'en Party. 1969.

Passenger to Frankfurt. 1970.

Nemesis. 1971.

The Golden Ball and Other Stories. 1971.

Elephants Can Remember. 1972.

Postern of Fate. 1973.

Poems. 1973.

Akhnaton. 1973.

Poirot's Early Cases. 1974.

Curtain. 1975.

Sleeping Murder. 1976.

An Autobiography. 1977.

The Mousetrap and Other Plays. 1978.

Miss Marple's Final Cases and Two Other Stories. 1979.

The Agatha Christie Hour. 1982.

Hercule Poirot's Casebook: Fifty Stories. 1984.

Miss Marple: Complete Short Stories. 1985.

Best Detective Stories. 1986.

Remembrance. 1988.

My Flower Garden. 1989.

Wilkie Collins
1824–1889

WILLIAM WILKIE COLLINS, elder son of the landscape painter William Collins, was born in London on January 8, 1824. He was educated for a few years at private schools in London, and between 1836 and 1838 traveled in Italy with his family. From 1841 to 1846 he worked briefly for a tea importer, but then his father allowed him to became a law student at Lincoln's Inn; he was later called to the bar, but never practiced.

Collins began writing in the early 1840s, his first work appearing in the *Illuminated Magazine* in 1843. In 1847 his father died, and Collins's biography of him, published in 1848, was his first book. It was followed in 1850 by his first novel, *Antonina; or, The Fall of Rome*. In 1851 Collins first met Charles Dickens, who became a close friend and collaborator. From then on he wrote numerous short stories and articles for Dickens's periodical *Household Words* (retitled *All the Year Round* in 1859), some of which were later collected in *After Dark* (1856), *The Queen of Hearts* (1859), and *My Miscellanies* (1863). Collins edited this journal from 1856 to 1863. He also produced a number of moderately successful plays, including dramatic adaptations of his own novels.

Most of the works for which Collins is now best known are novels and tales of mystery, suspense, and crime. These include *Basil: A Story of Modern Life* (1852), *Hide and Seek* (1854), *The Woman in White* (1860), *No Name* (1862), *Armadale* (1866), and *The Moonstone* (1868), considered one of the best mystery novels ever written. His two most famous novels, *The Woman in White* and *The Moonstone*, were serialized in *All the Year Round* in 1859–60 and 1868, respectively, before being published in book form. Although *The Moonstone* does not involve murder but only theft, Collins's later novel *The Law and the Lady* (1875) does indeed center on a murder, and could be called the first detective novel to do so.

Between 1870 and his death Collins wrote fifteen additional novels, including *The New Magdalen* (1873) and *The Law and the Lady* (1875); although popular during his lifetime, these works are now largely forgotten.

Collins also wrote a number of short stories of horror and the supernatural, including "A Terribly Strange Bed" and "The Dream-Woman."

Collins never married but lived for many years with Caroline Elizabeth Graves, whom he first met in 1859; after her marriage in 1868, Collins began a relationship with Martha Rudd, by whom he had three children. At some later date Caroline Graves, divorced from her husband, returned to live with Collins. Collins lived throughout his life in London, but also traveled extensively in France, Italy, and Switzerland, often with Dickens. For much of his life he suffered from rheumatic gout, for which he took ever larger doses of opium. He died in London on September 23, 1889.

▨ Critical Extracts

UNSIGNED   The *Woman in White* is the latest, and by many degrees the best work of an author who had already written so many singularly good ones. That mastery in the art of construction for which Mr. Wilkie Collins has long been pre-eminent among living writers of fiction is here exhibited upon the largest, and proportionately, the most difficult scale he has yet attempted. To keep the reader's attention fairly and equably on the alert throughout a continuous story that fills three volumes of the ordinary novel form, is no common feat; but the author of the *Woman in White* has done much more than this. Every two of his thousand and odd pages contain as much printed matter as three or four of those to which the majority of Mr. Mudie's subscribers are most accustomed, and from his first page to his last the interest is progressive, cumulative, and absorbing. If this be true—and it appears to be universally admitted—what becomes of the assertion made by some critics, that it is an interest of mere curiosity which holds the reader so fast and holds him so long? The thing is palpably absurd. Curiosity can do so much, but it cannot singly accomplish all that is imputed to it by this theory, for it is impossible that its intensity should be sustained without interruption through so long a flight. If the *Woman in White* were indeed a protracted puzzle and nothing more, the reader's attention would often grow languid over its pages; he would be free from the importunate desire that now possessed him to go through every line of it continuously; he would be content to take it up and lay it down at uncertain intervals, or be strongly tempted to skip to the end and find out the secret at once, without more tedious hunting through labyrinths devised only to retard his search, and not worth exploring for their own sake. But he yields to no such temptation, for the secret which is so wonderfully well kept to the end of the third volume is not the be-all and end-all of his interest in the story. Even Mr. Wilkie Collins himself, with all his constructive skill, would be at fault if he attempted to build an elaborate story on so narrow a basis— witness his tale of *The Dead Secret,* which is in some degree chargeable with this defect of construction, and therefore with a corresponding measure of prolixity. The strength and symmetry of the tale before us are marred by no such organic defect. Here the secret underlies, indeed, the whole tenour of the story, and its vital connexion with it is often more or less strongly surmised; but it is only at intervals that it is brought prominently into notice, and that direct efforts for its discovery become the sole business of the moment. Meanwhile there is other matter in hand sufficiently copious and exciting to keep the reader's mind perpetually occupied with a flow of varying emotions.

Unsigned, [Review of *The Woman in White*], *Spectator,* 8 September 1860, p. 864

GERALDINE JEWSBURY   When persons are in a state of ravenous hunger they are eager only for food, and utterly ignore all delicate distinctions of cookery; it is only when this savage state has been somewhat allayed that they are capable of discerning and appreciating the genius of the *chef.* Those readers who have followed the fortunes of the mysterious Moonstone for many weeks, as it has appeared in tantalizing portions, will of course throw themselves headlong upon the latter portion of the third volume, now that the end is really come, and devour it without rest or pause; to take any deliberate breathing-time is quite out of the question, and we promise them a surprise that will find the most experienced novel-reader unprepared. The unravelment of the puzzle is a satisfactory reward for all the interest out of which they have been beguiled. When, however, they have read to the end, we recommend them to read the book over again from the beginning, and they will see, what on a first perusal they were too engrossed to observe, the carefully elaborate workmanship, and the wonderful construction of the story; the admirable manner in which every circumstance and incident is fitted together, and the skill with which the secret is kept to the last; so that even when all seems to have been discovered there is a final light thrown upon people and things which give them a significance they had not before. The 'epilogue' of *The Moonstone* is beautiful. It redeems the somewhat sordid detective element, by a strain of solemn and pathetic human interest. Few will read of the final destiny of *The Moonstone* without feeling the tears rise in their eyes as they catch the last glimpse of the three men, who have sacrificed their cast in the service of their God, when the vast crowd of worshippers opens for them, as they embrace each other and separate to begin their lonely and never-ending pilgrimage of expiation. The deepest emotion is certainly resolved to the last.

> Geraldine Jewsbury, [Review of *The Moonstone*], *Athenaeum*, 25 July 1868, p. 106

T. S. ELIOT   *The Moonstone* is the first and greatest of English detective novels. We say *English* detective novels, because there is also the work of Poe, which has a *pure* detective interest. The detective story, as created by Poe, is something as specialized and intellectual as a chess problem; whereas the best English detective fiction has relied less on the beauty of the mathematical problem and much more on the intangible human element. In detective fiction England probably excels other countries; but in a *genre* invented by Collins and not by Poe. In *The Moonstone* the mystery is finally solved, not altogether by human ingenuity, but largely by accident. Since Collins, the best heroes of English detective fiction have been, like Sergeant Cuff, fallible; they play their part, but never the sole part, in the unravelling. Sherlock Holmes, not altogether a typical English sleuth, is a partial exception; but even Holmes exists, not solely because of his prowess, but largely because he is, in the Jonsonian sense, a humorous character, with his needle, his boxing, and his violin. But Sergeant Cuff, far more than Holmes, is the ancestor of the healthy generation of amiable, efficient, professional but fallible inspectors of fiction among whom we live today. And *The Moonstone*, a book twice the length of the "thrillers" that our contemporary masters write, maintains its interest and suspense at every moment. It does this by devices of a Dickensian type; for Collins, in addition to his particular merits, was a Dickens without genius. The book is a comedy of humours. The eccentricities of Mr. Franklin Blake, the satire on false philanthropy in the character of Mr. Godfrey Ablewhite (to say nothing of the Life, Letters and

Labours of Miss Jane Ann Stamper), Betteredge with his *Robinson Crusoe*, and his daughter Penelope, support the narrative. In other of Collins's novels, the trick of passing the narration from one hand to another, and employing every device of letters and diaries, becomes tedious and even unplausible (for instance, in *Armadale*, the terrific villain, Miss Gwilt, commits herself to paper far too often and far too frankly); but in *The Moonstone* these devices succeed, every time, in stimulating our interest afresh just at the moment when it was about to flag.

And in *The Moonstone* Collins succeeds in bringing into play those aids of "atmosphere" in which Dickens (and the Brontës) exhibited such genius, and in which Collins has everything except their genius. For his purpose, he does not come off badly. Compare the description of the discovery of Rosanna's death in the Shivering Sands—and notice how carefully, beforehand, the *mise-en-scène* of the Shivering Sands is prepared for us—with the shipwreck of Steerforth in *David Copperfield*. We may say, "There is no comparison!" but there *is* a comparison; and however unfavourable to Collins, it must increase our estimation of his skill.

T. S. Eliot, "Wilkie Collins and Dickens" (1927), *Selected Essays* (New York: Harcourt, Brace, 1950), pp. 413–14

DOROTHY L. SAYERS   Now, if you will examine carefully the first ten chapters of *The Moonstone*, written in 1868, you will find that practically every clue necessary to the unravelling of the mystery is as scrupulously set out in them as they would be in a story written yesterday by Freeman Wills Crofts. Judged by the standard of seventy years later, and across a great gap which acknowledged no fair-play standards at all, *The Moonstone* is impeccable. What has happened, in fact, is that *The Moonstone* set the standard, and that it has taken us all this time to recognize it. Having at last got so far, we observe the fair play of Wilkie Collins without reverence or surprise:

> Most can raise the flowers now,
> For all have got the seed.

Collins, however, had for models only the short stories of Edgar Allan Poe, and a couple of novels by Gaboriau, who is not by any means consistently fair in his methods. Nor, I think, was this quality in *The Moonstone* recognized in its own day for the admirable thing it was; the tendency of critics was rather to protest at being expected to remember details and dates, and to concentrate on the mere "thriller" surprises of the story. Collins, in fact, was called a master of "sensational fiction"; whereas his peculiar mastery was in the presentation of those clues for which the modern reader displays so keen an appetite.

Similarly, the actual scientific machinery used to fasten the theft of the moonstone, in the "classical" manner, on the most unlikely person is of a kind very familiar to us to-day; but it was Collins who first thought of it. And in this connection we may notice how many decades he is ahead of his followers in the scrupulous exactness of his medical, legal, and police details. When he wrote this book he was already using opium to relieve the agonies of rheumatic gout from which he suffered all his life; and his "clinical picture" of it is drawn from experience and drawn with care. The "law" of *The Moonstone* has been examined by experts and found correct; indeed, Collins was exact on these points in all his books, and painstakingly sought professional advice on all doubtful points. ⟨. . .⟩

⟨. . .⟩ To turn from a modern detective story and to open *The Moonstone* is to escape from a narrow artificial stage to the crowded reality of the marketplace. Collins's people do not exist simply and solely in order to make their moves on the chequer-board of intrigue; they have a full and lasting existence outside the story through which they pass; they are solid characters living in a real world. Collins, in short, is a writer of genuine creative imagination; and it is this which, quite apart from his "classic" contribution to detective development, gives to his work a perennial interest and a permanent literary value.

> Dorothy L. Sayers, "Introduction," *The Moonstone* by Wilkie Collins (London & New York: J. M. Dent/E. P. Dutton [Everyman's Library], 1944), pp. vi, xi

---

ROBERT P. ASHLEY   Contrary to popular belief, *The Moonstone* is not Collins's only detective novel. In *The Law and the Lady* (1875) Collins seems deliberately to have aimed at reproducing certain features of his two greatest successes, *The Woman in White* and *The Moonstone*, particularly the latter. ⟨. . .⟩

Almost as strikingly as *The Moonstone*, *The Law and the Lady* employed themes and motifs which were to become stock devices of the detective story. Prominent among these are the courtroom scenes, the attempt of the amateur (Valeria) to succeed where professionals (Eustace's lawyers) had failed, the endeavor to clear the name of a wrongly suspected person, and the piecing together of the fragments of a torn letter. In two respects *The Law and the Lady* comes much closer than *The Moonstone* to the twentieth-century detective story: the crime is murder, not theft, and the detective is the protagonist, not merely an important minor character.

As in *The Moonstone* suspicion is skillfully shifted from person to person—from Eustace to Mrs. Macallan to Mrs. Beauly to Dexter and back again. The eventual fastening of guilt upon a person previously stricken from the list of suspects provides an ingenious twist to the plot and represents another skillful employment by Collins of the least-likely person motif. Like Franklin Blake under the influence of opium, Miserrimus Dexter under the influence of approaching madness incriminates himself but leaves the mystery far from solved. The pseudo-scientific element of *The Moonstone* reappears in *The Law and the Lady*, with arsenic playing the role formerly played by opium.

The Law and the Lady resembles both *The Moonstone* and *The Woman in White* in its layers of mystery. No sooner is one secret revealed or one mystery solved than a new one arises: the first big mystery—what is the secret of Eustace's past?—is succeeded by the second—what happened at the trial?—which in turn gives way to the third—who killed Mrs. Macallan? Like both *The Woman in White* and *The Moonstone*, *The Law and the Lady* may owe some of its details of plot to a famous murder trial, the trial of Madeleine Smith for the murder of her lover, L'Angelier. Like Eustace Macallan, Madeleine Smith was proved to have bought arsenic but not to have administered it to the victim, and like Eustace she was set free by a verdict of "not proven."

Collins's attempt in *The Law and the Lady* to emulate his two masterpieces provides a revealing measure of his literary decline in the 'seventies. Despite this decline, *The Law and the Lady* is an ingenious and exciting detective story, and it is difficult to understand its having been so completely ignored by literary historians. If Sergeant Cuff is one of English fiction's first detectives, Valeria Macallan is one of its first detectivettes. Furthermore, if *The Moonstone* is the first detective novel in English, *The Law and the Lady* is the second. These are reasons enough for a place in detective fiction history.

Robert P. Ashley, "Wilkie Collins and the Detective Story," *Nineteenth-Century Fiction* 6, No. 1 (June 1951): 53–56

WILLIAM H. MARSHALL   The method which Collins brought near perfection in *The Woman in White*, by which the narrative is developed through the protagonist's editing of individual documents, was clearly suited to the needs of the kind of fiction given direction by *The Moonstone*. Encountering a group of dramatic monologues significantly arranged, the reader is able to learn more about the total situation than any one of the active characters knows. In *The Moonstone*, Franklin Blake, who is in love with his cousin Rachel Verinder, collects statements by those who have witnessed or participated in the episode of the disappearance of the Moonstone—the gem once stolen by Rachel's uncle, John Herncastle, from an idol in a Brahmin temple—on the night of Rachel's birthday, when, according to the terms of her uncle's will, it had been presented to her. Although each narrator brings to his story his own moral orientation, nothing is imposed upon the total narrative beyond the demonstration of the ultimate innocence of Franklin Blake himself—long suspected as the *premeditating* thief—and the identification of the real criminal. Despite the fact that the narrator of the Prologue, who details the original theft of the stone, foresees that the "crime brings its own fatality with it," the succeeding events result entirely from human agency. In the end, only Franklin Blake is in the position to impose meaning upon the full episode, but, perhaps with deference to the presumably equal judgment of his readers, he refrains.

The principal quality of the resulting narrative structure is the organic unity that is derived to a great degree from the exploitation of either the dramatic irony or the incomplete knowledge apparent in nearly every individual narration. Rachel Verinder writes to Ezra Jennings not long before the crucial experiment is conducted upon Franklin Blake: "I want to have something to do with it, even in the unimportant character of a mere looker-on" (Extracted from the Journal of Ezra Jennings). She here describes the situation to some degree of each of the participants in the episode: in terms of deducible meaning, none is really more than "a mere looker-on." Even the villain, Godfrey Ablewhite, begins his involvement by watching what is in front of him, and makes the significant commitment only somewhat later. Sergeant Cuff, in his letter of explanation to Franklin Blake—reconstructing the moment when the unknowingly drugged Blake took the Moonstone so that he might protect Rachel from the three Indians pledged to its recovery—remarks of the ultimate thief of the gem: "In that position he [Godfrey Ablewhite] not only detected you in taking the Diamond out of the drawer—he also detected Miss Verinder silently watching you from her bedroom, through her open door. He saw that *she* saw you take the Diamond too" (Sergeant Cuff's Narrative, Chapter IV). The very *seeing*, a form of *knowing*, gives each character a degree of power in relation to other characters, each of whom may in return have a species of knowledge about him. The structure of the total narrative resembles an arrangement of mirrors reflecting mirrors, no one of which directly reflects full reality.

William H. Marshall, *Wilkie Collins* (New York: Twayne, 1970), pp. 79–81

GAVIN LAMBERT   *The Woman in White* hinges on an elaborate deception carried out in the most correct surroundings and only gradually suspected by a series of astonished narrators. The crime is based on a French court case that Collins had read about, in which a woman was drugged, hidden away and eventually presumed dead so that her brother could inherit her estate. Collins grafts on to it his favourite substitution theme. The penniless Sir Percival Glyde marries Laura Fairlie, heir to a family fortune. Laura bears a marked resemblance to Anne Catherick, the Woman in White who has escaped from a private asylum as the story opens. Since Anne Catherick is weak in the heart as well as the head, ⟨Count⟩ Fosco conceives the idea of frightening her to death, then burying her as Lady Glyde. Laura is drugged and delivered back to the asylum as the Woman in White. In due course her estate will be delivered to Sir Percival.

The central crime leads into a maze of other revelations, emerging as each narrator supplies his testimony of events. Sir Percival's past is uncovered, the true identity of Anne Catherick revealed, the spectacular nature of Fosco himself exposed. Points of view shift, contradict each other, finally coincide. The voices—of aristocrats, servants, lawyers, a doctor, a whore turned respectable, an illiterate, an artist—are all distinct parts of a social composition. Their different levels of perception not only deepen the mystery but reflect Collins's own sympathies and antagonisms. Walter Hartright, the young art-teacher who begins and ends the story, is a low-key hero with some points of resemblance to Collins himself. His father was a successful artist, he is devoted to his widowed mother, his visual intelligence responds sharply to the lonely place and the incongruous image. The meeting with the Woman in White establishes a powerful uneasy atmosphere, pushed almost to the frontier of dreams—the walk home late at night through an empty heat-struck city, the solitary road, the silhouetted houses, the touch of a hand laid suddenly on Hartright's shoulder, the troubled apparition with 'her hand pointing to the dark cloud over London'. It reproduces almost exactly the encounter with Caroline Graves:

> We set our faces towards London, and walked on together in the first still hour of the new day—I, and this woman, whose name, whose character, whose story, whose objects in life, whose very presence by my side, at that moment, were fathomless mysteries to me . . . Had I really left, little more than an hour since, the quiet, decent, conventionally domestic atmosphere of my mother's cottage?

In a subdued way Hartright appears from the start as an alienated man, prepared for vertigo and dislocations, asking himself 'What shall I see in my dreams tonight?' Arriving at Limmeridge House in the north of England to teach drawing to Laura Fairlie and her half-sister Marian Halcome, he is immediately drawn to Laura. Fascinated by her resemblance to Anne Catherick, he responds to her gentle, obscurely frightened manner. To him, as to Collins, the victim-type is instantly appealing.

Gavin Lambert, "Enemy Country: Wilkie Collins," *The Dangerous Edge* (New York: Grossman Publishers, 1976), pp. 11–12

W. DAVID SHAW   The division between Sergeant Cuff's private and public lives, the key to his character, is continuous with his suspicion that other characters are not what they seem. Indeed Cuff, a detective by vocation, chooses roses as his avocation in order to create as wide a rift as possible between the two. "Show me any two things more opposite one from the other than a rose and a thief; and I'll correct my tastes accordingly" (first period, chap. 12). He cultivates oddity in order to exercise his keen distrust of any congruity between form and meaning. Cuff is even prepared to sacrifice to the shock effect of a witticism or a neatly turned antithesis the real complexities of the case. Like Browning's Gigadibs, he is in quest of such journalistic paradoxes as the tender murderer or superstitious atheist and is enamored of the perpetual contradictions that seem to characterize Blake.

Truth in criminal investigations is an imagination that succeeds, an intuition that happens to guess the art of deception in its practiced forms.

Cuff is a good psychologist and tactful diplomat, but many of his hunches are wrong. His deductions are therefore a tissue of true insight, partial apprehension, and outright error. From the correct assumption that the diamond has been lost, he passes too hastily to the surprising announcement that nobody has stolen the diamond (first period, chap. 12). That statement is untrue in the sense Cuff intends it but true in a sense that Cuff himself does not yet understand. Committed to the belief that signs are ambiguous and face several ways at once, Cuff may discern duplicity where it does not exist, in a character like Rachel. And he may miss the duplicity that is really there, in the split between conscious and unconscious experience in Franklin Blake.

What Betteredge says of Rachel's interpretation of Cuff might apply with equal propriety to Cuff's own methods of investigation: he interprets everything "in a glass darkly" (first period, chap. 13). Usually Cuff would prefer to be a Socratic midwife rather than a direct purveyor of information: thus when Betteredge asks for a name, Cuff encourages him to provide it himself. Like Sherlock Holmes, Cuff is also a master of mental broad jumps, able to connect a murder with "a spot of ink on a tablecloth" (first period, chap. 12). There is always a danger, however, that "detective-fever," as Betteredge calls it, may be a disease of Cuff's imagination, a merely fanciful use of the investigator's faculties. One symptom of "detective-fever" is a tendency to make everyone as subtle and suspicious as the detective. If the footsteps on the sand are confused, it is because their suspect wanted them to be confused. "I don't want to hurt your feelings," Cuff tells Betteredge, "but I'm afraid Rosanna is sly" (first period, chap. 15). Everyone is "sly" to Cuff, because duplicity is the idol of his cave. Cuff is so accustomed to secrecy and cunning in himself and others that he often withholds information when there is nothing to hide.

W. David Shaw, "The Critic as Detective: Mystery and Method in *The Moonstone*," *Victorians and Mystery: Crises of Representation* (Ithaca: Cornell University Press, 1990), pp. 295–96

CATHERINE PETERS   Wilkie Collins was himself to suffer severe emotional upheavals during the serialization of *The Moonstone*. He was much distressed by the death of his mother in the early months of 1868, and the interpolation of Lady Verinder's death, one of the few incidents in the novel which was clearly not planned in advance, may have been prompted by this. He was himself suffering an agonizing and unusually prolonged attack of his chronic disability, 'rheumatic gout', during her last illness, and was unable to attend her funeral. He was already dependent on opium, taken to relieve his symptoms, and the effects of the ever larger amounts he now had to take are vividly described in the novel. ⟨. . .⟩ Later that year Caroline Graves, the woman with whom he had lived for ten years but whom he had always refused to marry, left him to marry another man. In the same month a young woman, Martha Rudd, a shepherd's daughter from Norfolk who had worked as a servant, became pregnant by Collins with the first of their three children. Harriet Graves, Wilkie Collins' devoted adopted daughter, remained with him after her mother's marriage, and with her help he kept the story going, in spite of illness and unhappiness, dictating to her a short section of the novel (part of Miss Clack's narrative) he was too ill to write with his own hand.

The key to the mystery of *The Moonstone* is intimately bound up with the behaviour of two women; if they had behaved differently, the story would not only have taken an entirely different turn, it would have been over almost before it began. Without wishing to draw too many parallels between life and fiction, it seems possible that the situations of the seventeen-year-old Harriet Graves, loyal to a man whose behaviour she knew to be in many ways reprehensible, and that of the twenty-three-year-old servant Martha Rudd, in love with a gentleman whom the class system of Victorian England would seem to put out of her reach, may have suggested some aspects of the behaviour of Rachel Verinder and Rosanna Spearman in the novel.

The underlying significance of Wilkie Collins' detective story is, however, far wider than any reference to personal dilemmas, shortcomings and unhappiness. *The Moonstone* seems to offer the reader at least two books in one, integrated through an exploration of unconscious motivation and hidden processes of thought, essential to the final solution of the mystery. Beneath the detective puzzle lies a symbolic commentary on the theme of possession. The anonymous reviewer in *Nation* complained that 'as far as the real business of the plot is concerned, [the Moonstone] might as well have been a black bean or a horn button'. But it is partly the way the Moonstone operates as arbitrary sign, putting in question the concepts of value and ownership, that has ensured that Wilkie Collins' novel keeps its fascination when other detective stories have faded from our minds. The title is unusual for its period in directing the reader's attention to an object, rather than a person, a place, or a situation. The diamond, at once sacred and cursed, comes itself to possess those who possess or lust to possess it. The Moonstone acts as a catalyst, disturbing the life of the English country house, so placid on the surface. As it collects and then reflects the sunlight with a paradoxically 'moony gleam', so it also focuses the emotions of the characters in the story, laying hold on them, intensifying and making visible their unconscious, night-time hopes and fears. The solution to the mystery raises another question: possession of an object fades into insignificance compared with the possession of the self. If neither our emotions, nor even our actions, are under our conscious control, the safe boundaries of existence waver and dissolve.

Catherine Peters, "Introduction," The Moonstone by Wilkie Collins (New York: Alfred A. Knopf, 1992), pp. xii–xiv

▨ *Bibliography*

Memoirs of the Life of William Collins, Esq., R.A. 1848. 2 vols.

Antonina; or, The Fall of Rome: A Romance of the Fifth Century. 1850. 3 vols.

Rambles beyond Railways; or, Notes in Cornwall Taken A-Foot. 1851.

Mr. Wray's Cash Box; or, The Mask and the Mystery: A Christmas Sketch. 1852.

Basil: A Story of Modern Life. 1852. 3 vols.

Hide and Seek. 1854. 3 vols.

After Dark. 1856. 2 vols.

The Wreck of the Golden Mary (with Charles Dickens). 1856.

The Dead Secret. 1857. 2 vols.

The Lazy Tour of Two Idle Apprentices (with Charles Dickens). 1857.

The Perils of Certain English Prisoners (with Charles Dickens). 1857.

The Queen of Hearts. 1859. 3 vols.

The Woman in White. 1860. 3 vols.

No Name. 1862. 3 vols.

My Miscellanies. 1863. 2 vols.

Armadale. 1866. 2 vols.

The Frozen Deep (with Charles Dickens). 1866.

Armadale (drama). 1866.

No Thoroughfare (with Charles Dickens). 1867.

The Moonstone: A Romance. 1868. 3 vols.

Black and White: A Love Story (with Charles Fechter). 1869.

Man and Wife. 1870. 3 vols.

No Name (drama). 1870.

The Woman in White (drama). 1871.

Poor Miss Finch. 1872. 3 vols.

The New Magdalen. 1873. 2 vols.

Miss or Mrs.? and Other Stories in Outline. 1873.

Works. 1873–1902. 17 vols.

The Frozen Deep and Other Stories. 1874.

The Law and the Lady. 1875. 3 vols.

Miss Gwilt. 1875.

The Two Destinies: A Romance. 1876. 2 vols.

The Haunted Hotel: A Mystery of Modern Venice; to Which Is Added, My Lady's
        Money. 1878.

A Rogue's Life: From His Birth to His Marriage. 1879.

The Fallen Leaves. 1879. 3 vols.

Jezebel's Daughter. 1880. 3 vols.

The Black Robe. 1881. 3 vols.

Heart and Science: A Story of the Present Time. 1883. 3 vols.

"I Say No"; or, The Love-Letter Answered. 1884. 3 vols.

The Evil Genius: A Domestic Story. 1886. 3 vols.

The Guilty River. 1886.

Little Novels. 1887. 3 vols.

The Legacy of Cain. 1889. 3 vols.

Novels. 1889–1908. 29 vols.

Blind Love (with Walter Besant). 1890. 3 vols.

The Lazy Tour of Two Idle Apprentices; No Thoroughfare; The Perils of Certain
        English Prisoners (with Charles Dickens). 1890.

Works. 1900. 30 vols.

Tales of Suspense. Ed. Robert Ashley and Herbert Van Thal. 1954.

Tales of Terror and the Supernatural. Ed. Herbert Van Thal. 1972.

⊡ ⊡ ⊡

Freeman Wills Crofts
1879–1957

FREEMAN WILLS CROFTS was born on June 1, 1879, in Dublin. His father, a British army doctor, died when Crofts was a boy, and his mother later married an archdeacon of the Church of Ireland. He attended Methodist and Campbell College in Belfast and in 1896 was taken on as an apprentice by his uncle, Berkeley D. Wise, chief engineer of the Belfast & Northern Counties Railways. Crofts spent more than three decades with this company, eventually rising to the rank of chief assistant engineer. He married Mary Bellas Canning in 1912; they had no children.

Crofts began writing relatively late in life. In 1919 he suffered a serious illness that required a lengthy convalescence. During this period he became so bored that he occupied his time by writing down "what seemed the most absurd and improbable things I could think of." Looking at the work later and encouraged by the praise of his wife, he finished it and sent it to A. P. Watt, the literary agent, who marketed it to the publisher William Collins Sons; it appeared as *The Cask* (1920). (Crofts's account of his beginnings as a writer is found in his introduction to a 1939 reissue of the novel.)

The Cask has attained classic status as a detective story for its rigid adherence to the "fair play" tradition of laying out all clues before the reader and for the systematic way in which a seemingly unbreakable alibi is proven false. This latter feature would become a hallmark of Crofts's work. By 1939 *The Cask* had sold 100,000 copies.

Crofts began a steady stream of mystery novels, including an interesting attempt to combine the thriller and the detective tale, *The Pit-Prop Syndicate* (1922); but it was only in 1925, with *Inspector French's Greatest Case*, that he created his most popular detective. Inspector Joseph French of Scotland Yard is frequently called a "plodding" detective for his blandness of character (in stark contrast to the frequently eccentric "amateur" detectives of the Sherlock Holmes tradition), his careful attention to material clues, and his slow but painstaking pursuit of the criminal. French was featured in twenty-nine novels and many short stories throughout Crofts's career. These works are full of realistic details and frequently include plans of houses, railway timetables, and other factual information relevant to the solution of the mystery. As such, they established new levels of realism in the genre.

In 1929 Crofts retired from the Belfast & Northern Counties Railway, and he and his wife settled successively in various homes in southern England. Crofts became an active member of the Detection Club, contributing to several of its round-robin mystery novels. In 1939 he became a fellow of the Royal Society of Arts. During World War II he achieved great popularity with radio plays broadcast on the BBC, including a series entitled "Inspector French's Cases." After the war he wrote a detective story for young adults, *Young Robin Brand, Detective* (1947), as well as a retelling of the Gospels. Freeman Wills Crofts died on April 11, 1957.

▦ *Critical Extracts*

UNSIGNED   Innumerable detective stories are written and many are published, yet a really good one, ingeniously contrived, plausibly worked out, and so constructed as to be without quite evident flaws, is almost as rare as the proverbial black swan. There are a few, a very few, authors from whom we may confidently expect tales of this type, and to the list must now be added the name of Freeman Wills Crofts. This story ⟨The Cask⟩ with which he makes his bow to American readers is clever, interesting and well constructed.

Though much longer than the average tale of its kind, the narrative never drags for a moment; moreover, the manner in which the truth is finally discovered is entirely convincing, depending neither on mechanical devices, superhuman perspicacity, far-fetched coincidence nor extraordinarily good luck. And from first to last Mr. Crofts plays fair with the reader. All that his detectives—and there are no less than three of them—know is imparted at once to the reader, who follows them step by step, from complete perplexity to knowledge of the truth. It is a knowledge won by hard work, the careful investigating of every clue, the careful checking up of every statement.

Unsigned, [Review of *The Cask*], *New York Times Book Review*, 21 December 1924, p. 17

VINCENT STARRETT   Freeman Wills Crofts has written another detective story, *The Starvel Hollow Tragedy*, in which Inspector French of Scotland Yard again fares forth upon the trail of a gruesome mystery. There is nothing particularly brilliant about either Mr. Crofts or his detective, but for all that they are likable fellows. Like ⟨J. S.⟩ Fletcher, at his best, Mr. Crofts tells a straightforward story of crime and detection, filled with human, everyday characters and with careful attention to detail. The story, like its Inspector French forerunners, moves slowly and evenly from a logical beginning to a logical conclusion. It is the right sort of novel for the genuine detective-story addict, who likes to work on the case himself.

Vincent Starrett, "Varied Stories by Poe, Gobineau and Others," *New York World*, 6 November 1927, p. 11M

WILLARD HUNTINGTON WRIGHT   Fashions in detectives have changed greatly during the past decade or so. Of late the inspired, intuitive, brilliantly logical super-sleuth of the late nineteenth century has given place to the conservative, plodding, hard working, routine investigator of the official police—the genius of Carlyle's definition, whose procedure is based largely on a transcendent capacity of taking trouble. And it must be said that this new thoroughgoing and unimaginative detective often has a distinct advantage, from the standpoint of literary interest, over the flashy intellectual detective of yore. He is more human, more plausible, and often achieves a more satisfactory solution of the criminal mysteries to which he is assigned. The reader may follow him as an equal, and share in his discoveries; and at all times a sense of reality, even of commonplace familiarity, may be maintained by the author—a sense which is too often vitiated by the inspirational methods of the older detective.

The most skilful exponent of this style of detective story is Freeman Wills Crofts. His *The Cask* and *The Ponson Case* are masterpieces of closely-wrought construction, and *The Groote Park Murder, Inspector French's Greatest Case* and *The Starvel Hollow Tragedy*, stand as the foremost representatives of their kind—as much as do the novels of Gaboriau and the Holmes series of Conan Doyle. Indeed, for sheer dexterity of plot Mr. Crofts has no peer among the contemporary writers of detective fiction. His chief device is the prepared alibi, and this he has explored with almost inexhaustible care, weaving it into his problem with an industry matched only by the amazing industry of his sleuths.

Willard Huntington Wright, "Introduction," *The Great Detective Stories: A Chronological Anthology* (New York: Charles Scribner's Sons, 1927), pp. 27–28

H. DOUGLAS THOMSON   The realist having made his bed has got to lie in it. Of a necessity it must ever be sagging, for all the time he must be in the know. A knowledge of medicine and chemistry was indispensable to him even in the days of Sherlock Holmes. He must besides be as familiar with police methods as Mr. Edgar Wallace. Like Miss Sayers he must have common law and legal procedure at his finger tips. All this knowledge emanates without any gushing from Mr. Crofts. He is a criminologist and a cryptologist. I imagine he is a close student of the technical press, and files of *Police Journals* and *Reviews* adorn his shelves. He can tell one all about banking and brokerage; customs and excise; distilling; motor engines; seacraft, and a hundred and one different subjects. He approximates to the old-fashioned sleuth on whose omniscience emphasis was so plaintively but so necessarily laid.

In short, there are few writers in whom one could find such a wealth of interesting detail. If one were to count up to a hundred technical details in a story of his, one would be hard put to it to find a single flaw. I have heard that legal and medical experts have sat in judgement on his novels, prior to their publication and have picked out at the most three or four possible, but by no means certain, errors.

The *pièce de résistance* of his realism is his characterisation of the detective, that is of Inspector French, for the Burnleys, the Tanners and the Willises are only other editions of this favourite. The Inspector French that frowns on one from the insets of the dust wrappers seems quite an ordinary young man, clean-shaven, sharp of feature, well groomed and neatly dressed—just such a young man, in fact, as might adorn an advertisement of Austin Reed's or Three Nuns Tobacco. In the Elysian Fields he will assuredly be prejudged a gate-crasher by Sherlock Holmes and the super-detectives. His private life can boast no quixotry, no aesthetic capers. Being an ordinary sort of chap, it did not surprise us to learn that he was married. ⟨. . .⟩

In the circumstances it was natural that Mr. Crofts should have had no use for "the superior amateur." His detective is the professional expert, the

C.I.D. man, caring more for the material guerdon of advancement and an increase of salary than the fulsome flattery of a neighbour. So far he remains on the force (although merely from the point of view of realism Mr. Crofts must have recently considered French's resignation). He is energetic, ambitious, but not infallible; deferential to his superiors, he recognises the guiding genius of Chief-Inspector Mitchell and the Big Four.

The Inspector's methods are a true reflection of the man. He worries things out and is always "up against it." He never jumps to a conclusion, and that is the great difference between him and the Father Browns and Hanauds. If one theory fails, he tries another. This point is of some importance; for it is tantamount to the laying of all cards on the table. The fairplay method inaugurated by the fragmentary "Mystery of Marie Rogêt," and both tentatively and temporarily adopted by various hands, has at last found its complete expression. The data are given. The detective's inferences are assembled in detail and from time to time a résumé is presented demonstrating the point reached in the investigation, and the points remaining to be solved; the cruxes, as it were, underlined, and the "leads" tabulated. This is something to be going on with. This is business.

H. Douglas Thomson, "Mr. Freeman Wills Crofts," *Masters of Mystery: A Study of the Detective Novel* (London: William Collins Sons & Co., 1931), pp. 181–83

FREEMAN WILLS CROFTS   My mental picture of him (Inspector French) is as a rather stoutish man of slightly below middle height, blue eyed, with a pleasant, comfortable, cheery expression, though still looking very wide awake. He would not wear uniform and would not be distinguishable in dress from any other civilian. His manner would be suave and pleasant, even kindly, partly because he has found that if he sets those that he is interrogating at their ease he will get more out of them. He would be dressed in an ordinary lounge suit, with overcoat if necessary, and probably a soft hat of the "Homberg" type. He probably would not have a stick nor gloves. He has no peculiarities of motion.

I have tried to make French an ordinary man, carrying out his work in an ordinary way. It seemed to me that there were enough "character" detectives, such as Colonel Gethryn, Philo Vance, Poirot, etc. Thus he has no special characteristics except being thorough, painstaking, persistent and a hard worker. He makes mistakes, but goes ahead in spite of them.

My favourite detective story writer is Austin Freeman. After him I like John Rhode, Dorothy Sayers, Agatha Christie, etc. My plots are purely imaginary.

> Freeman Wills Crofts, Letter to Dodd, Mead (19 December 1932), cited in James Keddie, Jr., "Freeman Wills Crofts," *Armchair Detective* 2, No. 3 (April 1969): 138

E. R. PUNSHON   Many will agree that the detective novel loses something of its own peculiar flavour and attractiveness when the interest of the problem posed and logically solved is too much subordinated to the excitement of swiftly successive incident. It may be the influence of the holiday season, the feeling that their books will be read in lazy mood by the sea or in quiet country resorts, that at the moment seems to have induced many writers to rely less upon the interest of following a train of reasoning and more upon the record of event.

Mr. Freeman Wills Crofts, however, is, as always, faithful to the problem, and in his new tale, *Found Floating,* offers one as difficult as any even he has ever conceived. The story is set in the framework of a Mediterranean cruise, of which so attractive an account is given that probably it would pay the steamship companies to present a copy of the book to every prospective client. Add to that a crime completely puzzling in manner and in motive, and once again Mr. Crofts can claim to have given full measure to the lover of the detective novel.

> E. R. Punshon, "New Crime Tales," *Manchester Guardian*, 13 August 1937, p. 5

HOWARD HAYCRAFT   The first of modern writers to find fictional possibilities in the step-by-step methods of actual police routine was Freeman Wills Crofts. In the opinion of a vast number of readers and critics he has never been equaled, much less surpassed, in his particular field. ⟨. . .⟩

"In 1919," he writes, "I had a long illness, with a slow recovery, and to while away the time I got pencil and exercise book and began to amuse myself by writing a story. It proved a splendid pastime and I did a lot of it before getting about again. Then I put it away, never dreaming that it would see the light of day, but a little later I re-read it, thought that something might be made of it, and began to alter and revise. Eventually . . . to my immense delight it was published."

This story, as every devotee knows by now, was that masterpiece of practical crime detection, *The Cask* (1920). Mr. Crofts will presumably not object if one hazards the statement that not even he has succeeded in topping this well-nigh perfect example of its kind. In its quietly documented thoroughness, it is one of those timeless stories that improve rather than lose by the test of re-reading—preferably with pocket-atlases and maps of pre-Hitler London and Paris by the reader's side. Its central theme has become the trade-mark of Mr. Crofts' work in the field: the painstaking demolition of the "unbreakable" alibi. In fact, it has become almost a truism that the one character in a Crofts story who could not *possibly* have committed the crime will in the end be shown to have done just that!

If *The Cask* has a flaw, it is its failure to introduce Inspector French, the modest, believable police hero of most of the author's later works. This difficulty was remedied, however, with the appearance of *Inspector French's Greatest Case* (1925), a volume worthy in almost every way to find its place on the shelf beside *The Cask*. Unfortunately, not so much can be said of quite all the later Crofts books, for in recent years some impatient readers claim to have noticed evidences of weariness in the methodical Inspector's adventurings. Others feel that his narrator occasionally becomes too greatly preoccupied with time-tables and menus to serve the best interests of fiction. These complaints, one fears, are at one and the same time justified and inherent in the factual method when it gets out of hand. The detective story may not be an "art form," but in common with all fiction it partakes of the axiom that art can reproduce life only by being *selective*. 〈. . .〉

Whatever he may or may not produce in the future, Freeman Wills Crofts' permanent place in the history of detective fiction is already more than secure.

Howard Haycraft, *Murder for Pleasure: The Life and Times of the Detective Story* (New York: D. Appleton-Century Co., 1941), pp. 122–24

COLIN WATSON   Less concerned to indulge the public's appetite for revelation of how the wealthy lived, ex-engineer Freeman Wills Crofts was one of the few mystery writers of the period who told their stories in terms of routine police investigation. His Inspector French was a plodder, but an observant one. We learn from him that the household of a small London merchant of limited means consisted of father and daughter, two maids, a cook and a chauffeur, all living in a medium-sized house with furniture that had been good but now (in 1924) was shabby. In an apartment in St John's Wood, French found heavy, expensive furniture and fittings; good silk dresses; a carpet worth at least £120; and a half-empty box of Corona Coronas. Several well-bound 'standard works' were in a bookcase in the smoking room but only for decoration. In the sitting-room were several of 'the lighter type of novels, together with a number of French and Spanish with extremely lurid and compromising jackets'. The occupants' income, judged the inspector, would be between two and three thousand a year.

> Colin Watson, *Snobbery with Violence: Crime Stories and Their Audience* (New York: St. Martin's Press, 1971), p. 209

ERIK ROUTLEY   He was as regular and industrious in his methods as Trollope, and scrupulously fair in his laying of clues. He was ruthless in disposing of his murderers, who were never in any circumstances attractive or deserving of the reader's sympathy. Their motives were sometimes passionate, but far more often associated with greed, a vice peculiarly hated by puritans. There is no levity in his work. It is all sober, systematic slogging. And that is why he is the creator of the first great policeman in the business. ⟨. . .⟩

As a professional railwayman, Crofts was naturally the most eminent of railway-minded detective writers, and his timetables are one of the most conspicuous features of his stories. There is nothing sedentary about any of his policemen, who are never happier than when they are dashing about the country or the continent of Europe, always by train. Trains, symbol of the counterpoint between authority and adventure, appeal naturally to the puritan temperament of enterprise and moral rigour (I am told that in any railway society two of the best represented professions are likely to be low-church clergy and church organists).

⟨. . .⟩ There is no high life, apart from high business life, in Crofts. 'He was hanged on the 14th' is a perfectly possible final line in a Crofts short story. His accounts are unsensational enough to have pleased Holmes himself. And there, just as much as in Noël Coward, you see the spluttering bravura of the twenties. Coward is all style and champagne; Crofts is all no-nonsense moralism. It's all, to jaded eyes of the present, too good to be true, but in its way it's good all the same.

The Cask was a new kind of sober masterpiece, one of the finest first novels in detective history. Inspector French did not appear until 1925, in *Inspector French's Greatest Case*, which was quickly followed by *The Cheyne Mystery* (1926) and *The Starvel Tragedy* (1927). If you want the best example of the technique of arousing and holding a reader's interest in a specialised work-situation, worthy to stand alongside the best middle-period Sayers, it would be in *Death of a Train* (1946), one of his last books. Crofts found his length at once and held it. He knew just how to work within his limitations. He set many of his scenes in London or near the town where he lived (Guildford). With him you get moral relaxation in an ethical armchair that will never let you down, and a celebration of ordinariness that supplies adventure without any reference to Ruritania.

> Erik Routley, *The Puritan Pleasures of the Detective Story* (London: Victor Gollancz, 1972), pp. 124–27

JULIAN SYMONS   The plan of the house indicating where the body was found, the map of the grounds showing the garden and the summer-house, were standard accessories to the story of the period, and in many British books a timetable appeared too. This timetable, often of a railway or bus journey, was offered in preparation for the breaking of an alibi, and it was used in greatest detail and most often by Freeman Wills Crofts, who put his knowledge as a railway engineer to frequent although hardly varied use. In a Crofts story the murderer can often be identified at an early point by his apparently unbreakable alibi, which is duly broken by dogged Inspector (later Superintendent) French. Crofts's first book, *The Cask* (1920), which traces back in elaborate detail the way in which a cask came to contain gold coins and a woman's hand instead of a piece of statuary, has a grip and cleverness that he never quite repeated. His plotting became increasingly mechanical, particularly after the appearance in his fifth book of the plodding French. Crofts knew nothing about Scotland Yard, and did not feel it important that he should learn the details of police procedure, perhaps thinking that a detailed knowledge of railway timetables was enough. He succeeded so well in making his detective commonplace (in fact police detectives are markedly colourful characters) that he became uninteresting. *The Loss of the Jane Vosper* (1936) is one of the best French stories, showing Crofts's care in getting a background right, and his surprising ability to write scenes of action. *Inspector French's Greatest Case* (1925) can also be recommended.

Julian Symons, Bloody Murder: From the Detective Story to the Crime Novel: A History (1972; rev. ed. Harmondsworth, UK: Penguin, 1985), pp. 103–4

T. J. BINYON   For the first serious, professional police detective it was necessary to wait until 1920, when Freeman Wills Crofts made his début with *The Cask,* in which Inspector Burnley investigates the murder of a young Frenchwoman whose body has been discovered at London Docks in a cask supposedly containing statuary. The book is a milestone in the history of the detective novel. Although it retained some of the melodramatic qualities of its predecessors—of which Crofts was gradually to rid himself— at the same time it took over and developed the best qualities of Gaboriau. Crofts's policeman is the antithesis of the great detective; he has no Watson to astound with brilliant deductions, nor does he keep his ratiocinations concealed from the reader. His detection is solid, plodding, and logical, with an almost fanatical devotion to detail. The reader is privy to every step in the slow—at times almost agonizing—construction of a theory of the crime until the final solution is triumphantly reached. Crofts was a Northern Irishman who worked for the Belfast and Northern Counties Railway, rising to the position of chief assistant engineer; but in 1929 he resigned to become a full-time writer. It is not surprising, therefore, not only that some of his books should have a North of Ireland setting, but also that the plots of many of them turn on railway technicalities. Just as John Dickson Carr specialized in the locked-room mystery, so Crofts specializes in the unbreakable alibi, often built up, with virtuosity and imagination, from the railway timetable. His plots are put together with the care and precision of an engineer: indeed, Raymond Chandler has called him 'the soundest builder of them all'. His weaknesses are a certain predictability, in that it is often possible to identify the criminal early on as the suspect with the best alibi; an occasional dullness in narration; and a style which serves as a means of communication, but little else. After *The Cask* Crofts wrote three novels, *The Ponson Case* (1921), *The Pit-Prop Syndicate* (1922), and

The Groote Park Murder (1924), in each of which the detective is a different policeman. With his next novel, challengingly entitled *Inspector French's Greatest Case* (1925), however, he created his series detective, whom he went on to employ in nearly thirty novels and a number of short stories. Inspector Joseph French is stout, below middle height, with a clean-shaven, good-humoured face and dark blue eyes. Known behind his back at the Yard as 'Soapy Joe' because of the way he relies on the suavity of his manners, he is happily married, and often turns to his wife, Emily, for advice when he reaches a difficult stage in a case. He is fond of good food—his meals are often described in detail—and enjoys travel, whether on holiday or on duty. In fact, he differs from Crofts's earlier detectives only in that he is described more fully and given a home background; as far as method of detection goes, Crofts's policemen are indistinguishable from one another. They are all alike in other respects too: solid, bourgeois *fonctionnaires* who have come up through the ranks of the police force and have no pretensions to be other than they are. Nor is there the slightest hint that Crofts feels ill at ease in their company.

T. J. Binyon, *"Murder Will Out": The Detective in Fiction* (Oxford: Oxford University Press, 1989), pp. 82–83.

◈ Bibliography

The Cask. 1920.

The Ponson Case. 1921.

The Pit-Prop Syndicate. 1922.

The Groote Park Murder. 1924.

Inspector French's Greatest Case. 1925.

Inspector French and the Cheyne Mystery. 1926.

Inspector French and the Starvel Tragedy. 1927.

The Sea Mystery. 1928.

Inspector French's Case Book ⟨*Inspector French's Greatest Case, Inspector French and the Cheyne Mystery, Inspector French and the Starvel Tragedy*⟩. 1928.

The Box Office Murders ⟨*The Purple Sickle Murders*⟩. 1929.

Bann and Lough Neagh Drainage. 1930.

Sir John Magill's Last Journey. 1930.

Mystery in the Channel. 1931.

Sudden Death. 1932.

Death on the Way (Double Death). 1932.

The Freeman Wills Crofts Omnibus (The Cask, The Groote Park Murder, The
            Pit-Prop Syndicate, The Ponson Case). 1932.

The Hog's Back Mystery (The Strange Case of Dr. Earle). 1933.

The 12.30 from Croydon (Wilful and Premeditated). 1934.

Mystery on Southampton Water (Crime on the Solent). 1934.

Crime at Guildford (The Crime at Nornes). 1935.

The Loss of the "Jane Vosper." 1936.

Man Overboard! 1936.

Found Floating. 1937.

The End of Andrew Harrison (The Futile Alibi). 1938.

Antidote to Venom. 1938.

Fatal Venture (Tragedy in the Hollow). 1939.

Golden Ashes. 1940.

James Tarrant, Adventurer (Circumstantial Evidence). 1941.

A Losing Game. 1941.

Fear Comes to Chalfont. 1942.

The Hunt Ball Murder. 1943.

The Affair at Little Wokeham (Double Tragedy). 1943.

Mr. Sefton, Murderer. 1944.

Enemy Unseen. 1945.

Death of a Train. 1946.

Murderers Make Mistakes. 1947.

Young Robin Brand, Detective. 1947.

Silence for the Murderer. 1948.

The Four Gospels in One Story. 1949.

Dark Journey (French Strikes Oil). 1951.

Many a Slip. 1955.

The Mystery of the Sleeping Car Express and Other Stories. 1956.

Anything to Declare? 1957.

Sir Arthur Conan Doyle
1859–1930

ARTHUR CONAN DOYLE was born on May 22, 1859, in Edinburgh. He was educated at Hodder and Stonyhurst Academies and the University of Edinburgh, where he studied medicine. In 1880–81 he traveled to the Arctic and to West Africa as a ship's surgeon. He began a medical practice the next year at Southsea. In 1885 he married Louise Hawkins; they had two children.

Doyle had begun writing while in medical school in the 1870s, but took to it in earnest during the early years of his medical practice, when he had few patients. In 1891 he was able to abandon medicine for full-time writing because of the popularity of his Sherlock Holmes tales. In 1894 Doyle made an extensive lecture tour of the United States, and he also visited Switzerland and Egypt in an attempt to relieve his wife's tuberculosis. He attempted to enlist for combat duty in the Boer War in 1899, but was rejected because of his age; he instead served as a medical officer and also wrote several books about the conflict. In 1902, largely in recognition of his services in defending England's role in the war, he was knighted.

Doyle admitted that he had based the figure of Sherlock Holmes on Dr. Joseph Bell, one of his teachers in medical school. The Sherlock Holmes saga had begun in 1887 with the short novel *A Study in Scarlet* in *Beeton's Christmas Annual* (published as a book the following year) and attained immediate popularity. Many subsequent tales were published in the *Strand*, with distinctive illustrations by Sidney Paget, and were eventually collected in five volumes of short stories (*The Adventures of Sherlock Holmes*, 1892; *The Memoirs of Sherlock Holmes*, 1894; *The Return of Sherlock Holmes*, 1905; *His Last Bow*, 1917; *The Case-Book of Sherlock Holmes*, 1927) and three additional novels (*The Sign of Four*, 1890; *The Hound of the Baskervilles*, 1902; *The Valley of Fear*, 1915). Doyle, having wearied of Holmes, had killed him off in the final story of the *Memoirs*, but public outrage forced him to bring Holmes back to life for further adventures. As Poe had done with "The Mystery of Marie Rogêt," Doyle employed the ratiocinative methods he attributed to his detective in solving two real cases—those of George Edalji and Oscar Slater, both of which he wrote up in articles and books.

Doyle, however, considered his most serious work to be his historical novels, beginning with *Micah Clarke* (1889) and continuing with *The White Company* (1891), *Sir Nigel* (1906), and others. Doyle conducted scrupulous historical research in the writing of these novels. He also achieved popularity with a series of works involving an eccentric scientist, Professor Challenger: the short novels *The Lost World* (1912), *The Poison Belt* (1913), and *The Land of Mist* (1926), and some short stories. He wrote many other short stories of sport, medicine, the supernatural (including the celebrated "Lot No. 249"), and adventure.

Louise Doyle, who had been an invalid during the last decade of her life, died in 1906. Doyle had since 1897 maintained a platonic relationship with Jean Leckie, and married her in 1907; they had three children. Early in World War I Doyle was sent by the government to Italy on a mission, and throughout the war he wrote a history of the conflict, ultimately published in six volumes.

The horrors of the war turned Doyle from an agnostic into a spiritualist, and he began vigorously preaching the cause on tours throughout the world. He joined the Society for Psychical Research, established the Psychic Bookshop in London, and held séances in the homes of various illustrious people. He persisted in this interest in spite of the considerable amount of ridicule he suffered as a result of it. Sir Arthur Conan Doyle died on July 7, 1930.

The Sherlock Holmes tales are among the most widely imitated and parodied works in literary history. They definitively set the pattern for the idiosyncratic amateur detective, influencing almost every subsequent work of detective fiction up to the present day. The tales have been extensively dramatized and adapted for radio, film, and television. The early play *Sherlock Holmes* (produced 1899; published 1922) has been considered a collaboration between Doyle and William Gillette, but, although based on a now lost play by Doyle, it appears to have been entirely the work of Gillette.

◈ *Critical Extracts*

RONALD A. KNOX   Any studies in Sherlock Holmes must be, first and foremost, studies in Dr. Watson. Let us treat at once of the literary and bibliographical aspect of the question. First, as to authenticity. There are several grave inconsistencies in the Holmes cycle. For example the *Study in Scarlet* and the *Reminiscences* are from the hand of John H. Watson, M.D., but in the story of the 'Man with the Twisted Lip,' Mrs. Watson addresses her husband as James. The present writer, together with three brothers, wrote to ask Sir Arthur Conan Doyle for an explanation, appending their names in the proper style with crosses after them, and an indication that this was the sign of the Four. The answer was that it was an error, an error, in fact, of editing. 'Nihil aliud hic latet,' says the great Sauwosch, 'nisi redactor ignorantissimus.' Yet this error gave the original impetus to Backnecke's theory of the Deutero-Watson, to whom he assigns the *Study in Scarlet*, the 'Gloria Scott,' and the *Return of Sherlock Holmes*. He leaves to the proto-Watson the rest of the Memoirs, the *Sign of Four* and the *Hound of the Baskervilles*. He disputed the *Study in Scarlet* on other grounds, the statement in it, for example, that Holmes's knowledge of literature and philosophy was nil, whereas it was clear that the true Holmes was a man of wide reading and deep thought. ⟨. . .⟩

The 'Gloria Scott' condemned by Backnecke partly on the ground of the statement that Holmes was only up for two years at College, while he speaks in the 'Musgrave Ritual' of 'my last years' at the University; which Backnecke supposes to prove that the two stories do not come from the same hand. The 'Gloria Scott' further represents Percy Trevor's bull-dog as having bitten Holmes on his way down to Chapel, which is clearly untrue, since dogs are not allowed within the gates at either university. 'The bull-dog is more at home' he adds 'on the Chapel steps, than this fraudulent imitation among the divine products of the Watsons-genius.'

Ronald A. Knox, "Studies in the Literature of Sherlock Holmes" (1912), *Essays in Satire* (New York: E. P. Dutton, 1930), pp. 147–49

SIR ARTHUR CONAN DOYLE   People have often asked me whether I knew the end of a Holmes story before I started it. Of course I do. One could not possibly steer a course if one did not know one's destination. The first thing is to get your idea. Having got that key idea one's next task is to conceal it and lay emphasis upon everything which can make for a different explanation. Holmes, however, can see all the fallacies of the alternatives, and arrives more or less dramatically at the true solution by steps which he can describe and justify. He shows his powers by what the South Americans now call "Sherlockholmitos," which means clever little deductions which often have nothing to do with the matter at hand, but impress the reader with a general sense of power. ⟨. . .⟩

Sometimes I have got upon dangerous ground where I have taken risks through my own want of knowledge of the correct atmosphere. I have, for example, never been a racing man, and yet I ventured to write "Silver Blaze," in which the mystery depends upon the laws of training and racing. The story is all right, and Holmes may have been at the top of his form, but my ignorance cries aloud to heaven. I read an excellent and very damaging criticism of the story in some sporting paper, written clearly by a man who *did* know, in which he explained the exact penalties which would have come upon every one concerned if they had acted as I described. Half would have been in jail and the other half warned off the turf for ever. However, I have never been nervous about details, and one must be masterful sometimes. When an alarmed Editor wrote to me once: "There is no second line of rails at that point," I answered, "I make one."

Sir Arthur Conan Doyle, "Sidelights on Sherlock Holmes," *Memories and Adventures*
(Boston: Little, Brown, 1924), pp. 101–3

CHRISTOPHER MORLEY   The whole Sherlock Holmes saga is a triumphant illustration of art's supremacy over life. Perhaps no fiction character ever created has become so charmingly real to his readers. It is not that we take our blessed Sherlock too seriously; if we really want the painful oddities of criminology let us go to Bataille or Roughead. But Holmes is pure anesthesia. We read the stories again and again; perhaps most of all for the little introductory interiors which give a glimpse of 221B Baker Street. The fact that Holmes had earlier lodgings in Montague Street (alongside the British Museum) is forgotten. That was before Watson, and we must have Watson too. Rashly, in the later years, Holmes twice undertook to write stories for himself. They have not quite the same magic. No, we are epicures. We must begin in Baker Street; and best of all, if possible, let it be a stormy winter morning when Holmes routs Watson out of bed in haste. The doctor wakes to see that tall ascetic figure by the bedside with a candle. "Come, Watson, come! The game is afoot!" If that is not possible, then I prefer to find Holmes stretched on the sofa in a fit of the dumps; perhaps he is scraping on the violin, or bemoaning the dearth of imaginative crime and reaching for the cocaine (a habit he evidently outgrew, for we hear little of it in the later adventures). We have a glimpse of the sitting-room, that room we know so well. There are the great volumes of scrapbook records; the bullet marks on the walls; the mysterious "gasogene" which appears occasionally in English fiction and which I can only suppose to be some sort of syphon-bottle. (There is also a sort of decanter-holder called a "tantalus" now and then set out on the sideboard; another mystery for American readers, and now more than ever true to its name.) The Persian slipper for tobacco and the coal-scuttle for cigars don't appeal to me so much. They are more conscious eccentricities. In comes Mrs. Hudson with a message, or a "commissionaire" with a letter, and we are off. Gregson and Lestrade will get the credit, but we have the fun. Already we are in a hansom rattling through the streets to Waterloo or Charing Cross or Paddington. (Holmes rarely takes train at Euston or King's Cross or Liverpool Street.)

It is a kind of piety for even the least and humblest of Holmes-lovers to pay what tribute he may to this great encyclopaedia of romance that has given the world so much innocent pleasure. Already the grandchildren of Holmes's earliest followers are beginning upon him with equal delight. I was too young to know the wave of dismay that went round the English-reading world when Sherlock and Professor Moriarty supposedly perished together in the Reichenbach Fall, but I can well remember the sombre effect on my ten-year-old spirits when I first read the closing paragraphs of the Memoirs. The intolerable pathos of the cigarette-case on the rocky ledge; the firm clear handwriting of that last stoic message!

Christopher Morley, "In Memoriam: Sherlock Holmes," *The Complete Sherlock Holmes* by Sir Arthur Conan Doyle (New York: Literary Guild, 1936), pp. viii–ix

---

EDMUND WILSON   I will now confess ⟨. . .⟩ that, since my first looking into this subject last fall, I have myself become addicted, in spells, to reading myself to sleep with Sherlock Holmes, which I had gone back to, not having looked at it since childhood, in order to see how it compared with Conan Doyle's latest imitators. I propose, however, to justify my pleasure in rereading Sherlock Holmes on grounds entirely different from those on which the consumers of the current product ordinarily defend their taste. My contention is that Sherlock Holmes *is* literature on a humble but not ignoble level, whereas the mystery writers most in vogue now are not. The old stories are literature, not because of the conjuring tricks and the puzzles, not because of the lively melodrama, which they have in common with many other detective stories, but by virtue of imagination and style. These are fairy-tales, as Conan Doyle intimated in his preface to his last collection, and they are among the most amusing of fairy-tales and not among the least distinguished. ⟨. . .⟩

The writing, of course, is full of clichés, but these clichés are dealt out with a ring which gives them a kind of value, while the author makes speed and saves space so effectively that we are rarely in danger of getting bogged down in anything boring. And the clichés of situation and character are somehow made to function, too, for the success of the general effect. This effect owes its real originality not only to the queer collocation of elements ⟨. . .⟩ but also to the admirable settings: the somber overcarpeted interiors or the musty empty houses of London, the remote old or new country places, always with shrubbery along the drives; and the characters—the choleric big-game hunters and the high-spirited noble ladies—have been imbued with the atmosphere of the settings and charged with an energy sufficient—like the fierce puppets of a Punch-and-Judy show—to make an impression in their simple roles. ⟨. . .⟩

And it all takes place in ⟨. . .⟩ that atmosphere of "cozy peril," to quote a phrase from, I think, Mr. Morley, who, in his prefaces to the Sherlock Holmes omnibus and an anthology called *Sherlock Holmes and Dr. Watson*, has written so well on this subject. They will, of course, get safely back to Baker Street, after their vigils and raids and arrests, to discuss the case comfortably in their rooms and have their landlady bring them breakfast the next morning. Law and Order have not tottered a moment; the British police are well in control: they are the stoutest, most faithful fellows in the world if they can only be properly directed by Intellect in the form of a romantic personality possessed by the scientific spirit. All the loose ends of every episode are tidily picked up and tucked in, and even Holmes, though once addicted to cocaine, has been reformed by the excellent Watson. In this world, one can count on the client to arrive at the very moment when his case has just been explained, and Holmes and Watson always find it possible to get anywhere they want to go without a moment's delay or confusion.

Edmund Wilson, " 'Mr. Holmes, They Were the Footprints of a Gigantic Hound!' " (1945), *Classics and Commercials: A Literary Chronicle of the Forties* (New York: Farrar, Straus, 1950), pp. 267, 270–73

HESKETH PEARSON   It almost seems as if ⟨Doyle⟩ wrote history with the pen of Holmes, who preferred a scientific treatise to an exciting story; but he chronicled Holmes with the pen of Watson, who preferred an exciting story to a scientific treatise.

> So please grip this fact with your cerebral tentacle,
> The doll and its maker are never identical,

wrote Doyle to a critic who had suggested that Holmes's views on Poe's Dupin were those of his creator. We must be careful not to make the same error by assuming that Dr. Watson was Dr. Doyle. Nevertheless there was enough of Doyle in Watson to make it unnecessary for us to look further for a model. He frequently and unconsciously pictured himself in the character. "Your fatal habit of looking at everything from the point of view of a story instead of as a scientific exercise has ruined what might have been an instructive and even classical series of demonstrations," says Holmes to Watson, and it emphasizes what we have just been saying. Doyle was a born story-teller, and whenever he sacrifices action for accuracy his hold on the reader's attention weakens. Again Doyle was thinking of himself when he makes Holmes tell Watson: "You will realize that among your many talents dissimulation finds no place." Yet again: "My dear Watson, you were born to be a man of action. Your instinct is always to do something energetic." And when, in the adventure of "The Abbey Grange," Holmes decides to let the murderer off, he clinches our Watson-Doyle identification: "Watson, you are a British jury, and I never met a man who was more eminently fitted to represent one," which gives us Doyle's nature in a sentence.

The notion of writing a series of short stories round the character of Holmes came to Doyle when he read the monthly magazines that were then beginning to cater to the train-traveling public. "Considering these various journals with their disconnected stories, it had struck me that a single character running through a series, if it only engaged the attention of the reader, would bind that reader to that particular magazine. On the other hand, it had long seemed to me that the ordinary serial might be an impediment rather than a help to a magazine, since, sooner or later, one missed one number and afterwards it had lost all interest. Clearly the ideal compromise was a character which carried through, and yet instalments which were complete in themselves, so that the purchaser was always sure that he could relish the whole contents of the magazine. I believe that I was the first to realize this and *The Strand Magazine* the first to put it into practice." His agent, A. P. Watt, sent "A Scandal in Bohemia" to the editor of *The Strand*, Greenborough Smith, who liked it and encouraged Doyle to go ahead with the series. As he was uninterrupted by the arrival of a single patient throughout the whole of his time as an eye specialist, he spent his days writing, from ten in the morning till four in the afternoon. "My rooms in Devonshire Place," said he, "consisted of a waiting-room and a consulting-room, where I waited in the consulting-room and no one waited in the waiting-room."

Hesketh Pearson, Conan Doyle (New York: Walker & Co., 1961), pp. 127–29

DONALD J. WATT   The structure of *The Hound of the Baskervilles* is a tripartite one which stems from Doyle's use of Watson as a foil as well as a companion for Holmes. Doyle's uses of Watson in the Holmes repertoire ⟨. . .⟩ need not concern us here. What does concern us, though, is the fact that Doyle establishes Watson's position at the outset of the book and, at the same time, anticipates the overriding form of his presentation. In the opening chapter of the story Doyle, with typical economy, sets up the contrast between Holmes and Watson. Examining the stick left behind by Mortimer, Holmes invites Watson to deduce what he can about its owner. Holmes then proceeds to deflate Watson by extending and adjusting his inferences in a set of remarkable observations. Holmes's analysis is corroborated shortly by the appearance of Mortimer, at the end of the chapter, to seek assistance in the Baskerville mystery.

Doyle's first chapter thereby anticipates the process of the entire novel. Chapters 1–5 introduce the subject of the investigation (the mystery of Baskerville Hall); Chapters 6–11 bring Watson to Devonshire to learn what he can of the mystery; and Chapters 12–15 find Holmes on the scene to hone the truth out of Watson's uneven judgment of the case and to bring about his own unerring solution. In this sense, then, Doyle's first chapter

gives us a miniature mystery—the mystery of Mortimer's cane—which is a
microscopic reflection of the process he uses in resolving the far larger issue,
the mystery of Baskerville Hall.

Yet Doyle's structure is more subtle than this. Having impressed the
reader by Holmes's ability with the cane, Doyle must now suggest the prowess
of his opponent. Doyle accomplishes this in the first third of the book,
especially in Chapters 4 and 5, by creating another mystery, the mystery of
the stranger in London, which Holmes *fails* to solve. Holmes realises that
someone is following Sir Henry and attempts to discover the tracker's identity. He tries to pursue three lines or threads, three leads—the possibility
that the bearded man is Barrymore, Cartwright's search of London hotels
for cut sheets of *The Times*, and John Clayton's description of his spying
fare. Doyle concludes his chapter on "Three Broken Threads" with Holmes's
tribute to "a foeman who is worthy of our steel" and with his apprehensions
about sending Watson into a thoroughly dangerous situation in Devonshire.
Hence the first major structural division of Doyle's book gives us two mysteries which serve together as an introduction for the third, the generating
mystery of the tale.

> Donald J. Watt, "The Literary Craft of *The Hound of the Baskervilles*" (1972), *Sherlock
> Holmes by Gas-Lamp*, ed. Philip A. Shreffler (New York: Fordham University Press,
> 1989), pp. 194–95

SAMUEL ROSENBERG   In "The Man with the Twisted Lip,"
written shortly after "The Red-Headed League," we find that the compulsive
Conan Doyle has written a part for himself that is far from comic. This
time he is Neville St. Clair, the man with the twisted lip.

A former actor and expert of disguise (Doyle loved to wear disguises to
fool his friends), St. Clair, again like Doyle, is a writer. When his editor
assigns him to investigate London's beggars, St. Clair disguises himself as a
"crippled wretch of hideous aspect," complete with deep scars that twist
his lip, and finds that as a beggar he can easily earn more in a single day
than in a week of hard work as a serious writer.

Later, when he desperately needs £25 to pay an unrelenting creditor, he
"takes a holiday from work," resumes his begging, and in ten days earns the
needed £25. (Doyle left his work as doctor and serious writer to write *A
Study in Scarlet* for which he received exactly £25. When he asked, hat-in-

hand, for more money, he was turned down. Even the "ten days" is taken by Doyle from his own experience. Hesketh Pearson informs us that the average time required by Doyle, a prodigiously fast writer, for his £30 Sherlock Holmes stories was ten days.)

Then, like the real-life Doyle and the fictional Jabez Wilson, Neville St. Clair abandons his respected £2-a-week profession to lead a secret double life. During the day he is Hugh Boone, the loathsome crippled beggar who earns a yearly £700 or $3500, about $25,000 equivalent in modern value. At night, after removing his disguises in his dressing room in an "opium den," he entrains for a suburb where he is once again Neville St. Clair, a respected "investor in various companies." Confident in his deception, he marries the daughter of a prominent brewer, becomes the father of two children and continues to lead his double life for many years.

But one day when his wife is in London she accidentally sees St. Clair in the second-story window (symbolic place) of the opium den. He sees her too and makes agitated motions that lead her to assume he is the victim of foul play. She runs off and finds some constables, who enter the "dressing room" and find Hugh Boone, the beggar, but no trace of Neville St. Clair. When they find St. Clair's clothes (which he has thrown) in the Thames, they assume that the "beggar" killed St. Clair and threw him and his clothes into the water. (This is a forecast of the later struggle between two other Doylean doppelganger characters, which ended with their presumed death in the waters of Reichenbach Falls.)

When he is first hired by Mrs. St. Clair, Sherlock Holmes is baffled by this mystery. But soon his near-clairvoyant brain sorts things out. He goes to the jail, washes the grimy face of Hugh Boone with a large wet sponge, and reveals the missing St. Clair. When it becomes clear that no legal crime has been committed and that it would be best for the now-penitent St. Clair and his family if his story remained secret, Holmes uses his influence with the police and helps the man to give up his life as a beggar. (I wonder: Did he ever get back his £2-a-week job on the newspaper?)

We may deduce from this story—and the preceding "The Red-Headed League"—that Neville St. Clair is a projection of the self-flagellating Conan Doyle who is saying, in effect, "As a doctor and literary pretender I have earned practically nothing. But as a literary beggar who exploits the emotions of the passing throng, I have become respected and prosperous. I am no better than a beggar who abandons his station in life for the pennies thrown to him."

Here, as in every other Sherlock Holmes story, we find an internecine struggle (psychomachy) between two personified fractions of Doyle's imagination. One denizen of Doyle's "inner room" emerges to perpetrate a fraud against himself, his family, and society; but once again Doyle's relentless superego, Sherlock Holmes, exposes the imaginational alter ego of Conan Doyle and forces him to return to respectability.

> Samuel Rosenberg, *Naked Is the Best Disguise: The Death and Resurrection of Sherlock Holmes* (Indianapolis: Bobbs-Merrill, 1974), pp. 147–48

ALVIN E. RODIN and JACK D. KEY   More pertinent to the medical orientation of this book is the individual who served as the model for Sherlock Holmes. The front-ranker for this honor is Doctor Joseph Bell, Edinburgh surgeon and teacher of the student Conan Doyle, to whom Conan Doyle dedicated *The Adventures of Sherlock Holmes*. The evidence is quite clear, being provided by Conan Doyle himself in his autobiography of 1924.

> I thought of my old teacher, Joe Bell, of his eagle face, of his curious ways, of his eerie trick of spotting details. If he were a detective he would surely reduce this fascinating but unorganized business to something nearer to an exact science. . . . It is all very well to say that a man is clever, but the reader wants to see examples of it—such examples as Bell gave us every day in the wards.

He made a similar acknowledgement much earlier, during an interview in 1892. "The remarkable individuality and discriminating tact of my old master (Bell) made a deep and lasting impression on me, though I had not the faintest idea that it would one day lead me to forsake medicine for story writing."

A fellow student of Conan Doyle's, Doctor H. E. Jones, wrote in 1904 a similar account of Joseph Bell's acuity, and labeled him "the king of deduction." He also suggested that Conan Doyle's adaptation of Bell's skill to crime detection was influenced by another one of his professors. Sir Henry Littlejohn was Lecturer on Forensic Medicine and the City of Edinburgh Police Surgeon. Students flocked to murder trials at which he gave evidence.

In 1927, Conan Doyle provided additional insight into the genesis of his detective in a filmed interview.

It often annoyed me how in the old fashioned detective stories, the detective always seemed to get at his results by some sort of lucky chance or fluke or else it was quite unexplained how he got there. . . . I began to think about this and . . . of turning scientific methods . . . onto the work of detection. . . . I used as a student [to] have an old professor whose name was Bell who was extraordinarily quick at deductive work.

This is further evidence that Sherlock Holmes owes his creation to the medical training of Conan Doyle, and his overwhelming success, in part, to the author's medical knowledge.

Alvin E. Rodin and Jack D. Key, *Medical Casebook of Doctor Arthur Conan Doyle: From Practitioner to Sherlock Holmes and Beyond* (Malabar, FL: Robert E. Krieger Publishing Co., 1984), pp. 199–200

CHRISTOPHER CLAUSEN   Whether Holmes's methods and results in his detecting career really satisfy scientific standards of rigor is another question entirely. It has often been pointed out that many of his deductions are far from airtight. Although he frequently denounces guesswork, at times he seems alarmingly dependent on lucky intuitions. In one case, "The Musgrave Ritual," his solution depends on the assumption that an elm and an oak have not grown at all in two hundred and fifty years; but then, we have already been told that his knowledge of botany is variable. It would be possible to pick many holes in both his methods and his conclusions. The important point, however, is that he is conceived— and conceives of himself—as a man who applies scientific methods to the detection of crime, and that his success as a detective is due to those methods. He uses them more convincingly than most other fictional detectives, and he hews to them with a religious intensity. His reaction to Watson's first account of his exploits is not merely in character but deeply revealing: "Honestly, I cannot congratulate you upon it. Detection is, or ought to be, an exact science and should be treated in the same cold and unemotional manner. You have attempted to tinge it with romanticism, which produces much the same effect as if you worked a love-story or an elopement into the fifth proposition of Euclid." Like many other nineteenth-century enthusiasts, Holmes thinks of science as a purifying discipline whose chief goal is the clearing away of mysteries. The difference lies in the particular mysteries to which he applies it—and, perhaps, in the utter single-mindedness with which he devotes himself to his vocation. Tennyson's King Arthur was not the only kind of Victorian protagonist who represented "soul at war with sense."

Anyone who carries reason this far is bound to be rather solitary. In the second novel, *The Sign of Four* (1890), from which the above passage is quoted, we begin to see some of the sacrifices that Holmes has made in the pursuit of detachment, for it is in this story that Watson finds a wife. After what we have come to recognize as a typically brilliant series of deductions, Holmes is told of his collaborator's impending defection from Baker Street. "I feared as much," he responds. "I really cannot congratulate you." When Watson wishes to know whether he disapproves of the young woman, Holmes declares that, on the contrary, she is brilliant and charming. "But love is an emotional thing," he adds, "and whatever is emotional is opposed to that true cold reason which I place above all things. I should never marry myself, lest I bias my judgment." The price of his commitment is lifelong isolation and loneliness, and while these states are frequently mitigated by Watson himself (whose wife soon disappears) and by success and fame, they never cease to be the essential conditions of Holmes's existence. At the end of *The Sign of Four*, fame is in the future and Watson is about to disappear. Credit for the case having gone to the police, Watson wonders "what remains for you?" The answer, which ends the novel, is genuinely tragic: " 'For me,' said Sherlock Holmes, 'there still remains the cocaine-bottle.' And he stretched his long white hand up for it."

Christopher Clausen, "Sherlock Holmes, Order, and the Late-Victorian Mind," *The Moral Imagination: Essays on Literature and Ethics* (Iowa City: University of Iowa Press, 1986), pp. 57–59

APPLEWHITE MINYARD ⟨. . .⟩ from the start the detective stories were linked with Doyle's involvement in Spiritualism. When he was first attempting to establish himself as a medical doctor, one of his patients, General Drayson, was a believer in Spiritualism, and Doyle attended several séances at his home, eventually publishing his observances in the psychic journal *Light* in 1887, the same year that the first Holmes story appeared in *Beeton's Christmas Annual*.

Only once did Holmes directly address the issue of religion in the tales. In "The Naval Treaty" he said, "Nowhere is deduction so necessary as in religion. It can be built up as an exact science by the ideal reasoner." Doyle echoed nearly an identical sentiment in his *History of Spiritualism* when he said, "It [Spiritualism] founds our belief in life after death not upon ancient tradition or upon vague intuitions, but upon proven facts, so that a science of religion may be built up." ⟨. . .⟩

To unravel the moral and religious outlook of the great detective, it is necessary to look at what he actually said and relate that to Doyle's own statements. Holmes once recommended Winwood Reade's *The Martyrdom of Man* as "one of the most remarkable [books] ever penned." One of Reade's main premises in that book was that the destruction of Christianity and belief in a personal God were essential to the progress of man. This book had affected Doyle deeply when he read it and reinforced some of his own beliefs about the failure of organized religions to meet the moral and spiritual needs of rational men and women.

However, although Doyle decried orthodox religion, he never gave up on the idea of God. And there is also evidence in the Canon that Holmes believed in a supreme being. For example, in *The Stark Munro Letters*, a semi-autobiographical novel Doyle wrote in 1895, through the persona of Munro, Doyle said, "Nature is the true revelation of the Deity to man." And in his own autobiography, he made a nearly parallel statement when he said, "I had a very keen perception of the wonderful poise of the universe and the tremendous power and sustenance it implied." And Holmes said, in "The Cardboard Box," "It must tend to some end, or else our universe is ruled by chance, which is unthinkable." And in "The Veiled Lodger" he said, "If there is not some compensation hereafter, then the world is a cruel jest."

Applewhite Minyard, "The Religious Views of Sherlock Holmes," *Baker Street Journal* 39, No. 4 (December 1989): 198–201

ROSEMARY JANN   The myth of rationality that Doyle constructs in the Holmes stories relies heavily on the posited but seldom tested validity of indexical codes of body and behavior that allow Holmes infallibly to deduce character and predict actions from gesture and appearance. Doyle modeled Holmes's method on that used by his professor at the Royal Infirmary in Edinburgh, Dr. Joseph Bell, for diagnosing not just his patients' medical ills but also their recent or habitual behavior. Linking such "symptoms" to Freudian slips and the trademark techniques of particular artists, Carlo Ginzburg has underlined the importance of their being unconscious and difficult to dissemble, so that the body can't help but betray its secrets to the "scientific" specialist. Holmes "claimed by a momentary expression, a twitch of a muscle or a glance of an eye, to fathom a man's inmost thoughts. Deceit, according to him, was an impossibility in the case of one trained to observation and analysis." He is constantly searching for "traces of . . . individuality," but these are interpretable precisely because they can always be referred to quite deterministic codes of class, gender, and ethnicity that are always already there to render true "individuality" an illusion; Holmes "never make[s] exceptions. An exception disproves the rule." What Allan Sekula suggests about nineteenth-century physiognomy and phrenology is equally true of the more elaborate typologies based upon them in the Holmes stories: they create the distinctions that they purport to observe, in effect constructing categories of the normative while appearing merely to interpret them. Such typologies can be seen as playing an important part in the increasing specification of individuality that for Michel Foucault is directly proportional to the social control exercised in modern disciplinary systems; as power becomes more anonymous, those most subject to it become less so—they are in effect controlled by having all aspects of their identities subject to surveillance and measured against posited norms of behavior. By being able to reduce even the most bizarre details to their proper place in such typologies, Holmes helps enforce the fixity and naturalness of the social ordering that rests upon them. The effect of his "trade" in "facts" is to protect social order by a continual reiteration of normalcy. As D. A. Miller puts it, the detective's "super vision" creates "the prospect of an absolute surveillance under which everything would be known, incriminated, policed."

Rosemary Jann, "Sherlock Holmes Codes the Social Body," *ELH* 57, No. 3 (Fall 1990): 686–87

Bibliography

A Study in Scarlet. 1888.
The Mystery of Cloomber. 1889.

Micah Clarke. 1889.

Mysteries and Adventures ⟨*The Gully of Bluemansdyke and Other Stories*⟩. 1889,
     1893 (as *My Friend the Murderer and Other Mysteries and Adventures*).

The Captain of the Polestar and Other Tales ⟨*The Great Keinplatz Experiment
     and Other Stories*⟩. 1890.

The Firm of Girdlestone: A Romance of the Unromantic. 1890.

The Sign of Four. 1890.

The White Company. 1891. 3 vols.

The Doings of Raffles Haw. 1892.

The Adventures of Sherlock Holmes. 1892.

The Great Shadow. 1892.

The Refugees: A Tale of Two Continents. 1893. 3 vols.

The Great Shadow and Beyond the City. 1893.

Jane Annie; or, The Good Conduct Prize (with J. M. Barrie). 1893.

The Memoirs of Sherlock Holmes. 1894.

An Actor's Duel and The Winning Shot. 1894.

Round the Red Lamp: Being Facts and Fancies of Medical Life. 1894.

The Parasite. 1894.

The Stark Munro Letters. 1895.

The Exploits of Brigadier Gerard. 1896.

Rodney Stone. 1896.

Uncle Bernac: A Memory of the Empire. 1897.

The Tragedy of Korosko ⟨*A Desert Drama*⟩. 1898.

Songs of Action. 1898.

A Duet with an Occasional Chorus. 1899.

The Green Flag and Other Stories of War and Sport. 1900.

The Great Boer War. 1900, 1901, 1902.

The Immortal Memory. 1901.

The War in South Africa: Its Cause and Conflict. 1902.

The Hound of the Baskervilles: Another Adventure of Sherlock Holmes. 1902.

Works (Author's Edition). 1903. 13 vols.

The Adventures of Gerard. 1903.

A Duet (*A Duologue*). 1903.

The Return of Sherlock Holmes. 1905.

The Fiscal Question: Treated in a Series of Three Speeches. 1905.

An Incursion into Diplomacy. 1906.

Sir Nigel. 1906.

The Croxley Master: A Great Tale of the Prize Ring. 1907.

Waterloo. 1907.

The Story of George Edalji. 1907.

Through the Magic Door. 1907.

Round the Fire Stories. 1908.

The Crime of the Congo. 1909.

Divorce Law Reform: An Essay. 1909.

Songs of the Road. 1911.

Why He Is Now in Favour of Home Rule. 1911.

The Last Galley: Impressions and Tales. 1911.

The Case of Oscar Slater. 1912.

The Speckled Band: An Adventure of Sherlock Holmes. 1912.

The Lost World. 1912.

The Poison Belt. 1913.

The Adventure of the Dying Detective. 1913.

Divorce and the Church (with Lord Hugh Cecil). 1913.

Civilian National Reserve. 1914.

Great Britain and the Next War. 1914.

To Arms! 1914.

The World War Conspiracy: Germany's Long Drawn Plot against England. 1914.

In Quest of Truth (with H. Stansbury). 1914.

The German War. 1914.

Western Wanderings. 1915.

The Valley of Fear. 1915.

The Outlook on the War. 1915.

An Appreciation of Sir John French. 1916.

A Petition to the Prime Minister on Behalf of Roger Casement. 1916.

A Visit to Three Fronts: June 1916. 1916.

The British Campaign in France and Flanders. 1916–20 (6 vols.), 1928 (as *The British Campaigns in Europe 1914–1918*).

Supremacy of the British Soldier. 1917.

His Last Bow: Some Reminiscences of Sherlock Holmes. 1917.

The New Revelation. 1918.

Danger! and Other Stories. 1918.

The Vital Message. 1919.

The Guards Came Through and Other Poems. 1919.

Our Reply to the Cleric. 1920.

"*The Truth of Spiritualism*" (with Joseph McCabe). 1920.

Spiritualism and Rationalism: With a Drastic Examination of Mr. Joseph M'Cabe.
    1920.

The Wanderings of a Spiritualist. 1921.

D. D. Home: His Life and Mission by Mrs. Douglas Home (editor). 1921.

[*Sherlock Holmes* (with William Gillette). 1922.]

The Poems: Collected Edition. 1922.

Tales of the Ring and Camp. 1922.

Tales of Pirates and Blue Water. 1922.

Tales of Terror and Mystery. 1922.

Tales of Twilight and the Unseen. 1922.

Tales of Adventure and Medical Life. 1922.

Tales of Long Ago. 1922.

The Coming of the Fairies. 1922.

Spiritualism—Some Straight Questions and Direct Answers. 1922.

The Case for Spirit Photography (with others). 1922.

Three of Them: A Reminiscence. 1923.

Our American Adventure. 1923.

Our Second American Adventure. 1924.

Memories and Adventures. 1924.

The Spiritualists' Reader (editor). 1924.

The Mystery of Joan of Arc by Léon Denis (translator). 1924.

The Early Christian Church and Modern Spiritualism. 1925.

Psychic Experiences. 1925.

The Land of Mist. 1926.

The History of Spiritualism. 1926. 2 vols.

Pheneas Speaks: Direct Spirit Communications in the Family Circle. 1927.

The Case-Book of Sherlock Holmes. 1927.

Spiritualism. c. 1927.

What Does Spiritualism Actually Teach and Stand For? 1928.

A Word of Warning. 1928.

Sherlock Holmes: The Complete Short Stories. 1928.

An Open Letter to Those of My Generation. 1929.

Our African Winter. 1929.

The Roman Catholic Church: A Rejoinder. 1929.

The Maracot Deep and Other Stories. 1929.

The Conan Doyle Stories. 1929.

Sherlock Holmes: The Complete Long Stories. 1929.

The Edge of the Unknown. 1930.

Works (Crowborough Edition). 1930. 24 vols.

The Conan Doyle Historical Romances. 1931–32. 2 vols.

The Field Bazaar. 1934.

The Professor Challenger Stories. 1952.

The Complete Napoleonic Stories. 1956.

The Crown Diamond: An Evening with Sherlock Holmes. 1958.

Great Stories. Ed. John Dickson Carr. 1959.

Strange Studies from Life: Containing Three Hitherto Uncollected Tales. Ed. Peter Ruber. 1963.

The Annotated Sherlock Holmes. Ed. William S. Baring-Gould. 1967. 2 vols.

My Life with Sherlock Holmes: Conversations in Baker Street. Ed. J. R. Hamilton. 1968.

The Complete Adventures and Memoirs of Sherlock Holmes: A Facsimile of the Original Strand Magazine *Stories 1891–1893*. 1975.

The Hound of the Baskervilles: A Facsimile of the Adventure as It Was First Published in the Strand Magazine, London. 1975.

The Return of Sherlock Holmes: A Facsimile of the Adventure as It Was First Published in the Strand Magazine, London. 1975.

Sherlock Holmes: The Published Apocrypha (with others). Ed. Jack Tracy. 1980.

Best Science Fiction. Ed. Charles G. Waugh and Martin H. Greenberg. 1981.

Uncollected Stories. Ed. John Michael Gibson and Richard Lancelyn Green. 1982.

Essays on Photography. Ed. John Michael Gibson and Richard Lancelyn Green. 1982.

The Uncollected Sherlock Holmes. Ed. Richard Lancelyn Green. 1983.

Letters to the Press. Ed. John Michael Gibson and Richard Lancelyn Green. 1986.

◧ ◩ ◨

R. Austin Freeman
1862–1943

RICHARD FREEMAN (the "Austin" was added later) was born on April 11, 1862, in London's West End "Soho" section. Determined to rise above his working class family's station, he attended boarding school, where he excelled in Latin; later he was apprenticed as an apothecary. He became a licentiate of the Society of Apothecaries at London's Middlesex Hospital in 1886. In 1887 he became house physician and qualified for both the Royal College of Physicians and the Royal College of Surgeons. That same year he married his childhood sweetheart, Annie Elizabeth Edwards.

Freeman entered the Colonial Service shortly after his marriage and embarked upon an expedition to Africa's Gold Coast as assistant colonial surgeon, an experience that would later serve as the basis for his first book, *Travels and Life in Ashanti and Jaman* (1898), and first novel, *The Golden Pool* (1905). Four years into his stay in Africa he contracted blackwater fever, a pernicious type of malaria. He returned to London and was invalided out of the colonial service two months shy of qualifying for a pension.

Freeman held a number of medical positions over the next decade and became the father of two sons, Clifford John Austin in 1893 and Lawrence in 1897. While working as assistant medical officer at Holloway Prison he befriended the chief medical officer, John James Pitcairn. Writing pseudonymously as Clifford Ashdown, the pair produced a series of stories about a latter-day Robin Hood who preys on exploiters of others; they were serialized in *Cassell's Magazine* and later collected as *The Adventures of Romney Pringle* (1902). Additional stories were collected posthumously in *The Further Adventures of Romney Pringle* (1970).

Freeman's novel *The Red Thumb Mark* (1907) introduced Dr. John Evelyn Thorndyke, the first scientific detective and hero of twenty-nine novels and short story collections between 1907 and 1942. Created somewhat as a response to Conan Doyle's Sherlock Holmes, Thorndyke solved his mysteries not by deduction but by the scientific method. His adventures abounded with modern criminology methods and chemistry experiments, many of which Freeman had tried out himself to guarantee their efficacy.

Believing that readers of detective fiction were more interested in the actual machinery of detection than a suspenseful narrative, Freeman created the "inverted detective story" in *The Singing Bone* (1912), a collection of Dr. Thorndyke stories in which the crimes and criminals are revealed at the outset and the rest of the story is devoted to the detective's reconstruction of the crime from clues.

Although the immensely popular Dr. Thorndyke stories consumed most of his time, Freeman wrote other crime stories, including *The Unwilling Adventurer* (1913) and *The Exploits of Danby Croker* (1916). He also held a number of medical positions. An interest in eugenics led to his writing a social critique, *Social Decay and Regeneration* (1921), which denounced the worst consequences of capitalism and the Industrial Revolution. In failing health with Parkinson's disease for most of his final years, R. Austin Freeman died on September 28, 1943.

Critical Extracts

JOHN ADAMS   Three of the four books in which Dr. John Thorndyke is the central character are written in the orthodox way. They are intrinsically of very great interest, and, indeed, stand out as conspicuously above the ordinary story of this type. They are the work of a master in this somewhat difficult craft. The fourth volume, however, *The Singing Bone*, has all the attractions of an experiment in literary form. It is apparent that Mr. Freeman has been worried in his other books, as his readers must necessarily be, by the necessity of continually keeping back certain bits of information that might precipitate the *dénouement,* so he put to himself the question whether it would not be possible to write a detective story in which author and reader could play with the cards on the table. Accordingly, he set about writing the same story twice over—first from the point of view of the criminal, and then from the point of view of the detective. A by-product of this method is the elimination of the first personal form. The volume contains five such duplicated stories, and the result cannot be regarded as altogether successful. Were it not for Mr. Freeman's extraordinary power of telling a story the volume might have been a dismal failure. As it is, the author by a *tour de force* carries the reader right through the book, partly from sheer interest in the incidents, and partly from the interest in Thorndyke's methods. The objection to this duplicate method, which Mr. Freeman claims to have justified by its success, is that it emphasises the purely logical aspects of the different cases. It is not so much a series of stories as a set of exercises. A teacher might be tempted to use them as problems in applied logic. This logical interest is no doubt prominent in the other books, notably in the summing up at the symposium at the end of *The Eye of Osiris*, but in the short stories it is deliberately brought forward as the chief matter. Nothing but the author's remarkable skill in character delineation and graphic narrative could save the stories from being regarded as technical studies, such as find a suitable place in a course on forensic medicine.

Indeed, the whole position of Mr. Freeman depends upon the class of readers to whom he appeals. His work is certainly beyond the range of the ordinary devourer of "sleuth" novels. He makes very great demands on the attention of his readers. To read these books intelligently implies a definite exercise in the use of Mill's Canons of Inductive Logic, and the books might form a very practical means of testing the student's mastery of these canons. A very obvious and natural criticism of the stories is that they are too clever: they ask too much of the reader. But, unlike some clever writers, Mr. Freeman is clever enough to carry off his cleverness. His exposition is so clear, his arrangement of events so methodical, that the reader is led along with the minimum amount of effort consistent with a very definite exercise of the reason. Stupid and lazy readers may be warned off, but the ordinary intelligent reader may rely upon having from Mr. Freeman a course in mental gymnastics conducted under the pleasantest conditions.

John Adams, "Mr. R. Austin Freeman," *Bookman* (London) No. 259 (April 1913): 7

R. AUSTIN FREEMAN   The distinctive quality of a detective story, in which it differs from all other types of fiction, is that the satisfaction it offers to the reader is primarily an intellectual satisfaction. This is not to say that it need be deficient in other qualities appertaining to good fiction: in grace of diction, in humour, in interesting characterization, in picturesqueness of setting or in emotional presentation. On the contrary, it should possess all these qualities. It should be an interesting story, well and vivaciously told. But whereas in other fiction these are primary, paramount qualities, in detective fiction they are secondary and subordinate to the intellectual interest, to which they must be, if necessary, sacrificed. The entertainment that the connoisseur looks for is an exhibition of mental gymnastics in which he is invited to take part; and the excellence of the entertainment must be judged by the completeness with which it satisfies the expectations of the type of reader to whom it is addressed.

R. Austin Freeman, "The Art of the Detective Story," *Nineteenth Century and After* No. 567 (May 1924): 715–16

WILLARD HUNTINGTON WRIGHT   In R. Austin Freeman's Dr. Thorndyke the purely scientific detective made his appearance. Test tubes, microscopes, Bunsen burners, retorts, and all the obscure paraphernalia of the chemist's and physicist's laboratories are his stock in trade. In fact, Dr. Thorndyke rarely attends an investigation without his case of implements and his array of chemicals. Without his laboratory assistant and jack-of-all-trades, Polton,—coupled, of course, with his ponderous but inevitable medico-legal logic—he would be helpless in the face of mysteries which Sherlock Holmes and Monsieur Lecoq might easily have clarified by a combination of observation, mental analysis, and intuitive genius. Dr. Thorndyke is an elderly, plodding, painstaking, humorless and amazingly dry sleuth, but so original are his problems, so cleverly and clearly does he reach his solutions, and so well written are Dr. Freeman's records, that the Thorndyke books are among the very best of modern detective fiction. The amatory susceptibilities of his recording coadjutors are constantly intruding upon the doctor's scientific investigations and the reader's patience; but even with these irrelevant impediments most of the stories march briskly and competently to their inevitable conclusions. Of all the scientific detectives Dr. Thorndyke is unquestionably the most convincing. His science, though at times obscure, is always sound: Dr. Freeman writes authoritatively, and the reader is both instructed and delighted.

Willard Huntington Wright, "Introduction," *The Great Detective Stories: A Chronological Anthology* (New York: Charles Scribner's Sons, 1927), pp. 17–18

DOROTHY L. SAYERS   One fettering convention, from which detective fiction is only very slowly freeing itself, is that of the "love interest." Publishers and editors still labour under the delusion that all stories must have a nice young man and woman who have to be united in the last chapter. As a result, some of the finest detective-stories are marred by a conventional love-story, irrelevant to the action and perfunctorily worked in. The most harmless form of this disease is that taken, for example, in the works of Mr. Austin Freeman. His secondary characters fall in love with distressing regularity, and perform a number of conventional antics suitable to persons in their condition, but they do not interfere with the course of the story. You can skip the love-passages if you like, and nothing is lost.

Dorothy L. Sayers, "Introduction," *Great Short Stories of Detection, Mystery, and Horror* (London: Victor Gollancz, 1928), p. 39

H. DOUGLAS THOMSON   It is impossible to deny that Thorndyke is one of Fortune's favourites. He always finds some clue, or his microscope does—whether it is an infinitesimal piece of glass or a speck of dust. One's ignorance prevents one from questioning the probability of these finds. For example, in *A Wastrel's Romance* the criminal is traced to a certain locality from three different types of dust that are found in a discarded overcoat. In *The Red Thumb Mark* and *The Old Lag*, Dr. Freeman describes a very clever method of forging finger-prints by a line-block process. Yet I have heard an authority on process-engraving express grave doubts as to the chances of such forgery proving really misleading. Now and again Dr. Freeman has the last laugh, as in *The Moabite Cipher*, where the reader expects that one of the more complicated forms of "mathematical cipher" is to be solved, whereas the real message is written in invisible ink.

There are times, too, when Dr. Freeman can be attractively simple, as in *The Singing Bone*, where the main items in Thorndyke's deduction are as follows: A pipe is found near the body. But as the mouthpiece of this pipe indicates that its owner has a good strong set of teeth whereas the corpse certainly had not; and as the tobacco found inside the pouch was different from that found inside the pipe, the obvious conclusion—the one instance in a thousand where it is the right one—is that the pipe does not belong to the corpse. Then who else can be the owner but "the other?"

Simple, my dear Jervis. I bless Dr. Freeman for *The Singing Bone*, for it is the one and only Thorndyke story which I have prematurely solved *in detail.*

H. Douglas Thomson, "Dr. Austin Freeman," *Masters of Mystery: A Study of the Detective Story* (London: William Collins Sons & Co., 1931), pp. 174–75

AODH DE BLACAM   The first of the Thorndyke books, if memory serves, was *The Eye of Osiris*, appearing about 1910; and, about that time, short stories about Thorndyke appeared in the magazines.

The unusual hero of this book was Holmes with a difference. There was nothing fanciful about Dr. Thorndyke. He did not upset the landlady by peppering the walls with revolver shots; he did not solve problems in a musical trance; he was no boxer, or swordsman, and I cannot remember that he ever wore disguises or tricked his quarry by pretending to be dead. No, he was a sober-sided lawyer, specialising in Medical Jurisprudence. He lived in chambers, investigated cases for an insurance company, and acted on instructions from that plain, homely, unimaginative solicitor, Mr. Brodribb. His methods were methodical: a thing you could not say of Holmes. He tested evidence with the microscope, tabulated it, and reasoned in ponderous legal phraseology. He won his triumphs—defeated crime, vindicated the unjustly accused—always by solid scientific means and unwavering logic. St. Thomas Aquinas, if we can imagine the Angelic Doctor interesting himself in such mundane inquiries, would have approved of this syllogistic investigator.

Thorndyke's style, then, was pedestrian. True, but the tales are invariably full, engrossing and satisfying. The atmosphere and the characters, both are as racily English as in the works of Dickens: no gleam of Irish wit or whimsy disturbs the grave and homely life that he draws in the Temple and in the workshops in London. The people in them are delightful folk, all the more so because they are so realistic. When there is a love affair, it is as domestic and affectionate as reality demands.

The big man's assistant, crinkly-faced Polton, who is so happy in the workshop where he built instruments for Thorndyke's demonstrations: he is one of the most pleasing people we ever met in a story book. His appearances for years were brief, we longed to know more about him. At last, we were satisfied. In a book which is supposed to be Polton's autobiography, Freeman described this humble fellow's adventures as a clock-maker's assistant. It makes a truly Dickensian tale: Dickens would be proud of the picture of homely, droll, industrious common folk. The worthy craftsman became involved in a strange affair. He was charged with crime, and would have suffered, but that the benevolent Thorndyke interested himself in the affair, and found a clue in a clock, whereby Polton was exonerated. Hence Polton's life-long devotion to so kindly a master.

This is the most feeling of all the tales. We suffer the plain man's distress. A beautiful compassion bathes the pages. One reader in a score, perhaps, will advert to the fact that Polton, though he walks the valley of the shadow, never calls on God, and that Thorndyke's goodness shows no trace of a motive beyond natural good-will. When this is pointed out, however, an aspect of all the Freeman books is observed. The author, wholesome as he is, and free from the vulgarity and coarseness and sensationalism of most detective writers, may be said almost to boycott Christianity.

Aodh de Blacam, "The Detective as Philosopher," *Irish Monthly*, June 1945, pp. 262–64

RAYMOND CHANDLER   This man Austin Freeman is a wonderful performer. He has no equal in his genre and he is also a much better writer than you might think, if you were superficially inclined, because in spite of the immense leisure of his writing he accomplishes an even suspense which is quite unexpected. The apparatus of his writing makes for dullness, but he is not dull. There is even a gaslight charm about his Victorian love affairs, and those wonderful walks across London which the long-legged Dr Thorndyke takes like a stroll around a garden, accompanied by his cheerful and brainless Watson, Dr Jervis, whom no man in his senses would hire for any legal or medico-legal operation more exacting than counting the toes of a corpse.

Freeman has so many distinctions as a technician that one is apt to forget that within his literary tradition he is a damn good writer. He invented the inverted detective story. He proved the possibility of forging fingerprints and of detecting the forgeries long before the police thought of such a thing. His knowledge is vast and very real. The great scene would have been a courtroom battle between Thorndyke and Spilsbury, and for my money Thorndyke would have won hands down.

Raymond Chandler, Letter to Hamish Hamilton (13 December 1949), *Raymond Chandler Speaking*, ed. Dorothy Gardiner and Kathrine Sorley Walker (Boston: Houghton Mifflin, 1962), pp. 59–60

A. E. MURCH   In *The Singing Bone* (1912), Austin Freeman made an interesting experiment with a new technique of plot construction. When a detective story begins with the discovery of a murder, as so many do, one of the fundamental difficulties is the almost inevitable need to interrupt the progress of the story at some point to relate the events that led up to the crime. This can cause a tiresome break in continuity, yet unless the reader learns why, as well as how and by whom, the crime was committed, the tale is not fully told. Gaboriau made various attempts to overcome this artistic difficulty. Chavette handled the problem rather differently, without, however, finding a smooth way round. Even Conan Doyle, a master of technique, found the point a stumbling block, and in three of the four novels of Sherlock Holmes the recapitulation sharply disrupts the action.

In *The Singing Bone* Austin Freeman tried a new method of approach. First of all, the reader meets the criminal-to-be in his ordinary daily life, before the crime has even been thought of. Then the events that led to the murder are related, with all the circumstances placed before the reader. Finally, Dr. Thorndyke begins his investigation, gathering evidence here and there until his proofs are complete. This method leaves no room for 'red herrings,' and eliminates almost completely the valuable elements of surprise and mystification. Instead, the reader enjoys the novelty of knowing more than the detective; his attention is concentrated on the process of detection, rather than on what is discovered. As a result, stories told in this manner—'The Echo of a Mutiny,' for instance, or 'The Case of Oscar Brodski'—have a special atmosphere of their own, with the detective playing the rôle of Nemesis. Freeman did not repeat this experiment, and his next work, *A Silent Witness* (1914), reverts to the more conventional technique which he followed in the later tales of Dr. Thorndyke that continued to appear at fairly regular intervals until Austin Freeman's death in 1943. In most of these tales, the reader, though his interest and curiosity are adroitly kept at a high pitch of excitement, has no hope of solving the mystery for himself, unless he is skilled enough to deduce Dr. Thorndyke's line of enquiry from the type of experiment he employs, or possesses some highly-specialised knowledge of, for instance, the craft of making Japanese shadow-mirrors. Dr. Freeman's literary life extended almost to the middle of the twentieth century, but the leisurely, unsensational atmosphere of his stories, the romantic sensibility of his strong, silent heroes and gentle, ladylike heroines, the courteous manner of the cultured investigator himself, all are typical of the period befre the first World War, and Dr. Thorndyke's comfortable chambers in King's Bench Walk belong to much the same world as Sherlock Holmes's gas-lit rooms at 221b Baker Street.

A. E. Murch, *The Development of the Detective Novel* (London: Peter Owen, 1958), pp. 206–7

E. F. BLEILER   Freeman set out to create the most cerebral detective stories, and yet the reason that his work is read today is almost certainly not the factors that he rated most highly. The modern reader, who has come through the even more cerebral stories of Nicholas Blake and the Coles, the plot intricacies of J. D. Carr and Ellery Queen, the romantic realism of Hammett and Chandler, and the psychological brilliancies of T. S. Stribling is apt to marvel at Freeman's blind spot about what he was accomplishing, even in his own day.

Historically speaking, Freeman might be characterized as the antithesis to the work of Doyle, despite some superficial resemblances between the stories of the two men. Even more, Freeman embodied a reaction against the school of Doyle, such men and women as Richard Marsh, L. T. Meade and Robert Eustace, M. P. Shiel, B. Fletcher Robinson and the many lesser writers who contributed to *Pearson's, Strand, Windsor Magazine* and other periodicals. Doyle had established the pattern to which they usually conformed. This included an eccentric detective, nonchalant criminology, colorful adventures, and a naively weird pseudoscience: drugs with incredible properties, astonishing biological monsters, electrical machines, and, of course, highly romantic villains. It would be tempting to say that Freeman's work put the quietus to Indian idols who knifed gentlemen who pushed the wrong buttons, or beautiful mistress-minds of crime with disintegration devices, or memory-erasing drugs, but this may be claiming too much. Others were heading in the same direction. In England E. C. Bentley was trying to write a detective story of human relationships, in America M. D. Post was using the quirks of criminal law as the basis for stories, while Baroness Orczy was applying even more cerebral techniques to the solution of the mystery story, by abolishing everything except the explanation-denouement. The climate was generally tending away from romanticism. Let us simply say that Freeman was a major force in the evolution of the detective story, certainly today the most permanent and readable of his period.

E. F. Bleiler, "Introduction to the Dover Edition," *The Stoneware Monkey and The Penrose Mystery* by R. Austin Freeman (New York: Dover Publications, 1973), pp. iv–v

T. J. BINYON   That Freeman intended Thorndyke as a rival to
⟨Sherlock⟩ Holmes is clear from his remarks on the genesis of the character,
which contain open criticism not only of Holmes, but also of other contemporary detectives. After pointing out that Thorndyke was not based on any
real person, but deliberately invented, he continues:

> As mental and bodily characters are usually in harmony, I made
> him tall, strong, active and keen-sighted. As he was a man of
> acute intellect and sound judgement, I decided to keep him free
> from eccentricities, such as are usually associated with an
> unbalanced mind, and to endow him with the dignity of presence,
> appearance and manner appropriate to his high professional and
> social standing. Especially I decided to keep him perfectly sane
> and normal.

And in the short story 'The Anthropologist at Large' there is a not too
subtle but amusing dig at Holmes's methods when a client hands Thorndyke
a shabby billycock hat, saying that he understands that it is possible from
the examination of a hat to deduce 'not only the bodily characteristics of
the wearer, but also his mental and moral qualities, his state of health, his
pecuniary position, and even his domestic relations and the peculiarities of
his place of abode'—a pithy summing-up of the deductions Holmes makes
from the examination of Mr Baker's hat in 'The Adventure of the Blue
Carbuncle'. Thorndyke rises to the challenge, and, aided by his microscope,
produces hard evidence from the hat to suggest that it belongs to a Japanese
workman employed at a mother-of-pearl factory in the West India Dock
Road.

There can be no doubt that Thorndyke is by far the more convincing
of the two as a detective. Although Watson notes Holmes's 'profound'
knowledge of chemistry, we have evidence of it only once, at the beginning
of A *Study in Scarlet*, when Holmes announces that he has discovered a
new reagent 'precipitated by haemoglobin, and by nothing else'. This is
obviously fiction. By contrast, we see Thorndyke carrying out Reinsch's and
Marsh's tests for the presence of arsenic, and, in order to recover the lead
of a bullet from a body that has been cremated, heating the pulverized
remains in a crucible together with charcoal, sodium carbonate, borax, and
a couple of iron nails.

Holmes's inferences are brilliant and showy, but logically unsound; Thorndyke's arguments are rigorous, his thoughts logical and organized. ⟨. . .⟩
Thorndyke is more knowledgeable than Holmes: he can read Egyptian

hieroglyphics, identify at a glance two different types of duckweed, and explain the construction of Japanese magic mirrors. Nor does Freeman make the kind of factual mistake that occurs relatively frequently in Doyle: for example, when Holmes refers to a blue carbuncle as 'crystallized charcoal', when in fact it contains no carbon; calls the snake of 'The Adventure of the Speckled Band' a 'swamp adder . . . the deadliest snake in India', although the species does not exist; describes the Japanese system of wrestling as 'baritsu', a meaningless term; and asserts that it is possible from examining the tracks left by a bicycle to tell in which direction the cyclist was going.

> T. J. Binyon, "*Murder Will Out*": *The Detective in Fiction* (Oxford: Oxford University Press, 1989), pp. 17–18

◈ *Bibliography*

Travels and Life in Ashanti and Jaman. 1898.

The Adventures of Romney Pringle (with J. J. Pitcairn). 1902.

The Golden Pool: A Story of a Forgotten Mine. 1905.

The Red Thumb Mark. 1907.

John Thorndyke's Cases. 1909.

The Eye of Osiris: A Detective Romance ⟨*The Vanishing Man*⟩. 1911.

The Mystery of 31, New Inn. 1912.

The Singing Bone. 1912.

The Unwilling Adventurer. 1913.

The Uttermost Farthing: A Savant's Vendetta. 1914.

A Silent Witness. 1914.

The Exploits of Danby Croker: Being Extracts from a Somewhat Disreputable Autobiography. 1916.

The Great Portrait Mystery. 1918.

Social Decay and Regeneration. 1921.

Helen Vardon's Confession. 1922.

The Cat's Eye. 1923.

Dr. Thorndyke's Case-Book ⟨*The Blue Scarab*⟩. 1924.

The Mystery of Angelina Frood. 1924.

The Shadow of the Wolf. 1925.

The Puzzle Lock. 1925.

The D'Arblay Mystery. 1926.

A Certain Dr. Thorndyke. 1927.

The Surprising Adventures of Mr. Shuttlebury Cobb. 1927.

The Magic Casket. 1927.

As a Thief in the Night. 1928.

Flighty Phyllis. 1928.

The Famous Cases of Dr. Thorndyke ⟨*The Dr. Thorndyke Omnibus*⟩. 1929.

Mr. Pottermack's Oversight. 1930.

Dr. Thorndyke Investigates. 1930.

Pontifex, Son and Thorndyke. 1931.

When Rogues Fall Out ⟨*Dr. Thorndyke's Discovery*⟩. 1932.

Dr. Thorndyke Intervenes. 1933.

For the Defence: Dr. Thorndyke. 1934.

The Penrose Mystery. 1936.

Felo De Se? ⟨*Death at the Inn*⟩. 1937.

The Stoneware Monkey. 1938.

Mr. Polton Explains. 1940.

Dr. Thorndyke's Crime File. 1941.

The Jacob Street Mystery ⟨*The Unconscious Witness*⟩. 1942.

The Further Adventures of Romney Pringle (with J. J. Pitcairn). 1970.

The Queen's Treasure (with J. J. Pitcairn). 1975.

From a Surgeon's Diary (with J. J. Pitcairn). 1975.

Edgar Allan Poe
1809–1849

EDGAR ALLAN POE was born Edgar Poe in Boston on January 19, 1809, the son of traveling actors. Shortly after his birth his father disappeared, and in 1811 his mother died. He was taken into the home of John Allan (from whom Poe derived his middle name), a wealthy merchant living in Richmond, Virginia. In 1815 the Allans took Poe to England, where he attended the Manor House School at Stoke Newington, later the setting for his story "William Wilson." Poe returned to Richmond with the Allans in 1820. In 1826 he became engaged to Elmira Royster, whose parents broke off the engagement. That fall he entered the University of Virginia. At first he excelled in his studies, but in December 1826 John Allan took him out of school after Poe accumulated considerable gambling debts that Allan refused to pay. Unable to honor these debts himself, Poe fled to Boston, where he enlisted in the army under the name of Edgar A. Perry.

Poe began his literary career with the anonymous publication, at his own expense, of *Tamerlane and Other Poems* (1827), which because of its small print run and poor distribution has become one of the rarest volumes in American literary history. In 1829 Poe was honorably discharged from the army. Later that year he published a second collection of verse, *Al Aaraaf, Tamerlane, and Minor Poems,* containing revisions of poems from his first collection as well as new material. This volume was well received, leading to a tentative reconciliation with John Allan. In 1830 Poe entered West Point, but after another falling out with John Allan, who withdrew his financial support, Poe deliberately got himself expelled in 1831 through flagrant neglect of his duties. Nonetheless, he managed before leaving to gather enough cadet subscriptions to bring out his third collection of verse, *Poems* (1831). In 1833 Poe's final attempt at reconciliation was rejected by the ailing John Allan, who died in 1834 without mentioning Poe in his will.

In the meantime Poe's literary career was progressing. Having settled in Baltimore after leaving West Point, Poe won a prize in 1833 from the

Baltimore Saturday Visitor for one of his first short stories, "MS. Found in a Bottle." In 1835 he moved to Richmond to become editor of the recently established *Southern Literary Messenger*, which thrived under his direction. In 1836 Poe felt financially secure enough to marry Virginia Clemm, his fourteen-year-old cousin, but later that year he was fired from the *Messenger*, partly because of what appeared to be chronic alcoholism. In fact, Poe seems to have suffered from a physical ailment that rendered him so sensitive to alcohol that a single drink could induce a drunken state. Poe was later an editor of *Burton's Gentleman's Magazine* (1839–40), *Graham's Magazine* (1841–42), and the *Broadway Journal* (1845–46). In this capacity he wrote many important reviews—notably of Hawthorne, Dickens, and Macaulay— and occasionally gained notoriety for the severity and acerbity of his judgments. In particular he wrote a series of polemics against Henry Wadsworth Longfellow, whom he accused of plagiarism.

Meanwhile Poe continued to write fiction voluminously. His longest tale, *The Narrative of Arthur Gordon Pym* (apparently unfinished), is dated 1838 but appeared in the summer of 1837; *Tales of the Grotesque and Arabesque*, containing "The Fall of The House of Usher" and other important stories, was published in 1840; and *Tales* appeared in 1845. As a fiction writer Poe wrote not only tales of the macabre and the supernatural ("The Pit and the Pendulum," "The Black Cat," "The Tell-Tale Heart," "Ligeia") but also many humorous or parodic pieces ("King Pest," "Some Words with a Mummy"), prose poems ("Silence—a Fable," "Shadow—a Parable"), and what are generally considered the first true detective stories.

Poe's five detective tales lay down nearly all the conventions of the genre adopted by later writers. "The Murders in the Rue Morgue" (1841) is not only the first murder mystery but the first "locked room" story; it introduces Poe's nearly infallible detective, C. Auguste Dupin. In "The Mystery of Marie Rogêt" (1842) Poe attempted to solve a real murder case; and although he made breakthroughs in the analysis of the evidence, his reconstruction is not in fact correct. "The Gold-Bug" (1843) is one of the first stories to involve the decoding of a cipher. "The Purloined Letter" (1844) is perhaps Poe's purest tale of "ratiocination," or the application of intellect to a body of evidence. "Thou Art the Man" (1844) is believed to be the first comic detective story.

In 1844 Poe moved to New York, and in the following year he achieved international fame with his poem "The Raven," published in *The Raven and Other Poems* (1845). In 1847 Poe's wife Virginia, who had been seriously ill since 1842, died, leaving him desolate. For the few remaining years of his life he helped support himself by delivering a series of public lectures, including "The Poetic Principle" (published posthumously in 1850). Among his publications were the philosophical treatise *Eureka: A Prose Poem* (1848) and the lyric "Annabel Lee" (1849). His *Marginalia* was published serially from 1844 to 1849. After his wife's death Poe had several romances, including an affair with the Rhode Island poet Sarah Helen Whitman, and in 1849 he became engaged for a second time to Elmira Royster (then Mrs. Shelton). Before they could be married, however, Poe died in Baltimore on October 7, 1849, under mysterious circumstances.

▓ Critical Extracts

EDGAR ALLAN POE   You may remember a tale of mine published about a year ago in *Graham* and entitled the "Murders in the Rue Morgue". Its *theme* was the exercise of ingenuity in detecting a murderer. I am just now putting the concluding touch to a similar article, which I shall entitle "The Mystery of Marie Rogêt—a Sequel to 'The Murders in the Rue Morgue'." The story is based upon that of the real murder of Mary Cecilia Rogers, which created so vast an excitement, some months ago, in New-York. I have handled the design in a very singular and entirely *novel* manner. I imagine a series of nearly exact *coincidences* occurring in Paris. A young grisette, one *Marie Rogêt*, has been murdered under precisely similar circumstances with *Mary Rogers*. Thus under pretence of showing how Dupin (the hero of the Rue Morgue) unravelled the mystery of Marie's assassination, I, in fact, enter into a very rigorous analysis of the *real* tragedy in New-York. *No point* is omitted. I examine, each by each, the opinions and arguments of our press on the subject, and show (I think satisfactorily) that this subject has never yet been *approached*. The press has been entirely on a wrong scent. In fact, I really believe, not only that I have demonstrated the falsity of the idea that the girl was the victim of a gang, but have *indicated the assassin*. My main object, however, as you will readily understand, is the analysis of the *principles of investigation* in cases of like character. Dupin *reasons* the matter throughout.

Edgar Allan Poe, Letter to Joseph Evans Snodgrass (4 June 1842), *The Letters of Edgar Allan Poe*, ed. John Ward Ostrom (1948; rev. ed. New York: Gordian Press, 1966), Vol. 1, pp. 201–2

J. BRANDER MATTHEWS   In the detective story as Poe conceived it in the "Murders in the Rue Morgue," it is not in the mystery itself that the author seeks to interest the reader, but rather in the successive steps whereby his analytic observer is enabled to solve a problem that might well be dismissed as beyond human elucidation. Attention is centred on the unravelling of the tangled skein rather than on the knot itself. The emotion aroused is not mere surprise, it is recognition of the unsuspected capabilities of the human brain; it is not a wondering curiosity as to an airless mechanism, but a heightening admiration for the analytic acumen capable of working out an acceptable answer to the puzzle propounded. In other words, Poe, while he availed himself of the obvious advantage of keeping a secret from his readers and of leaving them guessing as long as he pleased, shifted the point of attack and succeeded in giving a human interest to his tale of wonder.

And by this shift Poe transported the detective story from the group of tales of adventure into the group of portrayals of character. By bestowing upon it a human interest, he raised it in the literary scale. There is no need now to exaggerate the merits of this feat or to suggest that Poe himself was not capable of loftier efforts. Of course the "Fall of the House of Usher," which is of imagination all compact, is more valid evidence of his genius than the "Murders in the Rue Morgue," which is the product rather of his invention, supremely ingenious as it is. Even though the detective story as Poe produced it is elevated far above the barren tale of mystery which preceded it and which has been revived in our own day, it is not one of the loftiest literary forms, and its possibilities are severely limited. It suffers to-day from the fact that in the half-century and more since Poe set the pattern it has been vulgarized, debased, degraded by a swarm of imitators who lacked his certainty of touch, his instinctive tact, his intellectual individuality. In their hands it has been bereft of its distinction and despoiled of its atmosphere.

Even at its best, in the simple perfection of form that Poe bestowed on it, there is no denying that it demanded from its creator no depth of sentiment, no warmth of emotion, and no large understanding of human desire. There are those who would dismiss it carelessly, as making an appeal not far removed from that of the riddle and of the conundrum. There are those again who would liken it rather to the adroit trick of a clever conjurer. No doubt, it gratifies in us chiefly that delight in difficulty conquered, which is a part of the primitive play impulse potent in us all, but tending to die out as we grow older, as we lessen in energy, and as we feel more deeply the tragi-comedy of existence. But inexpensive as it may seem to those of us who look to literature for enlightenment, for solace in the hour of need, for stimulus to stiffen the will in the never-ending struggle of life, the detective tale, as Poe contrived it, has merits of its own as distinct and as undeniable as those of the historical novel, for example, or of the sea tale. It may please the young rather than the old, but the pleasure it can give is ever innocent; and the young are always in the majority.

J. Brander Matthews, "Poe and the Detective Story," *Scribner's Magazine* 42, No. 3 (September 1907): 289

DOROTHY L. SAYERS   Putting aside his instructive excursions into the psychology of detection—instructive, because we can trace their influence in so many of Poe's successors down to the present day—putting these aside, and discounting that atmosphere of creepiness which Poe so successfully diffused about nearly all he wrote, we shall probably find that to us, sophisticated and trained on an intensive study of detective fiction, his plots are thin to transparency. But in Poe's day they represented a new technique. As a matter of fact, it is doubtful whether there are more than half a dozen deceptions in the mystery-monger's bag of tricks, and we shall find that Poe has got most of them, at any rate in embryo.

⟨. . .⟩ In "The Murders in the Rue Morgue," an old woman and her daughter are found horribly murdered in an (apparently) hermetically sealed room. An innocent person is arrested by the police. Dupin proves that the police have failed to discover one mode of entrance to the room, and deduces from a number of observations that the "murder" was committed by a huge ape. Here is, then, a combination of three typical motifs: the wrongly suspected man, to whom all the superficial evidence (motive, access, etc.)

points; the hermetically sealed death-chamber (still a favourite central theme); finally, the *solution by the unexpected means*. In addition, we have Dupin drawing deductions, which the police have overlooked, from the evidence of witnesses (superiority in inference), and discovering clues which the police have not thought of looking for owing to obsession by an *idée fixe* (superiority of observation based on inference). In this story also are enunciated for the first time those two great aphorisms of detective science: first, that when you have eliminated all the impossibilities, then, whatever remains, *however improbable*, must be the truth; and, secondly, that the more *outré* a case may appear, the easier it is to solve. Indeed, take it all round, "The Murders in the Rue Morgue" constitutes in itself almost a complete manual of detective theory and practice. ⟨. . .⟩

⟨. . .⟩ Poe stands at the parting of the ways for detective fiction. From him go the two great lines of development—the Romantic and the Classic, or, to use terms less abraded by ill-usage, the purely Sensational and the purely Intellectual. In the former, thrill is piled on thrill and mystification on mystification; the reader is led on from bewilderment to bewilderment, till everything is explained in a lump in the last chapter. This school is strong in dramatic incident and atmosphere; its weakness is a tendency to confusion and a dropping of links—its explanations do not always explain; it is never dull, but it is sometimes nonsense. In the other—the purely Intellectual type—the action mostly takes place in the first chapter or so; the detective then follows up quietly from clue to clue till the problem is solved, the reader accompanying the great man in his search and being allowed to try his own teeth on the material provided. The strength of this school is its analytical ingenuity; its weakness is its liability to dullness and pomposity, its mouthing over the infinitely little, and its lack of movement and emotion.

Dorothy L. Sayers, "Introduction," *Great Short Stories of Detection, Mystery, and Horror* (London: Victor Gollancz, 1928), pp. 17–18

EDWARD H. DAVIDSON   The tales of ratiocination are one direction of the artist's quest: by renouncing the actual world, Poe was free to construct a totally fictive playground of the mind which could still maintain workable likenesses to the world of common affairs. At the end, Poe came to a concept of God, part mind and part craftsman, who existed at one time in and then removed Himself from His creation. God and nature are thus dual; through nature, however, man essays to arrive at truth; but all the while he discovers in nature a frightening variety of discordant and cancelling propositions. "In their origin," Poe stated, "these laws were fashioned to embrace *all* contingencies which *could* lie in the future." Man perceives these laws as special in place and time, and thus he is forever confused by the jarring discrepancies between what is and what his mind tells him is "probability." What appears as an "accident" is merely a misapprehension of what is: "Modern science has resolved to *calculate upon the unforeseen.*" Poe's "Calculus of Probabilities" is a solution to his need of admitting that the mind is the only reality and that all it can know is itself and its operations which are concordant with the primal laws of the universe. The ratiocinative exercise of the detective is simply an allegory of how the mind may impose its interior logic on exterior circumstance. Dupin is the supreme artistic ego: everything external to himself can be made to fit the theoretical, the ideal logic.

Thus these tales of ratiocination were a number of expressions of Poe, the man and the artist. They were part of his struggle to conform by assuming more than a normal human share of certain faculties he otherwise held in contempt: he could assume the roles of natural scientist and "success," and then he could go much further and accomplish much more than the mere "businessman" of the nineteenth century could gain. He would go so far, in fact, that he would be contemptuous of the money he found in the pirate hoard in "The Gold-Bug" and care only for the imaginative exercise which made mere gold ludicrous. These tales are Poe's war on his age: he could not front his age in any truly critical terms, as did Hawthorne and Melville; he could only ridicule by pretending to take seriously certain values and then destroy them at the very moment of treating them with reverence.

Edward H. Davidson, *Poe: A Critical Study* (Cambridge, MA: Harvard University Press, 1957), pp. 220–22.

RICHARD WILBUR   "The Murders in the Rue Morgue" has pleased millions of readers as a description—to quote one of Poe's letters—of "the exercise of ingenuity in detecting a murderer." Yet anyone who reads it in a chair, rather than a hammock, is likely to feel teased into "participating," into trying to account for a sense that he is reading more than a tale of detection. In the first place, Dupin is far more than a hero of "ingenuity"—a term which, within the story, is treated with scorn. Though sometimes depicted as a reasoner, he is the embodiment of an idea, strongly urged in *Eureka* and elsewhere, that poetic intuition is a supra-logical faculty, infallible in nature, which includes and obviates analytical genius. As Kepler guessed his laws, the dreamer Dupin guesses his solutions, making especial use of a mind-reading power so sure that it can divine the thought sequences of persons he has never met. Dupin's divinations are instantaneous, as some say the Creation was instantaneous, and his recital to the narrator of his "chain of reasoning" is, like Genesis, a sequential shadowing-forth of something otherwise inexpressible.

Denis Marion and others have noted that Dupin's logic, as reported in "The Murders in the Rue Morgue," is not inevitable, either when he "reads" a long concatenation of the narrator's thoughts, or when he reconstructs the "reasoning" which led to his solution of the crime. The ear-witnesses of the murder have heard two voices within Mme. L'Espanaye's chambers, one exclaiming in French and the other in a tongue conjectured to be this or that, but in all cases unintelligible to the particular witness. Because an Italian, an Englishman, a Spaniard, a Hollander, and a Frenchman have all declared the second voice to be foreign to them, Dupin makes the "*sole proper deduction*" that the voice is that of a beast. This is to brush aside, as Marion says, several possibilities: that the speaker was Turkish or Bantu, that he had a speech defect, or that some or all of the witnesses were mistaken. Again, Dupin draws from the fact that the killer did not take Mme. L'Espanaye's gold the conclusion that the crime was without motive; but theft is not the only possible motive for murder. The fact is that Dupin's logic, proceeding with a charmed arbitrariness toward the solution which seems to justify it, has what Poe called an "*air* of method," but is really intuition in disguise.

Richard Wilbur, "The Poe Mystery Case," *New York Review of Books*, 13 July 1967, p. 26

STUART LEVINE   ⟨. . .⟩ the detective stories should not be considered as an isolated handful of experiments in a totally different genre. Rather, they fit in perfectly well with the pattern which we have seen operating in so many of Poe's stories. If we were to arrange Poe's fiction along sort of a scale, running from those in which the narrator has a relatively difficult time in perceiving to those in which he has no trouble at all, the Dupin stories would come near the end of our list. At the other end of the scale would go tales such as "Ligeia," "Berenice," "The Fall of the House of Usher," "The Pit and the Pendulum," and "A Descent into the Maelstrom." What they have in common is that to "get through" to whatever "vision" he is to experience, the perceiver in each of them has to go through a process far more arduous than do Ellison ⟨in "The Domain of Arnheim"⟩ or Dupin. The patterns of crime which Dupin perceives will "take" the usual adjectives. They are ornate, complex, bizarre, but Dupin himself does not have to undergo a harrowing experience in order to see them.

Stuart Levine, *Edgar Poe: Seer and Craftsman* (DeLand, FL: Everett/Edwards, 1972), pp. 166–67

J. GERALD KENNEDY   Like his adversary in "The Purloined Letter," Dupin is both poet and mathematician. As a mathematician he understands the "Calculus of Probabilities" which ordinarily governs natural phenomena. As a poet, though, he recognizes the surprising paradoxes of human experience which make an "ordinary" case sometimes more difficult to solve than one "excessively outré." According to Poe's epistemology, the two modes of cognition are inextricably related; "the *truly* imaginative [are] never otherwise than analytic," he writes in "The Murders in the Rue Morgue." But both methods of knowing are ancillary to the kind of pure reasoning to which Dupin alludes in his remark about the letter thief: "As poet *and* mathematician, he would reason well; as mere mathematician, he could not have reasoned at all." The detective's ability to combine imagination and analysis causes the narrator of "The Murders in the Rue Morgue" to recall "the old philosophy of the Bi-Part Soul" and imagine a "double Dupin—the creative and the resolvent." In the same tale Poe reminds us that "intuition" has nothing to do with the analyst's solutions, which are obtained "by the very soul and essence of method." Dupin's method typically involves both a meticulous examination of physical evidence (involvement in the world of men) and a dispassionate consideration of the case as a whole (withdrawal to the realm of abstract thought). Out of this dialectical tension between involvement and detachment, poetry and mathematics, emerges the Truth which is the detective's goal.

Significant though Dupin's conquest of the unknown may seem in the context of Poe's artistic quest for a rational vision of experience, the fact remains that the author discarded his detective hero after "The Purloined Letter." A partial explanation comes from Poe himself, who wrote to Philip Pendleton Cooke in 1846: "These tales of ratiocination owe most of their popularity to being something in a new key. I do not mean to say that they are not ingenious—but people think them more ingenious than they are— on account of their method and *air* of method. In the 'Murders in the Rue Morgue,' for instance, where is the ingenuity of unravelling a web which you yourself (the author) have woven for the express purpose of unravelling?" That Poe came to see the detective story as a rather superficial and mechanical exercise in mystification also appears to inform "The Oblong Box," where the narrator's failure illustrates the speciousness of an intellectual system out of touch with the problems of human fallibility and mortality. Poe's fundamental vision of the human condition, the vision which even through ratiocination he could not at last escape, saw man as the predestined victim of the Conqueror Worm. In abandoning the detective story, Poe finally acknowledged that ratiocination answers no questions of genuine importance, clarifies nothing about the hopes and fears of humankind. For a brief period in Poe's career, ratiocination perhaps offered a distraction from the recurring nightmare of death and disintegration. But he could never fully recover, through his fictional man of reason, the reassuring eighteenth-century myth of a rationally designed universe; the inescapable terrors of the imagination made that task impossible.

J. Gerald Kennedy, "The Limits of Reason: Poe's Deluded Detectives," *American Literature* 47, No. 2 (May 1975): 195–96

DAVID KETTERER   Poe's prizewinning story "The Gold-Bug," which first appeared in the *Dollar Newspaper* for June 21 and 28, 1843, contains many slips, as pointed out by Woodrow J. Hassell; but they simply do not matter, thanks to the tale's imaginative momentum. As Hassell concludes, it is a product of the skillful fusion of the poet and the reasoner. In this tale, Poe is making artistic capital out of the cryptographic ability he prized so jealously. Now the reward is not a year's subscription to *Graham's Magazine* and the *Saturday Evening Post* but Captain Kidd's treasure. Legrand, the protagonist, even uses the same slogan that Poe used: "It may well be doubted whether human ingenuity can construct an enigma of the kind which human ingenuity may not, by proper application, resolve." Poe claims in *Graham's Magazine*, "Human ingenuity cannot concoct a cipher which human ingenuity cannot resolve." The treasure, like the money that Dupin insisted on and received for his services, may be interpreted as the reward of arabesque vision afforded to the analytic imagination. ⟨. . .⟩

"The Gold-Bug" is actually just as much a crime story as any of the Dupin tales. In each case, the crime represents the perception of arabesque reality. However, "The Gold-Bug"—one of Poe's finest tales—is not a detective story in the strictest sense because "every shred of the evidence on which Legrand's brilliant deductions are based is withheld from the reader until *after* the solution is disclosed" ⟨Howard Haycraft⟩. Similarly, "Thou Art the Man," which was published in *Godey's Lady's Book* for November, 1844, and seems to be almost a parody of Poe's ratiocinative tales, does not play fair because the information that the bullet passed *through* the horse is withheld. Neither is the narrator honest concerning "Old Charley" Goodfellow's threat upon being knocked down by Mr. Pennifeather: "He arose from the blow, adjusted his clothes, and made no attempt at retaliation at all—merely muttering a few words about 'taking summary vengeance at the first convenient opportunity,'—a natural and very justifiable ebullition of anger, which meant nothing, however, and, beyond doubt, was no sooner given vent to than forgotten." At the conclusion of the tale, the narrator reveals, "I was present when Mr. Pennifeather had struck him, and the fiendish expression which then arose upon his countenance, although momentary, assured me that his threat of vengeance would, if possible, be rigidly fulfilled."

Nevertheless, "Thou Art the Man" does have its logical place in the chronological development of Poe's ratiocinative tales. When Old Charley speaks of "disinterring the treasure," opening the box, he is anticipating the discovery that the box contains a corpse; but he is also recalling the action of "The Gold-Bug." The similarity cannot be pursued. If "The Gold-Bug" is one of Poe's best tales, "Thou Art the Man," although a forerunner of the "murder-in-a-small-town" theme, is among his least interesting productions. Balancing the look back to the previous ratiocinative tale is a look forward to the next. The employment of the "least-likely-person" theme in "Thou Art the Man" anticipates the "overlooked-obvious" theme in "The Purloined Letter."

David Ketterer, *The Rationale of Deception in Poe* (Baton Rouge: Louisiana State University Press, 1979), pp. 248–51

BRUCE I. WEINER   It may be ⟨. . .⟩ that crime in the Dupin stories disrupts the ostensible order of things to permit a glimpse of an ideal world beyond, but Dupin is not directly engaged with the ideal. He is as ardent a student of Transcendentalism as the narrator of "Ligeia," but the mysteries he solves are material. They are *outré* but not occult, brutal or clever but not, like the mystery of the Man of the Crowd, deep. Indeed, the paradox upon which Poe builds his detective tales nullifies the problem of the unsolved mysteries. "Truth is not always in a well," Dupin tells the narrator in "Murders," but "as regards the more important knowledge, I do believe that she is invariably superficial." So much for the mystery of Ligeia's eyes, "more profound than the well of Democritus." Contrary to what Dupin suggests when he scoffs at the police for holding the object of their investigation too close, or failing to realize that a star is more clearly seen when looked at askance, this is more than a difference of how we look at truth. The cosmic mystery in "Ligeia" is reduced in "Murders" to the dimensions of the typical whodunit. Dupin circumscribes the mystery himself when he dismisses the possibility of the occult: "It is not too much to say that neither of us believe in praeternatural events. Madame and Mademoiselle L'Espanaye were not destroyed by spirits. The doers of this deed were material, and escaped materially."

Still Poe tries to have it both ways with Dupin. By confining him to an investigation of material crimes, Poe satisfies those doubts about the power of human understanding that prevail in the unsolved mysteries, but he characterizes Dupin's analysis as a "moral activity which disentangles," which partakes of the reciprocal laws of physics and metaphysics. The true analyst displays "a degree of *acumen* which appears to the ordinary apprehension praeternatural. His results, brought about by the very soul and essence of method, have, in truth, the whole air of intuition." In these propositions about the faculty of analysis, Poe attempts to bridge the distinction, current in the psychology of his day, between the rational and imaginative faculties, between the discriminating powers that tie us down to the material world and the creative intuition that elevates us to the ideal. The method of the true analyst, according to Poe's narrator in "Murders," is the converse of the artist's creative process. The question remains, though, whether Dupin's analysis in practice is the "metaphysical acumen" it is supposed to be in theory. Donald Stauffer maintains that it is. Dupin's solutions "are actually flashes of intuition" which "approach that vision of the ultimate unity of all things which [Poe] was to set down in its final form in *Eureka*."

Stauffer asks us to suspend our disbelief, however, in an illusion that Poe himself discredits. In "The Mystery of Marie Rogêt" his narrator admits that Dupin's solution of the Rue Morgue murders "was regarded as little less than miraculous" only because the "simple character of those inductions by which he disentangled the mystery" were never explained to the police or the public. Although Dupin's "analytic abilities acquired for him the credit of intuition," his "frankness would have led him to disabuse every inquirer of such prejudice." Ironically, the narrator himself is guilty of promoting such prejudice, for he functions chiefly to convey the impression that Dupin's solutions are miraculous flashes of intuition. Poe's strategy in the detective tales, to paraphrase the narrator of "Murders," is to make Dupin's solutions *appear* preternatural to the ordinary intellect, to give them the whole *air* of intuition, while revealing that they are, in fact, brought about by the very soul and essence of logical method. The effect is achieved by Dupin's unexpected announcement to the bewildered narrator that he has solved the mystery, making it seem like clairvoyance. Then Dupin backtracks to explain the chain of reasoning that led to his conclusion. Not preternatural, Dupin's analysis seems no less marvelous, for even when explained it appears abstruse to ordinary intellects like the narrator.

Bruce I. Weiner, " 'That Metaphysical Art': Mystery and Detection in Poe's Tales," *Poe and Our Times*, ed. Benjamin Franklin Fisher IV (Baltimore: Edgar Allan Poe Society, 1986), pp. 38–39

ROBERT GIDDINGS   Dupin is an epic character in so far as he epitomizes the spirit of his time and the character of his nation. He is very American, and very much a man of his period. The quoted passage at the opening of 'The Murders in the Rue Morgue', the story which introduces Dupin to us, is from Sir Thomas Browne's *Urn-Burial*, and associates Dupin immediately with Achilles. His mental characteristics are given us as emphatically analytical, rational and reflective. But these qualities are harnessed to *usefulness*. This is a very American quality. 〈. . .〉 He is young, and though of good old family stock, the family fortunes have declined and he has to shift for himself in the world. He cares only for the basic necessities of life. His individualism shows itself in the way he abjures most social contacts.

Although no less than Oedipus and Hamlet Dupin finds himself entangled in the resolution of mysteries, there are several important qualities which mark Dupin out as a new departure. Each of the three tales which feature Poe's analytic hero is unique unto itself, but there are some common features which are very important in qualifying the essence of Dupin, and establishing that there is much more to be yielded by examining them than simply demonstrable Freudianism. One obvious difference is that Dupin is not personally involved in the problems he solves. They are not a matter of life and death to him. Nor does he set out—as Oedipus had—to solve a problem which affected the whole community. Nor, as was the case with Hamlet, does he wrestle with problems of kingship, succession, conscience, heaven and hell. The importance of the mysteries lies in the very fact that he is the one who solves them by exercising his particular gifts. This is one of the first points Poe makes about him.

> Robert Giddings, "Was the Chevalier Left-Handed? Poe's Dupin Stories," *Edgar Allan Poe: The Design of Order*, ed. A. Robert Lee (London: Vision Press, 1987), pp. 97–98

CHARLES E. MAY   "The Mystery of Marie Rogêt" is, most agree, the weakest of the three Dupin stories, primarily because it is so lacking in narrative interest. And indeed it is lacking in narrative interest because it is so bound to an actual murder that Poe, in the Dupin guise, hopes to resolve. As a result, the detective here is so firmly ensconced in his armchair that the readers of the story take little interest in his attempts to lay bare the mystery. But the piece is worth looking at briefly not only for its further illustration of the motifs of the analytical, but also because Poe poses it as a classic example of a fiction being superimposed over a reality. The prefatory note from Novalis suggests the issue that interests Poe here: "There are ideal series of events which run parallel with the real ones. They rarely coincide. Men and circumstances generally modify the ideal train of events, so that it seems imperfect, and its consequences are equally imperfect." The narrator then provides a brief exposition on coincidence by which he justifies the paralleling of the ideal (i.e., the fictional events of Marie Rogêt) with the real (i.e., the actual events of Mary Rogers). The parallel between the names and the exact parallel between the events make it clear, of course, that there is no coincidence here, at least not as we understand that term in everyday reality. What people call coincidence in everyday reality, Poe wishes to remind us, is in fiction the artistic calculation of putting things together in a unified, parallel fashion.

Dupin's method in "The Mystery of Marie Rogêt" is similar to that of the Rue Morgue case in that he investigates the crime by studying actual texts, that is, newspaper accounts; thus, he is dealing with events already at a textual remove from actuality. The story differs from "The Murders in the Rue Morgue" in that it has nothing of the outré about it; it is ordinary and is for that reason all the more difficult. However, the main reason it is more difficult than the Rue Morgue case is that there can be no "Bi-Part" Dupin/Poe here, one who both creates and resolves. The event is ordinary precisely because it is real, not fictional, and thus has no aesthetic pattern. What Dupin must do in this case is just the opposite of what he did in the Rue Morgue case. In the first, he had to create an unusual pattern to fit the events of the case; that is, he had to create a fiction. In this case, he has to expose the fictions that the newspapers have created about the events. For example, the idea of one newspaper that Marie Rogêt is still alive, Dupin attributes to the appeal of both the epigrammatic nature of its "pungent contradiction" and its melodramatic nature, not its plausibility. That is, Poe/Dupin exposes the fictional conventions of the newspapers, although it is precisely fictional conventions that he himself used in "The Murders in the Rue Morgue" to create that story. Thus, what Poe does in "Marie Rogêt" is to expose the methods he used in "Rue Morgue."

Charles E. May, Edgar Allan Poe: A Study of the Short Fiction (Boston: Twayne, 1991), pp. 89–90

Bibliography

Tamerlane and Other Poems. 1827.

Al Aaraaf, Tamerlane, and Minor Poems. 1829.

Poems. 1831.

The Narrative of Arthur Gordon Pym of Nantucket. 1838.

The Conchologist's First Book; or, A System of Testaceous Malacology. 1839.

Tales of the Grotesque and Arabesque. 1840. 2 vols.

Prospectus of The Penn Magazine. 1840.

Prose Romances: The Murders in the Rue Morgue; The Man That Was Used Up. 1843.

Tales. 1845.

The Raven and Other Poems. 1845.

Mesmerism "in Articulo Mortis" ⟨"The Facts in the Case of M. Valdemar"⟩. 1846.

Prospectus of The Stylus. 1848.

Eureka: A Prose Poem. 1848.

Works. Ed. Rufus W. Griswold. 1850–56. 4 vols.

Tales of Mystery and Imagination. 1855.

Works. Ed. John H. Ingram. 1874–75. 4 vols.

Works. Ed. Richard Henry Stoddard. 1884. 8 vols.

Works. Ed. Edmund Clarence Stedman and George Edward Woodberry. 1894–95. 10 vols.

Complete Works. Ed. James A. Harrison. 1902. 17 vols.

Last Letters to Sarah Helen Whitman. Ed. James A. Harrison. 1909.

Complete Poems. Ed. J. H. Whitty. 1911.

Poems. Ed. Killis Campbell. 1917.

Letters. Ed. Mary Newton Stanard. 1925.

Best Known Works. Ed. Hervey Allen. 1931.

Complete Poems and Stories. Ed. Arthur Hobson Quinn. 1946. 2 vols.

Letters. Ed. John Ward Ostrom. 1948 (2 vols.), 1966.

Selected Prose, Poetry, and Eureka. Ed. W. H. Auden. 1950.

Literary Criticism. Ed. Robert L. Hough. 1965.

Poems. Ed. Floyd Stovall. 1965.

Collected Works. Ed. Thomas Ollive Mabbott et al. 1969–78. 3 vols. (incomplete).

The Science Fiction of Edgar Allan Poe. Ed. Harold Beaver. 1976.

Collected Writings. Ed. Burton R. Pollin et al. 1981– .

The Annotated Edgar Allan Poe. Ed. Stephen Peithman. 1981.

Poetry and Tales. Ed. Patrick Quinn. 1984.

Essays and Reviews. Ed. G. R. Thompson. 1984.

Melville Davisson Post
1869–1930

MELVILLE DAVISSON POST was born on April 19, 1869, into a West Virginia family whose roots extended back to America's colonial days and whose lands had come from a direct grant by George III. Both his rural background and his parents' deep religiousness were strong influences on his writing.

Post obtained an A.B. from the University of Virginia in 1891 and his LL.B. from the school the following year. Upon graduating, he practiced general and criminal law in a partnership in Wheeling, West Virginia. In 1896 he distilled his professional experiences into *The Strange Schemes of Randolph Mason*, a collection of stories about an amoral New York City attorney who practices law by the book and uses legal loopholes to have his clients acquitted. With two more collections of Randolph Mason stories, *The Man of Last Resort; or, The Clients of Randolph Mason* (1897) and *The Corrector of Destinies* (1908), Post helped bring about badly needed changes in the law and established his reputation as the most original writer of crime fiction in America since Edgar Allan Poe.

Post became a corporate lawyer in 1901; that same year he published his first novel, the regional adventure *Dwellers in the Hills*. In 1903 he married Ann Bloomfield Gamble, with whom he had a son, Ira C. Post II, in 1905. Ira's death from typhoid at eighteen months left Post and his wife devastated, precipitating the dissolution of his law practice and several years of overseas travel.

In 1911 the *Saturday Evening Post* published "The Broken Stirrup Leather," Post's first tale of Uncle Abner, a highly spiritual cattleman on the Virginia frontier who combines superior detective skills, biblical ethics, and homespun philosophy to solve rural mysteries. The twenty-two Uncle Abner stories, collected as *Uncle Abner, Master of Mysteries* (1918) and *The Methods of Uncle Abner* (1974), were recognized as the first uniquely American variations on the crime and detective story formula as promulgated by Poe and Arthur Conan Doyle. Post also gained renown as a critical theorist through two essays, "The Blight" (1914) and "The Mystery Story" (1915), in which he defended the literary legitimacy of the mystery or "problem" story and emphasized the importance of "mathematically accurate" plots and characters and incidents taken from real life for the success of such stories.

Over the next fifteen years Post worked out his theories for the mystery story through the collected adventures of several series characters, including Scotland Yard inspector Sir Henry Marquis (*The Sleuth of St. James's Square*, 1920; *The Broadmoor Murder*, 1929), Paris police prefect M. Jonquelle (*Monsieur Jonquelle, Prefect of Police of Paris*, 1923), American Secret Service agent Captain Walker (*Walker of the Secret Service*, 1924), and Virginia lawyer Colonel Braxton (*The Silent Witness*, 1930).

Post became increasingly reclusive and his literary output reduced following Ann's death in 1919 and the death of his father in 1923. He died of complications from a fall from his horse on June 23, 1930.

▨ *Critical Extracts*

UNSIGNED   If there is anything new to be found under the sun, Melville Davisson Post has come very near it in *The Strange Schemes of Randolph Mason*, which is a series of short stories, the central figure whereof, Randolph Mason, is introduced as a shrewd, crafty, remarkably ugly man, utterly devoid of moral principle. A lawyer of unusual ability, he has prostituted his talent to the pursuit of his favorite theory, which is, that the most horrible wrongs may be planned and executed in such a manner, that they are not crimes before the law. To this end he makes himself familiar with the most minute technicalities of state laws, and this knowledge enables him to advise his clients with the utmost certainty. Through his devilish cunning, murderers, embezzlers and forgers are enabled to walk out of court scot-free, in the face of judge and jury convinced of their guilt, but powerless to convict. Though far from profitable reading, and utterly improbable, this work opens up a new line of thought, and offers a startling commentary on the apparent vulnerability of some of our laws.

Unsigned, [Review of *The Strange Schemes of Randolph Mason*], *Critic*, 27 March 1897, p. 218

UNSIGNED   Randolph Mason may not be humanly possible—an embodied characteristic is rarely so; but there is a certain stern charm in so austere a conception as the incarnate essence of justice untinctured with sympathy. The character of his interest in the destinies he regulates is aptly sketched by one who remarks concerning him:

> Write to him the sort of note that you would write to a famous
> archaeologist if you wished him to call and examine a rare
> Egyptian pot . . . invite him to the examination of a case of rare
> and interesting injustice.

It is open to question, of course, whether he and his secretary would ever have seen the light had it not been for Sherlock Holmes and Dr. Watson; but that in an imitative age matters little, so the work be well done. Most of the stories hang upon points of law more interesting to the technician than to the outsider; the "Virgin of the Mountain" plumbs deeper waters, calling into play the reader's personal sense of justice apart from the law. Whether one agree with Mason's solution of the problem or not, it is an interesting case, and to the perverse especially piquant as an unique chance to find a joint in the hero's armor of infallibility.

Unsigned, [Review of *The Corrector of Destinies*], *Nation*, 19 November 1908, p. 498

UNSIGNED   Mr. Post is one of those natural story-tellers who are not made, but born with the narrative gift. His is a fecund imagination, and if he makes use of the wonderful jewels, secret codes, spies and counterfeiters familiar to detective fiction, there is always something, or nearly always, something novel in his way of manipulating his material, some new turn or twist which gives freshness to the narrative. All those who like to be first puzzled and then surprised will heartily enjoy reading of the experiences and exploits of *The Sleuth of St. James's Square*.

Unsigned, [Review of *The Sleuth of St. James's Square*], *New York Times Book Review and Magazine*, 20 December 1920, p. 23

MELVILLE DAVISSON POST   A well-constructed plot should be single in its issue. It should present one moving event in its complete unity. It should be so constructed that it unfolds itself or builds itself up by a natural and orderly moving of events. Every event should follow the preceding one in inevitable sequence, and the explanation should appear suddenly.

The element of surprise must come swiftly at the end. When the story is ended the reader will not wait for explanations. Everything he must know or ought to know should be given to him before the explanation. The complications must be cleared in a few words. It is here that most mystery stories fail. The reader is interested in the first half of the story, but when the other half is devoted to explanations of the mystery, which he already understands, he will not read it.

Hence the plot for the mystery, problem or detective story must now be constructed better than it used to be. Even Poe's long explanations, as in "The Murders in the Rue Morgue," are no longer tolerated. After the reader discovers who the criminal agent was he does not wish to read the long explanation.

The important thing in the structure of stories now is to get every explanation of every character before the reader in advance of the revelation of the mystery, and to uncover the mystery, with a rush, at the end. This is manifestly more difficult than the old-fashioned method; but the reader demands it and the writer must do it.

In this respect he can no longer follow Poe, Gaboriau, Doyle, and their like. An illustration of this new method is in one or two mild little stories by Thomas Bailey Aldrich—"Marjorie Daw," and "Our Neighbors at Ponkapog"; for in those stories, when the mystery is revealed, no explanation follows.

In short, if the mystery depends on the identity of a criminal agent the story must end immediately after the reader discovers the criminal agent. Whatever the mystery may be, the moment it is made known to the reader the story ends at once. Therefore the first requisite of such a story is that everything necessary for the reader to know must precede this discovery.

Melville Davisson Post, "The Mystery Story," *Saturday Evening Post*, 27 February 1915, p. 22

BLANCHE COLTON WILLIAMS   Mr. Post recognizes that in a story, the story's the thing, that no degree of literary excellence can atone for lack of plot. He addresses himself at once to the popular and critical reader. If there lives a writer of stories who is the "critic's writer," he is the man. He expressed himself unmistakably in "The Blight" (*Saturday Evening Post*, 26 December 1914): "The primary object of all fiction is to entertain the reader. If, while it entertains, it also ennobles him this fiction becomes a work of art; but its primary business must be to entertain and not to educate or instruct him." In answering the question, "What sort of fiction has the most nearly universal appeal?" he holds that the human mind is engaged almost exclusively with problems, and that "the writer who presents a problem to be solved or a mystery to be untangled will be offering those qualities in his fiction which are of the most nearly universal appeal." Men of education and culture—but never critics of stories!—have taken the position that literature of this character is not of the highest order. He cites Aristotle's *Poetics:* "Tragedy is an imitation, not of men, but of an action of life . . . the incidents and the plot are the end of tragedy." The plot is first; character is second. The Greeks would have been astounded at the idea common to our age that "the highest form of literary structure may omit the framework of the plot." The short story is to our age what the drama was to the Greeks and Poe knew this. And he is the one literary genius America has produced.

Yet Mr. Post's ideal of plot is no mere mechanical contrivance. He once expressed his pleasure to the present writer that "there are people who see that a story should be clean cut with a single dominating germinal incident upon which it turns as a door upon a hinge, and not built up on a scaffolding of criss-cross stuff." In all these underlying principles of his work, principles stated with the frankness of Poe, Melville Post strikes an answering chord in the critic who finds in his stories the perfect application of the theories he champions.

Mr. Post also holds a brief for his large employment of tragic incident: "Under the scheme of the universe it is the tragic things that seem the most real." He pleases the popular audience because he writes of crime. He knows, as Anna Katherine Green knows, its universal appeal.

Blanche Colton Williams, "Melville Davisson Post," *Our Short Story Writers* (New York: Dodd, Mead, 1922), pp. 299–300

GRANT OVERTON   Poe had replaced the god from the machine with the man from the detective bureau, but further progress seemed for some time to be blocked. All that anyone was able to do was to produce a crime and then solve it, to build up a mystery and then explain it. This procedure inevitably caused repetition. The weakness was so marked that many writers tried to withhold the solution or explanation until the very end, even at the cost of making it confused, hurried, improbable. Even so, no real quality of drama characterized the period between the crime at the commencement and the disclosure at the finish of the tale. I do not know who was the first to discover that the way to achieve drama was to have the crime going on, to make the tale a race between the detective and the criminal. The method can, however, be very well observed in Mary Roberts Rinehart's first novel, *The Circular Staircase* (1908); and of course it is somewhat implied in the operations of Count Fosco in Wilkie Collins's *The Woman in White*, many years earlier. But this discovery constituted the only technical advance of any importance since Poe. As a noticeable refinement upon this discovery Melville Davisson Post has invented the type of mystery or detective-mystery tale in which the mysteriousness and the solution are developed together. Not suitable for the novel, which must have action, this formula of Mr. Post's is admirable for the short story, in which there is no room for a race with crime but only for a few moments of breathlessness before a dénouement.

This refinement of Mr. Post's whereby repetition is avoided, the development of the mystery and its solution side by side, is usually hailed as his greatest achievement. I happen to think that he has in certain of his tales achieved something very much greater. It seems to me that in some of his work Mr. Post has put the *deus ex machina* back in place; has by a little lifted the mere detective story to the dignity of something like the old Greek tragedy, and in so doing has at least partially restored to the people the purge of pity and the cleansing of a reverent terror.

For, whatever tribute one may pay him on the technical side—and every book of his increases the tribute that is his due—the thing that has remained unremarked is his use of plot for ennobling the heart and mind of the reader. He is right, of course, when he says that the primary business of the writer must be to entertain; but more rightly right when he adds that it is possible to do the something more in a work which may aspire to be called a work of art.

Grant Overton, "Melville Davisson Post and the Use of Plot," *Bookman* (New York) 59, No. 4 (June 1924): 427

WILLARD HUNTINGTON WRIGHT   One of the truly out-
standing figures in detective fiction is Uncle Abner, whose criminal adventures are recounted by Melville Davisson Post in *Uncle Abner: Master of
Mysteries*, and in a couple of short stores included in the volume, *The Sleuth
of St. James's Square*. Uncle Abner, indeed, is one of the very few detectives
deserving to be ranked with that immortal triumvirate, Dupin, Lecoq and
Holmes; and I have often marveled at the omission of his name from the
various articles and criticisms I have seen dealing with detective fiction. In
conception, execution, device and general literary quality these stories of
early Virginia, written by a man who thoroughly knows his *métier* and is
also an expert in law and criminology, are among the very best we possess.
The grim and lovable Uncle Abner is a vivid and convincing character,
and the plots of his experiences with crime are as unusual as they are
convincing. Mr. Post is the first author who, to my knowledge, has used
the phonetic misspelling in a document supposedly written by a deaf and
dumb man as a proof of its having been forged. (The device is found in the
story called "An Act of God.") If Mr. Post had written only *Uncle Abner*
he would be deserving of inclusion among the foremost of detective fiction
writers, but in *The Sleuth of St. James's Square*, and especially in *Monsieur
Jonquelle*, he has achieved a type of highly capable and engrossing crime-
mystery tale. The story called "The Great Cipher" in the latter book is,
with the possible exception of Poe's "The Gold-Bug," the best cipher story
in English.

> Willard Huntington Wright, "Introduction," *The Great Detective Stories: A Chronologi-
> cal Anthology* (New York: Charles Scribner's Sons, 1927), pp. 23–24

HOWARD HAYCRAFT   Post, who received record prices for his
magazine work, considered himself the champion of plot-technique in the
short story. Indeed, he is probably the most creditable exponent of the
formularized short story that America has developed; and his skill in this
direction, however detrimental it may have been to his "artistic" reputation,
brought to the detective story a new technical excellence that was to have
far-reaching effects. His clipped, economical style was admirably suited to
the form, and his deft, selective plot manipulation was a strong and healthy
contrast to the rambling diffuseness of most of his countrymen who were
active in the field at the time.

Nevertheless, in his preoccupation with plot formulas, Post underestimated some of his own greatest talents. The Abner stories are still read and re-read after more than a quarter-century less for the intensive plots of which their author was so proud—strikingly original in their time but mostly hackneyed by imitation to-day—than for the difficult-to-define quality that separates the sheep from the goats in any form of literature: in Post's case, as nearly as can be expressed, his richly sentient realization of character, place, and mood. Had he been willing to emphasize this side of his talent more, his stature as a true literary artist might have been greater than now seems likely. As it was, his never quite expressed serious abilities were sufficient to set him, in the less pretentious form of the detective story, head and shoulders above his contemporaries and to make him the peer of almost any practitioner of the genre who has written since. ⟨. . .⟩

Superlatively fine as they are, the Uncle Abner stories have not altogether escaped criticism. Their most serious fault, in the opinion of certain critics, is the author's failure in a few of the tales to make all the evidence explicit. In at least one instance ⟨"An Act of God"⟩ this criticism is justified beyond any doubt. But in other cases, one wonders if a basic misunderstanding on the part of the critics themselves may not be at fault? Certainly, we must insist on fair play. But the detective story, whether long or short, does not exist in which there is not *some* "off-stage" work—if only in the detective's mind. To have matters otherwise would be to deprive us of our puzzle in mid-career. In nearly every case, Post's offense is merely the logical extension of this principle; and one feels, somehow, that the writer of the *short* detective story (handicapped and restricted in ways that the author of a novel never knows) should be allowed the widest possible discretion and latitude in this respect. Had Post met the demands of the quibblers to catalogue and label every clue, there would in many instances have been no mystery and no story. . . . It is not without reason that, for all Post's genius in physical device, Abner's detection in the final analysis nearly always hinges on *character*. It is his judgment of men's souls that leads him to expect and therefore to find and interpret the evidence, where lesser minds (including perhaps, the literal ones of his decriers) see naught.

Howard Haycraft, *Murder for Pleasure: The Life and Times of the Detective Story* (New York: D. Appleton-Century, 1941), pp. 95–97

ANTHONY BOUCHER   If the Mason stories point out weaknesses in our social fabric and stress the evil of which man is capable, the stories of Abner affirm (far more ringingly than any course in American History and Institutions) the incomparable breadth and depth and truth of the American concept of society and injustice, and the dignity and potential greatness of man, whose father is God.

Rome has never issued an official pronouncement concerning a patron saint of detectives; but one can have little doubt that it is the prophet Daniel, who so skillfully solved (in the Catholic Bible and the Protestant Apocrypha) the puzzles of the falsely accused Susanna and of the mysteriously voracious idol of Bel. If the prophet Daniel is the patron, his favorite son must be Abner, who combines acute deductive skills with an Old Testament moral grandeur which makes him seem to speak at times with the very voice of the Lord.

> Anthony Boucher, "Introduction," *Uncle Abner: Master of Mysteries* (1962; rpt. in *The Complete Uncle Abner*, San Diego: University of California, 1977), p. 418

CHARLES A. NORTON   Post had been writing and publishing tales about his finest character, Uncle Abner, for seven years before they were collected into the deservedly famous *Uncle Abner, Master of Mysteries*. It is not only the best of Post's work, but one of the truly great collections of mystery and detective stories of all time. The chief contributions made here by Post are through his character, Abner. Here is the first great "non-detective" who solves crimes. Also with Abner, we find a character who does not wait upon the law, but administers justice as he sees it in accordance with the powers of Providence—although he often cooperates with the law in a manner justified in the frontier setting of the tales. Perhaps Abner's method of solving crimes is one of the most important contributions, for he operates not only on shrewd intelligence in sorting out significant clues, but he has the added ability to read human nature. In these Abner stories, in nearly every instance, Post has devised plots that have various aspects of the tragic drama. Many good things have been said about these stories and many more remain to be said—they are a supreme accomplishment.

> Charles A. Norton, "A Final Evaluation," *Melville Davisson Post: Man of Many Mysteries* (Bowling Green, OH: Bowling Green University Popular Press, 1973), p. 230

ALLEN J. HUBIN   The stature of the Abner narratives was recognized early; by 1941 (in his *Murder for Pleasure*) Howard Haycraft was observing that "posterity may well name [Uncle Abner], after Dupin, the greatest American contribution to the form," and in 1942 (in his *The Detective Short Story*) Ellery Queen was stating firmly that *Uncle Abner* was "the finest book of detective short stories written by an American author since Poe." There has long been a critical consensus, at least in the United States, that the Abner tales constitute a magnificent achievement—and one that was seemingly born fully developed rather than—like the hard-boiled story—evolving over several years.

Is this the reason why Uncle Abner appears to be *sui generis*, why no subsequent American writers—with the possible exception of William Faulkner in *Knight's Gambit*—attempted to build upon, imitate, or develop further the Abner model? Has there been a general recognition that the Uncle Abner stories, and Abner himself, were and are complete in themselves?

The various fictional cleric-detectives (such as Father Brown) that have dotted the ratiocinative landscape might be cited in rebuttal. But Uncle Abner was not a clergyman, and in the intensity of his religious beliefs, in his passion for justice, in his identification with the people and the land, I believe he stands uniquely apart.

Uncle Abner is also more distinctly American in acceptance than the hard-boiled story, which in the hands of Hammett as well as less able American practitioners was quickly recognized as a salable commodity in England and elsewhere. It is a matter of record that, although Post reportedly enjoyed a literary reputation in England through the appearance of his first novel (*Dwellers in the Hills*), *Uncle Abner* (U.S., 1918) was not brought out in Britain until a small publisher, now defunct, issued the book in 1972.

Further, England's Julian Symons says in his highly regarded *Mortal Consequences* (1972; *Bloody Murder* in England) that "the attraction the stories have for Americans simply does not exist for others. To English readers, Uncle Abner is likely to seem a distant and implausible figure." I find this curious, for the ties of Abner and his people to England are clearly evident in the stories, and Abner is twice described as "a man who might have followed Cromwell." Abner is profoundly a man of his Virginia country and mid-nineteenth-century period; but can it be true that no such character, strong and devout and wise, could have tramped the farther hills of England during the last century?

Yet, the fact of Abner's low appeal to the English remains, and he stands to this day as peculiarly American.

Allen J. Hubin, "Introduction," *The Complete Uncle Abner* (San Diego: University of California, 1977), pp. viii–ix

---

OTTO PENZLER   In Randolph Mason, Post created one of the first and greatest rogues in mystery fiction. His adventures mark the creation of a totally new kind of crime story. In the past, as in most traditional forms of detective fiction, even to the present day, criminals had concerned themselves with eluding capture. In the Randolph Mason stories, the paramount factor is avoiding punishment.

Mason is an unscrupulous lawyer who recognizes that justice and the law are often unrelated, so he advises his clients to conduct their affairs in a manner that will elude the arms of the law. In one instance, he informed a client that the only solution to his problem was for him to murder his wife.

In his introduction to *The Strange Schemes of Randolph Mason*, the first book about the lawyer who later gave his name to Erle Stanley Gardner's more famous criminal lawyer, Perry Mason, Post wrote: "The law provides a Procrustean standard for all crimes. Thus a wrong, to become criminal, must fit exactly into the measure laid down by the law, else it is no crime; if it varies never so little from legal measure, the law must, and will, refuse to regard it as criminal, no matter how injurious a wrong it may be. There is no measure of morality, or equity, or common right that can be applied to the criminal case."

Mason once described his philosophy, which is a monument of amorality: "No man who has followed my advice has committed a crime. Crime is a technical word. It is the law's term for certain acts which it is pleased to define and punish with a penalty. What the law permits is right, else it would prohibit it. What the law prohibits is wrong, because it punishes it. The word moral is a purely metaphysical one."

While criticized for faulty construction, the Randolph Mason stories were terrifically powerful in their time, on occasion resulting in badly needed changes in the law. In concept, as well as stylistically, they remain as shocking and memorable today as when they were written—nearly ninety years ago.

Otto Penzler, "Collecting Mystery Fiction: Melville Davisson Post," *Armchair Detective* 18, No. 2 (Spring 1985): 168

▣ *Bibliography*

The Strange Schemes of Randolph Mason. 1896.

The Man of Last Resort; or, The Clients of Randolph Mason. 1897.

Dwellers in the Hills. 1901.

The Corrector of Destinies: Being Tales of Randolph Mason as Related by His Private Secretary, Courtlandt Parks. 1908.

The Gilded Chair. 1910.

The Nameless Thing. 1912.

German War Ciphers. 1918.

Uncle Abner, Master of Mysteries. 1918.

The Mystery at the Blue Villa. 1919.

The Sleuth of St. James's Square. 1920.

The Mountain School-Teacher. 1922.

Monsieur Jonquelle, Prefect of Police of Paris. 1923.

Walker of the Secret Service. 1924.

The Man Hunters. 1926.

The Revolt of the Birds. 1927.

The Broadmoor Murder: Including the Remarkable Deductions of Sir Henry Marquis of Scotland Yard (The Garden in Asia). 1929.

The Silent Witness. 1930.

The Methods of Uncle Abner. Ed. Tom and Enid Schantz. 1974.

The Complete Uncle Abner. Ed. Allen J. Hubin. 1977.

Mary Roberts Rinehart
1876–1958

MARY ROBERTS RINEHART was born Mary Ella Roberts on August 12, 1876, in Allegheny, Pennsylvania. Her father, Thomas Roberts, was an unsuccessful salesman and unlucky inventor who finally committed suicide in 1895, and the family was somewhat poor, although never desperately so. Mary graduated from a local high school in the midst of the depression of 1893, but luckily a well-to-do uncle offered to pay for her to attend medical school. She was interested in medicine (a career her family deemed inappropriate for women), but at age sixteen she was too young to be admitted and decided instead to attend nursing school at the Homeopathic Medical and Surgical Hospital and Dispensary. The squalor of late nineteenth-century medicine dissuaded Mary from pursuing a medical career. (During her second day of nursing school she was handed a bucket in an operating room and told to dispose of its contents. Inside was a severed foot.) However, her medical experience gave her a great deal of material for future stories (most notably the "Tish" detective-nurse stories). Mary graduated from nursing school in 1896, married Dr. Stanley Marshall Rinehart (with whom she had three sons) soon after, and began to suffer from a breakdown in health that would plague her for the rest of her life.

In the early 1900s Rinehart began to write fiction and poetry, and in 1904 her first published work, a poem, appeared in a local newspaper. Rinehart quickly became successful, serializing the mystery *The Man in Lower Ten* in the magazine *All-Story* in 1906 and doing the same with *The Circular Staircase* a year later. In 1908 *The Circular Staircase* was published in book form; it was an instant hit and was quickly followed by many others. Rinehart ultimately would rule the best-seller list for twenty-seven years, having books on the list continuously from 1909 to 1936.

A remarkably prolific writer who habitually wrote nine hours a day every day, Rinehart also wrote nonfiction (she was a war correspondent during World War I); plays, most notably *The Bat* (1920), an adaptation of *The Circular Staircase* that was a huge Broadway success; and nonmystery novels, including the autobiographical *K* (1915). But her most popular writings were her mysteries, generally told in the first person by an unmarried female narrator who is reminiscing about a murder or, more commonly, several murders. Rinehart's writing was influenced by Gothic literature and emphasized the terror felt by the narrator as she solves the grisly crimes with little or no help from the police. Ogden Nash labeled Rinehart's style the "Had I But Known" or "H.I.B.K." school of writing, a label that has stuck and is frequently used by critics, friendly and otherwise, in describing Rinehart's fiction.

The success of Rinehart's fiction made her quite wealthy, and despite lavish spending habits she was able to maintain herself and her family luxuriously for the rest of her life. Her later life was a constant mix of intensive bouts of writing followed by more intensive bouts of illness (she woke up in an oxygen tent after completing one particularly involving novel). Her autobiography, *My Story*, was published in 1931 and updated in 1948. Mary Roberts Rinehart died of a heart attack on September 22, 1958.

Critical Extracts

UNSIGNED   "As charming as a débutante"—these are the first words of the publishers' announcement as to the heroine of *The Amazing Adventures of Letitia Carberry*, by Mary Roberts Rinehart. It would be a treat to hear Letitia's own comment on this faint praise. It is, indeed, the irony of fate. On the one hand is the novel-reading public, unutterably bored by the endless stream of stories about débutantes; and here, on the other hand, is a novel with a refreshingly different kind of heroine—a delightful old maid of fifty, adventurous, witty, entirely unashamed of her spinsterhood—and the first phrase that occurs to her friends who are heralding her is "as charming as a débutante!" Well, at any rate, the book soon makes one forget that phrase.

The first tale, which comprises more than half the pages, is a rather farcical detective story. The scene of action is a hospital, in which "Tish" is a very impatient patient. A man who has died quietly in his bed disappears an hour later from the mortuary and is found hanged to a chandelier in a vacant room. The authorities "don't seem to care whether their corpses walk around at night or not," but a few days later an actual murder takes place under strikingly similar circumstances, and "Tish," having played volunteer detective from the start with great spirit and energy, has accumulated a number of clues.

The joke is, however, that her clues seem to point in different directions, and that, though she solves the mystery in the end, she does it not by "examining the dust with a microscope"—which is her generic term for orthodox detective work—but by extracting the facts from the pretty little nurse who knows them all. The others have refused to question the girl because they are afraid she is implicated, and they like her too much to be willing to track her down; the girl herself has kept silent in order to shield another nurse from the consequences of carelessness. Letitia, who simply wants the facts, succeeds in getting them, and incidentally clears the girl of suspicion. The solution of the mystery—the murderer proves to be a maniac—is not very interesting, and there are some things that remain unaccounted for. But the tale is told in such a lively, humorous manner, and there is such infectious, spontaneous pleasure in the telling, that the reader is not inclined to be critical.

> Unsigned, "A Delightful Spinster," *New York Times Book Review*, 7 January 1912, p. 9

GRANT MARTIN OVERTON   Next to the vitality, the variety of Mrs. Rinehart's work is most noticeable. Her first novel, *The Circular Staircase*, was a mystery tale, and so was her second, *The Man in Lower Ten*. She has, from time to time, continued to write excellent mystery stories. *The Breaking Point* is, from one standpoint, a first class mystery story; and then there is that enormously successful mystery play, written by Mrs. Rinehart in conjunction with Avery Hopwood, *The Bat*. Nor was this her first success as a playwright for she collaborated with Mr. Hopwood in writing the farce *Seven Days*. Shall I add that Mrs. Rinehart has lived part of her life in haunted houses? I am under the impression that more than one of her residences has been found to be suitably or unsuitably haunted. There was that house at Bellport on Long Island—but I really don't know the story. I do know that the family's experience has been such as to provide material for one or more very good mystery novels. My own theory is that

Mrs. Rinehart's indubitable gift for the creation of mystery yarns has been responsible for the facts. I imagine that the haunting of the houses has been a projection into some physical plane of her busy subconsciousness. I mean, simply, that instead of materialising as a story, her preoccupation induced a set of actual and surprising circumstances. Why couldn't it? Let Sir Oliver Lodge or Sir Arthur Conan Doyle, the Society for Psychical Research, anybody who knows about that sort of thing, explain! ⟨. . .⟩

⟨. . .⟩ one could go on with other samples of Mrs. Rinehart's abundant variety. I think, however, that the vitality of her work, and not the variety nor the success in variety, is our point. That vitality has its roots in a sympathetic feeling and a sanative humour not exceeded in the equipment of any popular novelist writing in America today.

Grant Martin Overton, "The Vitality of Mary Roberts Rinehart," *When Winter Comes to Main Street* (New York: George H. Doran Co., 1922), pp. 114–16

MARY ROBERTS RINEHART   ⟨. . .⟩ writing is work. It is long, arduous and incessant work. It cuts out many of the pleasant things of life. The author lives with one foot in an everyday world and the other feeling about anxiously for a foothold in another more precarious one. And still he cannot analyze entirely either why he writes instead of making scrubbing brushes; or why, having chosen to write, he writes the things he does. ⟨. . .⟩

The books have covered about every phase of life I know, and some—like one aboard a sailing vessel, where I placed a bridge where no bridge should ever have been—about things of which I knew very little. But it sometimes startles me to think that I have written so much about murder. I have no criminal side to my nature. I am really one of those people who return books and umbrellas, and insist on giving up my railroad ticket if I am overlooked.

Even most of my progenitors seem to have lived long lives, although there is a legend that the pirate, Bartholomew Roberts, was one of them.

But I have written fifteen books about crime. Not thrillers, which bear no relation to life or plausibility, but stories of murder, committed with normal weapons by people otherwise normal. And I am frank to say that I have had a lot of trouble doing it.

The plain fact is that a properly written and developed crime book is really a novel, plus an intricate and partially hidden plot. The writer, in doing one, has pretty nearly as hard a time as the criminal himself. For not only must the characters be real, the setting recognizable and the crime logical. The intricacy of the plot makes it necessary to hold a dozen or a hundred threads in the mind. In doing one I take notes as I go along, but alterations often make these useless; and also I frequently mislay them. ⟨. . .⟩

Yet, in its essence, the crime story is simple. It consists of two stories. One is known only to the criminal and to the author himself. It is usually simple, consisting chiefly of the commission of a murder and the criminal's attempt to cover up after it; although quite often he is driven to other murders to protect himself, thus carrying on the suspense.

The other story is the one which is told. It is capable of great elaboration, and should, when finished, be complete in itself. It is necessary, however, to connect the two stories throughout the book. This is done by allowing a bit, here and there, of the hidden story to appear. It may be a clue, it may be another crime. In any case, you may be certain that the author is having a pretty difficult time, and that if in the end he fails to explain one of these appearances, at least five hundred people will discover it and write him indignant letters.

Mary Roberts Rinehart, *Writing Is Work* (Boston: The Writer, 1939), pp. 22–24

HOWARD HAYCRAFT   The dividing line between the *physical* type of detective story and the pure mystery story is often difficult to distinguish. The conclusive test might well be whether, in the final analysis, the solution is accomplished by incident (mystery story) or deduction (detective story). Even by this test, it is not easy to decide in which of these categories the dramatic and highly popular murder stories of Mary Roberts Rinehart belong. They fall almost exactly on the border-line. (But it is possibly not without some significance that the average uncritical American reader, asked to list important writers of the "detective story," will almost invariably place Mrs. Rinehart's name first.) Examined in the light of careful scholarship, some of the Rinehart tales would likely be found to belong to the one type, some to the other. One day, perhaps, the academic world will forego its preoccupation with the dead bones of the past long enough to perform this practical service to literature! ⟨. . .⟩

Virtually all the Rinehart crime novels have detectives of a sort, which is one reason they are so difficult to classify. Most of them have two: an official detective of more or less astuteness; and the first-person narrator, usually a woman, most often a romantic spinster engaged in protecting young love from unjust suspicion, who alternately complicates the plot and aids detection in unpremeditated fashion—a combination of participating (usually interfering!) Watson, and detective-by-accident.

This is the readily recognizable "Rinehart formula," still delightful when practised by its originator, but becoming increasingly tedious in the hands of her far-too-numerous imitators among American women writers. It is, in fact, only Mrs. Rinehart's superlative talent as one of the great story-tellers of the age (and the intensely human quality of her writing) that induces us to overlook in her own tales breaches of detective etiquette we could excuse in nobody else: what Waldo Frank calls her "carpentry." Foremost in any catalogue of these flaws must be the manner in which romantic complications are allowed to obstruct the orderly process of puzzle-and-solution. Similarly, the plots are always being prolonged by accidents and "happenstances"—not honest mistakes of deductive judgment by the investigator, which would be a legitimate part of the game, but unmotivated interferences and lapses on the part of the characters, who are forever blundering into carefully laid traps and springing them prematurely, or "forgetting" to tell the official detective of important clues. ("Four lives might have been spared if I had only remembered. . . .") Only too frequently, it must be confessed, these clues turn out at the dénouement to have had no bearing on the puzzle anyway! ⟨. . .⟩

Unfortunately, it is too often these weaknesses that Mrs. Rinehart's imitators are prone to mimic, rather than her points of strength—of which there are many. For the "formula" she devised possesses immense technical advantages, quite apart from its inventor's personal narrative skill. Chief among them, as pointed out by the late Grant Overton, are the reader's participation in the adventure by self-identification with the narrator; and the "forward action" of the plot, the direct antithesis of the over-intellectualized puzzle story. In a Rinehart murder novel the initial crime is never the be-all and end-all but only the opening incident in a progressive conflict between the narrator and the criminal. As Overton further observed: "Here [is] no put-the-pieces-together formula; here [is] an out-guess-this-unknown-or-he'll-out-guess-you, life-and-death struggle." Sometimes this dramatic approach goes too far and carries the story past the border-line of detection and into the realm of mere mystery-adventure; but kept within bounds it is a technique that practitioners of the cut-and-dried Static School might profitably study. In Mrs. Rinehart's own skilled hands it results in a mood of sustained excitement and suspense that renders the reader virtually powerless to lay her books down, despite their logical shortcomings.

Howard Haycraft, *Murder for Pleasure: The Life and Times of the Detective Story* (New York: D. Appleton-Century, 1941), pp. 87, 89–91

RUSSEL NYE   Mrs. Rinehart's formula in *The Circular Staircase* was a good one. She used it again in *The Man in Lower Ten* (1909), and over and over again, down to *The Swimming Pool* in 1952. The society she wrote about was the comfortable, orderly society of 1912, temporarily disturbed by a crime but perfectly capable of rearranging itself after the guilty were apprehended. Cooks were Irish, chauffeurs Negro, gardeners crotchety old men named Amos, chambermaids not very bright and easily frightened. The clean-cut young people were named Jim and Judy, and the police who called were always Inspectors and Captains.

Mrs. Rinehart's style was old-fashioned and leisurely, fitted to long evenings of reading at home. *The Door* (1921), one of her most popular, opened with a fifteen-hundred word essay on the psychology of crime ("What is it that lies behind the final gesture of the killer?") followed by a three-thousand word description of the narrator's home, location, furnishing, staff of five servants, and the ramifications of the family's relationships. The "Had I but known" theme is introduced quietly:

> It is one of the inevitable results of tragedy that one is always harking back to it, wondering what could have been done to avert it. I find myself going over and over the events of that night, so simple in appearance, so dreadful in result. Suppose I had turned on Sarah's light that night? Would I have found her murderer in the room? Was the faint sound I heard the movement of her curtain in the wind, as I had thought, or something much more terrible?
>
> Again, instead of sending Joseph upstairs to search, what if I had had the police called and the house surrounded?
>
> Still, what could I have done for Sarah? Nothing. Nothing at all.

Russel Nye, "Murderers and Detectives," *The Unembarrassed Muse: The Popular Arts in America* (New York: Dial Press, 1970), pp. 246–48

ARNOLD R. HOFFMAN   In ⟨Rinehart's⟩ mysteries the narrators often survey the world of a waning—or better, moribund—Victorian upper class, sometimes from within, sometimes from the viewpoint of the genteel poor, and sometimes through the eyes of the middle class. In an aura of nostalgia that ebbs and flows, one sees old fortunes dwindling through too many heirs, no heirs at all, or mere waste. One sees social refinements, the proprieties, being stubbornly maintained by one generation and glaringly ignored by its successor. The generation gap is never more strikingly evident or more sensitively depicted than in *The Breaking Point* where the old man looks to God and trusts and the young man acknowledges a vague Providence but insists on searching. In a succession of images generally so deftly executed that they complement rather than obscure a good story—and Mrs. Rinehart always thought of herself as a storyteller, not as a literary figure—we watch the quickening pace of the workaday world and leisure life bring in cigarettes to replace pipes and cigars, fast driving to replace a walk or a picnic, and fifteen minutes alone for a young couple instead of five (*The Case of Jennie Brice*).

Significantly, Mrs. Rinehart avoided a hard didactic line on any of the social issues. In 1908 she was *not* a young rebel advocating social upheaval. In 1934 she was *not* a middle-aged law giver. And in 1952 she was *not* an entrenched old woman railing against the encroachments of the young and the new. Rather, from the outset of her career Mrs. Rinehart manifested a feeling for both sides of the issue. Her detractors might say she simply knew what would sell to most people, but ⟨. . .⟩ I would say she observed and recorded the topical with an objective sensibility.

Arnold R. Hoffman, "Social History and the Crime Fiction of Mary Roberts Rinehart," *New Dimensions in Popular Culture*, ed. Russel B. Nye (Bowling Green, OH: Bowling Green State University Popular Press, 1972), pp. 167–68

JAN COHN   As Rinehart learned to make the richest use of the buried story ⟨. . .⟩, so she found in her long-time fascination with identity the second crucial element for these mysteries. Once the structure for the buried story had been worked out, the formal problem became the linking of the surface and buried stories, the discovery of a way to carry some passionate past action into the present, to create one or more characters who so disguised their passionate past as to fit into a tranquil world. The solution lay in lost, mistaken, and especially assumed identity. When a character could pretend to be (or even believe himself to be) other than what he really was, he could fit into a world he did not really belong to. Then, when the disclosure came or was threatened, violence was triggered.

Mysteries, of course, have long been vehicles for disguise, and Rinehart's earlier mystery novels presented characters in disguise of one kind or another from the beginning. It is important, however, to distinguish between a disguise and an assumed identity here. A disguise is put on; it is a mask that conceals the real person while he or she must pretend to be someone else. In her mature mysteries Rinehart occasionally has a character in the surface story put on such a disguise, often to aid in solving the crime. But for Rinehart assumed identity was something much deeper: a character *becomes* someone else. Assumed identity always stems from the buried past and is always reserved for evil or tragic personalities. A character usually assumes a new identity because he wishes to remake himself, to be recreated, but sometimes a character actually loses his old identity through amnesia and the recreation is innocent, though dangerous. More often though, the assumption of identity is malevolent and typically involves the adoption of a false set of class and family credentials.

With a young woman of low social origins who assumes the identity of an upper class woman, Rinehart discovered both the connection she needed between the surface and buried stories and the conception of evil that would control the mysteries of this period. Evil lay in the problem of sexuality. Whether Rinehart ever recognized the thematic burden of her buried stories is unclear; she certainly never mentioned it in writing about her work. But what these stories warn of is the evil effects of romantic misalliance, of affairs or marriages across class lines and under false pretenses. Most typically, a young man of good family is sexually drawn to a beautiful, vulgar, unprincipled woman acting in a false character, an assumed identity. For example, she may come from a small midwestern town and then, moving east, change her name and the facts of her past. Afterwards, having married into society, she lives under the assumed identity of an aristocrat, for decked out in borrowed feathers, she does not belong. Rinehart located the source of evil quite specifically in the intrusion of such a woman into a refined and ethical and aristocratic world. ⟨. . .⟩

The corrective to the buried story and its vicious cross-class marriages lies in the surface story. Here the romantic interest typically centers on a young woman of good family and a man who at least appears to be from "the people," clearly reversing the class affiliations of the buried story. With the Depression Rinehart's best families are often in economic straits, at least relatively so, and her young women must assume responsibility for something more than their clothing and party invitations. In some cases, they must work. Usually these women are older than the girls in Rinehart's early stories. The eighteen year olds of that period were pretty, innocent, sometimes endangered, and usually engaged to the wrong man. In the 30s the hero no longer needs to fight his way over a rival for the girl's affection. What keeps the lovers apart is real or apparent class differences along with the complications arising from the mystery which they both work at solving. As a result of these changes in her young women, Rinehart created heroines with considerably more character and a far more interesting "voice" than in her earlier work, and in them she found particularly suitable narrators for several of the mysteries of her mature period.

Jan Cohn, "Mary Roberts Rinehart," *10 Women of Mystery*, ed. Earl F. Bargainnier (Bowling Green, OH: Bowling Green State University Popular Press, 1981), pp. 198–99

KATHLEEN L. MAIO   Mary Roberts Rinehart (1876–1958) is the "mother" of HIBK. Although there was a large body of first-person-female narrative mystery fiction before Rinehart (Anna Katharine Green's "Amelia Butterworth" novels are charming examples), it is Rinehart who clearly developed the narrative technique into a formula that went beyond pure detection. Rinehart's first nonserial novel, *The Circular Staircase* (1908), is the cornerstone work of HIBK. The narrator, spinster Rachel Innes, rents a summer country house called Sunnyside and is soon embroiled in a plot of multiple murder (five die) and general mayhem. She is clearly an innocent bystander to the original plot. But soon the reputations of her niece and nephew, and her own safety, are threatened. For a while she waits for the police to resolve things, but she soon finds their inaction "deadly," and the situation increasingly dangerous. In self-defense she becomes a detective, ferreting clues and suppressing those that implicate her household.

The official sleuth, Mr. Jamieson, his band of detectives, and the confused innocents involved all stumble at cross-purposes through a plot that becomes more deadly and dangerous with every moment. Miss Innes makes most of the key discoveries because she is not plagued by the need for "logical" (linear) thinking like the classic male sleuth. She does not expect human behavior to be a rational process. She does not expect physical evidence to tell the whole story. Curiosity and leaps of insight stand her in good stead. She tells us:

> Halsey always says: "Trust a woman to add two and two together and make six." To which I retort that if two and two plus x make six, then to discover the unknown quantity is the simplest thing in the world. That a household of detectives missed it entirely was because they were busy trying to prove that two and two makes four.

Rinehart would later freely admit that "*The Circular Staircase* was intended to be a semi-satire on the usual pompous self-important crime stories."

The Circular Staircase was followed by many more Rinehart mysteries, and almost all are within the HIBK formula. Rinehart was masterful in the use of the older woman as spinster-heroine and narrator. While these women are sharp, fiercely independent, and skeptical about men, they often help foster the obligatory romance by playing fairy-godmother-as-vindicating-sleuth for one or more sets of young lovers. Other mysteries feature younger (but still mature) women as central figures. In *The Wall* (1938) and *The Great Mistake* (1940), young women are actively brave in working to rid their households of danger.   They are rewarded with romance and a happy ending. But theirs is a happy ending tempered by the need to look back, to reevaluate, and even to regret the past.

Kathleen L. Maio, "Had-I-But-Known: The Marriage of Gothic Terror and Detection," *The Female Gothic,* ed. Julianne E. Fleenor (Montreal: Eden Press, 1983), pp. 84–85

⊠ *Bibliography*

The Circular Staircase. 1908.
The Man in Lower Ten. 1909.
When a Man Marries. 1909.
The Window at the White Cat. 1910.
The Amazing Adventures of Letitia Carberry. 1911.
Where There's a Will. 1912.

The Case of Jennie Brice. 1913.

The After House: A Story of Love, Mystery and a Private Yacht. 1914.

The Street of Seven Stars. 1914.

K. 1915.

Kings, Queens and Pawns: An American Woman at the Front. 1915.

Tish. 1916.

Through Glacier Park: Seeing America First with Howard Eaton. 1916.

Bab, a Sub-Deb. 1917.

Long Live the King! 1917.

The Altar of Freedom. 1917.

Twenty-three and a Half Hours' Leave. 1918.

Tenting To-night: A Chronicle of Sport and Adventure in Glacier Park and the Cascade Mountains. 1918.

The Amazing Interlude. 1918.

Dangerous Days. 1919.

Love Stories. 1919.

A Poor Wise Man. 1920.

"Isn't That Just Like a Man!" ⟨with *"Oh, Well, You Know How Women Are!"* by Irvin S. Cobb⟩. 1920.

The Truce of God. 1920.

Affinities and Other Stories. 1920.

Sight Unseen and The Confession. 1921.

More Tish. 1921.

The Breaking Point. 1922.

The Out Trail. 1923.

Temperamental People. 1924.

The Red Lamp ⟨*The Mystery Lamp*⟩. 1925.

The Bat (with Avery Hopwood). 1926.

Tish Plays the Game. 1926.

Nomad's Land. 1926.

Lost Ecstasy ⟨*I Take This Woman*⟩. 1927.

Two Flights Up. 1928.

This Strange Adventure. 1929.

The Romantics. 1929.

The Door. 1930.

Mary Roberts Rinehart's Mystery Book ⟨*The Circular Staircase, The Man in Lower Ten, The Case of Jennie Brice, The Confession*⟩. 1930.

Seven Days (with Avery Hopwood). 1931.

Mary Roberts Rinehart's Romance Book ⟨K, *The Amazing Interlude, The Street*
   of Seven Stars⟩. 1931.
My Story. 1931, 1948.
A Woman Goes to Market. 1931.
The Bat (drama; with Avery Hopwood). 1932.
Miss Pinkerton: Adventures of a Nurse Detective ⟨*The Double Alibi*⟩. 1932.
Mary Roberts Rinehart's Crime Book. 1933.
The Album. 1933.
The State versus Elinor Norton. 1934.
Mr. Cohen Takes a Walk. 1934.
The Doctor. 1936.
Married People. 1937.
Tish Marches On. 1937.
The Wall. 1938.
Writing Is Work. 1939.
The Great Mistake. 1940.
Familiar Faces: Stories of People You Know. 1941.
Haunted Lady. 1942.
Alibi for Isabel and Other Stories. 1944.
The Yellow Room. 1945.
The Curve of the Catenary. 1945.
A Light in the Window. 1948.
Episode of the Wandering Knife: Three Mystery Tales. 1950.
The Swimming Pool. 1952.
The Frightened Wife and Other Murder Stories. 1953.
The Best of Tish. 1955.

Dorothy L. Sayers
1893–1957

DOROTHY LEIGH SAYERS, the only child of an Anglican clergyman, was born in Oxford on June 13, 1893. She spent three difficult and awkward years at the Godolphin School for Girls in Salisbury before matriculating at Somerville College, Oxford, in 1912. At Oxford Sayers was an excellent student of modern languages who also showed an interest in literature, debating, and theatre. She earned an M.A. with First Class Honours in 1915, but did not receive her degree until five years later when Oxford decided to grant degrees to women.

After Oxford Sayers taught briefly at the Hull High School for Girls. She then took a job at the publishing firm Basil Blackwell, which issued Sayers's first book, the poetry collection *Op. I* (1916). In 1919 she left to take a teaching position in France, returning to London the next year to begin her writing career in earnest. To support herself she worked for an advertising agency, Benson's, from 1922 to 1931; this experience would serve as the basis for the novel *Murder Must Advertise* (1933).

In 1923 Sayers's first detective novel, *Whose Body?*, was published to favorable reviews. In this sophisticated mystery Sayers introduces the debonair sleuth Lord Peter Wimsey. She continued writing about Wimsey's intrigues throughout the 1920s and 1930s in both novels (notably *Have His Carcase*, 1932; *The Nine Tailors*, 1934; *Gaudy Night*, 1935; and *Busman's Honeymoon*, 1937, initially written as a play with Muriel St. Clare Byrne) and short story collections (*Lord Peter Views the Body*, 1928; *Hangman's Holiday*, 1933). Several of her later novels feature a sensitively portrayed romance between Wimsey and the writer Harriet Vane, who was introduced in *Strong Poison* (1930) and is commonly thought to be modeled on herself. Sayers also helped to found the Detection Club, and she published several noteworthy anthologies of mystery and horror tales that featured her scholarly introductions on the rise and development of these genres.

Notwithstanding her literary success, Sayers's personal life was troubled. In 1924 she gave birth to an illegitimate son, John Anthony. Although she later adopted him, her true relationship to him was not revealed until almost twenty years after her death. Sayers married a journalist, Captain Oswald Atherton "Mac" Fleming, in 1926, and he agreed to lend his name to Sayers's fatherless son; but the marriage was turbulent because of Fleming's irresponsibility and alcoholism. He died in 1950.

In the late 1930s Sayers abandoned mystery writing and turned her attention toward more scholarly pursuits. She wrote several religious plays, including the celebrated BBC radio performance of *The Man Born to Be King*, as well as numerous critical and theological essays. During her final years she worked on a translation of Dante's *Divine Comedy*, finishing her renditions of the *Inferno* and *Purgatorio* as well as parts of the *Paradiso* before her death. In 1950 she received an honorary degree from the University of Durham and in 1952 she became a churchwarden at St. Thomas's in London. Although she devoted the last twenty years of her life to religious and scholarly writings, Sayers is today best remembered for her mystery novels of the 1920s and 1930s, which have recently been widely adapted on television. She died suddenly at her home in Witham on December 17, 1957.

▨ *Critical Extracts*

Q. D. LEAVIS   Th⟨e⟩ odd conviction that ⟨Sayers⟩ is in a different class from Edgar Wallace or Ethel M. Dell apparently depends on four factors in these novels. They have an appearance of literariness; they profess to treat profound emotions and to be concerned with values; they generally or incidentally affect to deal in large issues and general problems (*e.g. Gaudy Night* in so far as it is anything but a bundle of best-selling old clothes is supposed to answer the question whether academic life produces abnormality in women); and they appear to give an inside view of some modes of life that share the appeal of the unknown for many readers, particularly the life of the older universities.

Literature gets heavily drawn upon in Miss Sayers' writings, and her attitude to it is revealing. She displays knowingness about literature without any sensitiveness to it or any feeling for quality—*i.e.* she has an academic literary taste over and above having no general taste at all (there can hardly be any reader of Donne beside Miss Sayers who could wish to have his poetry associated with Lord Peter's feelings). Impressive literary excerpts, generally 17th century (a period far-off, whose prose ran to a pleasing quaintness and whose literature and thought are notoriously now in fashion) head each chapter. She—I should say Harriet Vane—proudly admits to having 'the novelist's habit of thinking of everything in terms of literary allusion.' What a give-away! It is a habit that gets people like Harriet Vane firsts in English examinations no doubt, but no novelist with such a parasitic, stale, adulterated way of feeling and living could ever amount to anything. And Miss Sayers' fiction, when it isn't mere detective-story of an unimpressive kind, is exactly that: stale, second-hand, hollow. Her wit consists in literary references. Her deliberate indecency is not shocking or amusing, it is odious merely as so much Restoration Comedy is, because the breath of life was never in it and it is only the emanation of a 'social' mind wanting to raise a snigger; you sense behind it a sort of female smoking-room (see the girlish dedication to *Busman's Honeymoon*) convinced that this is to be emancipated.

Q. D. Leavis, "The Case of Miss Dorothy Sayers," *Scrutiny* 6, No. 3 (December 1937): 335–36

RAYMOND CHANDLER   In her introduction to the first *Omnibus of Crime*, Dorothy Sayers wrote: "It [the detective story] does not, and by hypothesis never can, attain the loftiest level of literary achievement." And the reason, as she suggested somewhere else, is that it is a "literature of escape" and not "a literature of expression." I do not know what the loftiest level of literary achievement is: neither did Aeschylus or Shakespeare; neither does Miss Sayers. Other things being equal, which they never are, a more powerful theme will provoke a more powerful performance. Yet some very dull books have been written about God, and some very fine ones about how to make a living and stay fairly honest. It is always a matter of who writes the stuff, and what he has in him to write it with.

As for "literature of expression" and "literature of escape"—this is critics' jargon, a use of abstract words as if they had absolute meanings. Everything written with vitality expresses that vitality: there are no dull subjects, only dull writers. All men who read escape from something else. Some escape into Greek or astronomy or mathematics; some into weeding the yard or playing with the children's toys or getting tight in little bars. But all men must escape at times from the deadly rhythm of their private thoughts. That is part of the process of life among thinking beings. It is one of the things that distinguish them from the three-toed sloth; he apparently—one can never be quite sure—is perfectly content hanging upside down on a branch, not even reading Walter Lippmann.

I think what was really gnawing at Miss Sayers's mind was the slow realization that her kind of detective story was an arid formula which could not even satisfy its own implications. If it started out to be about real people (and she could write about them—her minor characters show that), they must very soon do unreal things in order to form the artificial pattern required by the plot. When they did unreal things, they ceased to be real themselves. They became puppets and cardboard lovers and papier-mâché villains and detectives of exquisite and impossible gentility.

The only kind of writer who could be happy with these properties was the one who did not know what reality was. Dorothy Sayers's own stories show that she was annoyed by this triteness; the weakest element in them is the part that makes them detective stories, the strongest the part which could be removed without touching the "problem of logic and deduction." Yet she could not or would not give her characters their heads and let them make their own mystery. It took a much simpler and more direct mind than hers to do that.

Raymond Chandler, "The Simple Art of Murder," Atlantic Monthly 174, No. 6 (December 1944): 56–57

MARTIN GREEN　　⟨. . .⟩ Dorothy Sayers was, to put it mildly, attracted to Lord Peter. Yet she felt she could afford to deny him all physical glamour and natural dignity explicitly; nor did she miscalculate. Any English reader will acknowledge the glamour of that image, however much he may dislike it. The lack of natural power is designed to bring out vividly the intellectual and artificial power of Lord Peter's taste, his brains, his position, his breeding, his learning, his sophistication, his analytical intelligence; all that is symbolized in the monocle. Artificial power seemed to Dorothy Sayers a better quality in a man than natural power—because it was safer, obviously. But don't let the safeness obscure the fact that this was power.

This blond, chinless, burbling type was prominent in English culture between the wars. Dorothy Sayers herself compared Lord Peter to P. G.

Wodehouse's Bertie Wooster, and to the roles created by Ralph Lynn in the Aldwych farces; and she used other characters from those imaginative worlds. Bunter is plainly modelled on Jeeves, and the Dowager Duchess of Denver could have come out of one of Ben Travers's farces. There are parallels, moreover, with some of Evelyn Waugh's characters. But Lord Peter is more interesting, as a cultural image, than any of his rivals or models: partly because he was put into significant relation to such a range of English reality—social and intellectual—but more because he was a figure of power. Bertie Wooster and Ralph Lynn were not such fools as they seemed, but the power did finally reside with Tom Walls or Jeeves. Lord Peter seems just as silly, but is masterful. And once we have met him, the other versions seem lacking in important ways. We feel that Dorothy Sayers had found the true, full form of this image. The reason is surely that this was a national image of the Englishman. He was in implicit contrast with the Australian or the American, so much richer in natural power and tough experience, so much younger nationally. We identified ourselves with upper-class effete figures because we knew that that was the way we must seem to the rest of the world. We took an interest in the difficulties and triumphs of people born to high estate and no income, with elegant educations and no useful knowledge of the modern world, because we all of us felt a bit like that when confronted with American or Australian cousins. Even within England, educated people felt they made the same contrast with the insurgent lower class. But we did not want to admit ourselves to be really weak and silly. A weak endowment by nature, but tremendous artificial power—socially and intellectually subtle, sophisticated, ruthless: that was how we saw ourselves, and that was why Lord Peter represented us.

Martin Green, "The Detection of a Snob," *Listener*, 14 March 1963, p. 464

JOHN G. CAWELTI   Sayers's best work, *The Nine Tailors*, uses the classical detective story structure to embody a vision of the mysteries of divine providence. This moral and religious aspect of the story by no means prevents it from having an effective and complex structure of detection and mystification, but this structure relates to the other interests of character, atmosphere, and theme in a very different way than is typical of Christie. For one thing, to a considerable extent we experience the inquiry as Lord Peter Wimsey does. Indeed, he remains mystified about the central crime in much the same way that we do and the way in which he finally arrives at the true solution is shown to us in much the same light as it appears to him. In other words, the detective and the reader do not part company two-thirds of the way through the tale but share in the process of discovery throughout. Character, also, assumes a kind of prominence in the story that is almost unknown to Christie. While the cast of characters is much the same as one would expect to find in a Christie story and has a decided stereotypical quality, they are not simply functional adjuncts of the detec-tion-mystification structure. For instance, there are a number of characters who are never presented to us as possible suspects and who yet play important parts in the story. This is almost never the case with Christie, except in her less successful tales. Finally, there is a great deal of material that charac-terizes or explains important aspects of the social setting without significantly contributing to the development of the mystery. The most notorious instance of this is Sayers's elaborate treatment of the art and ritual of change-ringing. While the bells do have an important role in the mystery, it was obviously not necessary to present a treatise on campanology in order to account for that circumstance. 〈. . .〉

〈. . .〉 in *The Nine Tailors*, Dorothy Sayers effectively integrates the formu-laic structure of the classical detective story with the additional narrative interests of religious theme and social setting. The mixture works effectively in this case without breaking the bounds of the formula because the mystery and the structure of inquiry through which it is presented are unified with the central theme of the mystery of God's providential action. Though this is a high accomplishment in the art of the classical detective story, some of its limitations become immediately apparent if we place *The Nine Tailors* in comparison with some of the great novels that deal with the religious aspects of murder, such as *Crime and Punishment* or *The Brothers Karamazov*. In *The Nine Tailors* God's will rather too comfortably aligns itself with a noticeably limited vision of English class justice. Compared with Dostoev-sky's treatment of the purging and redemption of Raskolnikov one becomes too easily aware that in Sayers's English village evil seems to be defined more in terms of nasty, aggressive members of the lower classes trying to punch their way up the social scale than as the more universally meaningful sense of mystery and evil that Dostoevsky so powerfully delineates. To enjoy fully and be moved by *The Nine Tailors* one must be able temporarily to accept the snobbish, class-ridden, provincial world of Fenchurch St. Paul as a microcosm of the world; otherwise one will inevitably agree with those readers who find the religious symbolism of the book pretentious and inappropriate. Whether these limitations of vision represent the attitudes of Miss Sayers or the formulaic boundaries of the classical detective story— and they are probably a combination of both—does not greatly matter. The fact that Sayers was able to work comfortably within the basic patterns of the classical formula suggests that her own religious commitments made sense in this way. Nonetheless, those who are willing to accept the stringent limitations of this fictional universe for the sake of such curious pleasures as the final twist by which it becomes apparent that God is the least likely person, are grateful to Dorothy Sayers for this embodiment of her art.

John G. Cawelti, *Adventure, Mystery, and Romance: Formula Stories as Art and Popular Culture* (Chicago: University of Chicago Press, 1976), pp. 120, 124–25

DAWSON GAILLARD   When she wrote *Strong Poison*, Sayers may have had in mind *Trent's Last Case*, a novel in which the detective falls in love and retires from detective work. She admired E. C. Bentley's achievement in that 1913 novel. She told readers that they may recognize its charm and brilliance and yet "have no idea how startlingly original it seemed when it first appeared. It shook the little world of the mystery novel like a revolution, and nothing was ever quite the same again. Every detective writer of today owes something, consciously or unconsciously, to its liberating influence." Bentley brought a real human being into his novel to replace the infallible Holmes and the infallible and abstract Dupin.

Like Sayers later, Bentley was discontent with the overly mechanical detective story. He admired Holmes but did not admire his exaggerated unreality. When he began to write his novel, therefore, Bentley intended to depart from the Holmes model. The result was a novel that showed writers that they could break the pattern of the infallible, austere detective and still construct a unified plot. Sayers's discussion of *Trent's Last Case* praises its unity of plot and tone. Without violating its unity, she said, Bentley approached the detective novel as a novelist, not as a short-story writer of puzzles.

Although some people look to Sayers's friend Eric Whelpton as the model for Lord Peter, a more reasonable direction is toward Trent. His parodies of quotations ("the dun deer's hide on fleeter foot has never tied" and "drain not to its dregs the urn of bitter prophecy") resemble Wimsey's speech. As

Trent's foolishness amuses Inspector Murch, Wimsey's amuses—and often annoys—Charles Parker. Not to push these comparisons too far, we need be aware only that when Sayers began to write, she looked to literature as well as to life for her models.

Before Lord Peter departed from her fiction, Sayers carefully operated on him to transform him from a puppet into a believable, three-dimensional character complete with genealogy and progeny. In 1937, she ruefully described her success: "I discover with alarm that his children are coming tumbling into the world before I have time to chronicle these events, and I am distracted and confused by the friendly letters of readers, giving him and Harriet the best advice upon child-welfare."

Dawson Gaillard, *Dorothy L. Sayers* (New York: Ungar, 1981), pp. 50–51

P. D. JAMES   Although Dorothy L. Sayers did as much as any writer in the genre to develop the detective story from an ingenious but lifeless puzzle into an intellectually respectable branch of fiction with serious claims to be judged as a novel she was an innovator of style and intention not of form. She was content to work within the convention of a central mystery, a closed circle of suspects each with his or her motive for the crime, a superman amateur detective, superior in talent and intelligence to the professional police, and a solution which the reader could arrive at by logical deduction from clues planted with deceptive cunning but essential fairness. The novels, too, are very much of their age in the complexity and ingenuity of the methods of murder. Readers of the 1930s expected that the puzzle would be dominant and that the murderer would demonstrate in his villainy an almost supernatural cunning and skill. Those were not the days of the swift bash to the skull followed by 60,000 words of psychological insight. The murder methods she devised are, in fact, over-ingenious and at least two are doubtfully practicable. A healthy man is unlikely to be killed by noise alone, a lethal injection of air would surely require a suspiciously large hypodermic syringe, and the methods of murder in *Have His Carcase* and *Busman's Honeymoon* are unnecessarily complicated, particularly for the crude and brutal villains of these stories. But if she was sometimes wrong she was never wilfully careless and her papers bear witness to the scholarly trouble she took to get her details right. She was adept at the technical tricks of her trade: the manipulation of train timetables, the drawing of red herrings skilfully across trails, the devising of plots that depended on clocks, tides, secret codes and mysterious foreigners. But she used these ploys with a freshness, wit and panache which reinvigorated even the tritest of conventions.

P. D. James, "Foreword," *Dorothy L. Sayers: A Biography* by James Brabazon (New York: Charles Scribner's Sons, 1981), pp. xiv–xv

---

ALZINA STONE DALE   By the mid-thirties Lord Peter Wimsey had become such a well-known character that any number of people were eager to adapt him to stage or screen. ⟨Muriel St. Clare⟩ Byrne herself had been approached to write a Wimsey play, but refused, while Sayers was inundated with scripts written by other people. She asked for Byrne's help in screening these scripts, which Byrne gave with her usual efficiency, but she found all of them dreadful and began to urge Sayers to write a play herself.

Sayers's theatrical experience had been limited to Somerville theatricals and an unsold film scenario written in the twenties. During 1934, however, she was struggling to write a film script for a Wimsey movie, which appeared in 1935 as *The Silent Passenger*. The film did not contain a word of her script, and Lord Peter was cast as a swarthy Italian-waiter type. This project convinced her that films were not worth the money they offered.

It is a testament to their belief in one another's capabilities and their capacity to work together that early in 1935 Sayers finally agreed to try and write a Wimsey stage play with Byrne's help. Two things probably encouraged her the most: Sayers and Byrne were equally ardent theater-goers and they both liked hard work, so long as it was work they considered "their job." They needed to enjoy this project, which was a very ambitious one to complete together with their regular professional obligations. Between February and May 1935, they produced a finished three act play, even though they made changes in it over that summer. ⟨. . .⟩

Byrne says that the play ⟨*Busman's Honeymoon*⟩ was not actually completed before the end of summer 1935 when it was sent off to theatrical producer Maurice Browne, who kept it until January 1936 trying to find financial backing. As a result, despite the speed with which it was written, *Busman's Honeymoon* did not open in London until December 1936. (Sayers meanwhile had gone to work writing the novel of the play, which was completed by the time the play opened.) ⟨. . .⟩

Sayers makes it plain in ⟨her⟩ notes that the murderer was a forerunner of her Judas, the modern man, when she writes that "he is definitely of the post-war brood . . . the only one who resents Peter's wealth and standing." Of Lord Peter himself Sayers writes that "to the villagers . . . he presents no problems; they recognize him at once as a hereditary ruler & are not embarrassed by his eccentricities, which are exactly what they would expect from a gentleman of his condition." Then she makes an equally revealing comment about Harriet and Peter's romance, saying that "the fact that they both have the same educational background is probably a considerable factor in the establishment of a common understanding; & though you might think that they are the last people who should ever have married one another, Oxford will in the end be justified of her children." These passages not only remind the reader of Harriet's thoughts in the novel *Busman's Honeymoon* when she realizes she has "married England," but they also reinforce the intentional symbolic importance of their courtship in Oxford and link the writing of *Gaudy Night* and *Busman's Honeymoon* more closely with Sayers's consideration of the fruits of a university education.

Alzina Stone Dale, "Introduction," *Love All: A Comedy of Manners; Together with Busman's Honeymoon: A Detective Comedy* by Dorothy L. Sayers and Muriel St. Clare Byrne (Kent, OH: Kent State University Press, 1984), pp. xviii, xx, xxv

---

MITZI BRUNSDALE   Dorothy Sayers's intimate portrait of Pym's Publicity ⟨in *Murder Must Advertise*⟩ is often praised as this novel's greatest strength, but the "criticism of life" that she attempted here also hints at the advocacy of Christian morality that dominates her later work. She deliberately set the false worlds of advertising and drugs side by side to point up their common denominator of deceit, offering illusory escape from real-life problems at a cost that devours the soul. As the rich man who had everything a hungry writer in 1921 had wanted, Lord Peter had never appreciated until he worked at Pym's the "enormous commercial importance" of the lower middle class, who hungered for luxuries and leisure they could never enjoy and who "could be bullied or wheedled" into wasting hard-earned money on momentary and illusory gratification. Peter's social conscience had begun to stir.

Murder Must Advertise also contains a lightly sketched self-portrait of Dorothy Sayers as Miss Meteyard, sometime scholar of Somerville, famous for the "vulgarest limericks ever recited within [Pym's] chaste walls." Like Dorothy, Miss Meteyard had problems with the income tax, a striking rather than a conventionally pretty countenance, and a powerful devotion to the doctrine of fair play that unravels this crime, in which the victim asks for his own catastrophe: when a person starts "to worry about whether he's as good as the next man," Miss Meteyard firmly states, he sets off an "uneasy snobbish feeling and makes himself offensive." With Mac, Dorothy Sayers lived day in, day out with that kind of insecurity, often a major element in alcoholism. She tried to cope with Mac's feelings of inferiority by encouraging his sporadic creative forays, like the *Gourmet's Book of Food and Drink* he published in 1933, but its offhand dedication to Dorothy, "who can make an Omelette," seems almost grounds for a wife to reach for a blunt instrument.

Mitzi Brunsdale, *Dorothy L. Sayers: Solving the Mystery of Wickedness* (New York: Berg, 1990), pp. 116–17

CATHERINE KENNEY   *The Documents in the Case* was daring because it took artistic—and, it would be fair to assume, financial—risks. With a popular series detective and a successful record of writing fairly conventional detective stories behind her, DLS decided to try a book without her great sleuth and with much greater thematic complexity than before. Thus, she risked not only disaffecting her readership, but also the possibility of failing to achieve more ambitious goals. Under the influence of Wilkie Collins's considerable stylistic charms, she adopted the epistolary form for this, her fifth novel, which is also the pivotal book in her development as a novelist. Although she had experimented with letters in *Unnatural Death*, this old standby for writers of fiction was essentially a new narrative form for DLS in 1930. James Brabazon regards the epistolary form as a natural choice for her, given her legendary letter-writing ability, as well as her love for another novel in letters, Richardson's *Sir Charles Grandison*. That she even attempted all these things is admirable, but more impressive is the book that resulted, which is far and away the best novel she had done to this point.

From the letters DLS wrote to her collaborator, Eustace Barton, we know that the idea, that is, the detective premise, for this novel was suggested by Barton. What is interesting is how Sayers took this rather conventional, if clever, detective idea, and turned it into the basis of a serious novel of rich social criticism and psychological complexity. I do not know at what point she decided to use the epistolary form for this story, but the decision was felicitous. As Barton had foreseen, the theme of the book is the nature of reality, its detective problem hinging upon the difference between real and synthetic poison. The letter form, which dramatizes the way that individual perceptions shape reality, is a perfect vehicle for the novel's theme; in a sense, it *embodies* the theme. The form also allows for extended discussions of such subjects as sexual politics, middle-class respectability, the relationship between art and life, and the possibility for belief in an increasingly secular world—quite a bit for a detective story to take up—but all rendered believable by the epistolary form, which allows the letter-writer to function effectively as both narrator and essayist. Letters permit the leisure, reflection, and subtlety that are necessary to the unfolding of this multidimensional novel of ideas, as well as the intimacy appropriate to the presentation of the kind of domestic tragedy the story relates.

    Catherine Kenney, *The Remarkable Case of Dorothy L. Sayers* (Kent, OH: Kent State University Press, 1990), pp. 141–42

S. T. JOSHI   Lord Peter Wimsey is of the English aristocracy. True, he is a younger son and therefore not a peer, but he is an aristocrat nonetheless. This fact in itself does not make Wimsey a snob: many critics have failed to make a distinction between Wimsey's attitude and Sayers' attitude, a distinction of great importance. Wimsey, in fact, is not a snob at all—he gets along quite well with all classes of society. But Sayers, in making Wimsey an aristocrat, takes care to allay criticism of him on this count by making him appear to break the mould. His celebrated first utterance, "Oh, damn!", is a not very subtle attempt to show that he is no stuffed shirt (like his elder brother, Gerald, Duke of Denver). Moreover, although he feigns an air of foolishness, he is nevertheless the one who solves the crime. No idle aristocrat he!

    The trump card in all this is that Wimsey is smart—he belongs not only to the aristocracy of blood, but the aristocracy of intellect. Sayers let us know this in very blunt and sometimes silly ways: Wimsey is a knowledgeable collector of incunabula; he plays Bach and Scarlatti effortlessly on the piano (but of course would prefer a harpsichord); at one point he even "whistles a complicated passage of Bach under his breath" (not a simple passage and not out loud); his knowledge of the arcane art of bell-ringing serves him well in The Nine Tailors; he seems a born advertising copywriter in Murder Must Advertise; and his knowledge of chemistry helps him solve the mystery in Strong Poison.

The degree to which Wimsey differs from one's average (and contemptuous) conception of the British aristocrat can be gauged by the degree to which he differs from his obvious inspiration, P. G. Wodehouse's Bertie Wooster. Sayers makes no secret of this inspiration: in Murder Must Advertise a character in an advertising agency, not realising that Wimsey is himself on the staff under an assumed name, explicitly compares him to Wooster as the type of the dim-witted scion of ageing blood; a few paragraphs later we are given the perfectly irrelevant detail that another character is reading a Wodehouse novel. And although Wimsey himself declares in The Five Red Herrings, "I was born looking foolish and every day in every way I am getting foolisher and foolisher", all this is only on the surface. It is not merely his intelligence that segregates him from the Woosters of the world; it is that his every motion testifies to his good breeding. ⟨. . .⟩

So here we are: Wimsey, though an aristocrat (Sayers never lets us forget it), is nevertheless not your usual aristocrat. How, then, does Sayers prove herself to be a snob? I repeat that Wimsey himself is not a snob; but this very fact is only one more trick whereby Sayers can convince us that Wimsey, and therefore certain others of the upper classes—like the flighty Hon. Frederick Arbuthnot, the real Bertie Wooster in Sayers (do British people really say "billy-ho" or "chappie"?)—are really just regular guys. Wimsey can be a real card sometimes: he terrifies Harriet Vane by driving fast in a motorcar; he shocks even the decadent young people in Murder Must Advertise by his antics at a wild party; he light-heartedly proposes to Harriet every April Fool's Day until she finally relents and accepts his hand. But Sayers gives herself away by little false notes and gaffes: in particular, her harping on the fact that Wimsey has all the money he could possibly want and that everything he owns costs a lot of money (he has a suitcase "of expensive-looking leather"; the Duke of Denver is "the wealthiest peer in England") reveals Sayers' fundamentally middle-class mentality. Snobbishness is really a middle-class failing: it is the aping of the outward motions and habits of true aristocracy by those who are not of its number; and it is a failing because it is so irremediably vulgar.

Her portrayal of the "lower classes" confirms this notion: whereas Wimsey, Vane, and others speak like normal people, the working-class characters in Sayers' novels can never make an utterance without countless grammatical mistakes—reduplicated plurals, double negatives, mispronunciation of difficult words, disagreement between subject and verb—and, of course, the ubiquitous dropped *h*. *These* people certainly never went to Oxford, like Wimsey and Harriet; or if they did it is only as servants and janitors. Whereas normal people are addressed by civilised names, the lower classes are addressed either by last names or by patronising diminutives like "Annie". In two stories—"The Undignified Melodrama of the Bone of Contention" and "The Incredible Elopement of Lord Peter Wimsey"—the supernatural is hinted at, but in such a flippant way as to suggest a certain polite laughter at the ignorant and superstitious yokels who get taken in by what turns out to be mere jiggery-pokery. On the other side, Sayers writes with pious reverence when talking about the aristocracy. She cannot resist unearthing an archaic procedure whereby the House of Lords must try one of their own—the Duke of Denver—for murder (*Clouds of Witness*); and the mere recital of hoary and pompous titles—Lord High Steward, Clerk of the Crown in Chancery—acts like an intoxicant to Sayers.

But let us give Wimsey, and Sayers, their due. It is frequently Wimsey's sheer frivolity, especially when he archly catches someone in a lie or reveals a guilty secret, that becomes frustrating and even harrowing to his antagonists; and he is clever, there is no denying it. What is more, Wimsey becomes truly humanised not by the little tricks Sayers pulls in her early novels, but by his long courtship of Harriet Vane; and it is hardly to be questioned that Sayers' four novels of the Wimsey-Vane saga are her most impressive achievement.

> S. T. Joshi, "Dorothy L. Sayers: The Highbrow Detective Story," *Million* No. 14 (March–June 1993): 14–15

Bibliography

Op. I. 1916.
Catholic Tales and Christian Songs. 1918.

Whose Body? 1923.

Clouds of Witness. 1926.

Unnatural Death. 1927.

The Unpleasantness at the Bellona Club. 1928.

Lord Peter Views the Body. 1928.

Great Short Stories of Detection, Mystery, and Horror ⟨The Omnibus of Crime⟩
      (editor). 1928.

Tristan in Brittany by Thomas the Troubadour (translator). 1929.

Strong Poison. 1930.

The Documents in the Case (with Robert Eustace). 1930.

The Five Red Herrings. 1931.

*Great Short Stories of Detection, Mystery, and Horror: Second Series ⟨The Second
      Omnibus of Crime⟩* (editor). 1931.

Have His Carcase. 1932.

Murder Must Advertise. 1933.

Hangman's Holiday. 1933.

The Nine Tailors. 1934.

*Great Short Stories of Detection, Mystery, and Horror: Third Series ⟨The Third
      Omnibus of Crime⟩* (editor). 1934.

Gaudy Night. 1935.

Papers Relating to the Family of Wimsey. 1936.

Tales of Detection (editor). 1936.

Busman's Honeymoon: A Detective Comedy (with Muriel St. Clare Byrne).
      1937.

Busman's Honeymoon: A Love Story with Detective Interruptions. 1937.

The Zeal of Thy House. 1937.

An Account of Lord Mortimer Wimsey, the Hermit of the Wash. 1938.

The Greatest Drama Ever Staged. 1938.

In the Teeth of the Evidence and Other Stories. 1939.

The Devil to Pay. 1939.

Strong Meat. 1939.

He That Should Come. 1939.

Begin Here: A War-time Essay. 1940.

Creed or Chaos? 1940.

The Mind of the Maker. 1941.

The Mysterious English. 1941.

Why Work? 1942.

The Other Six Deadly Sins. 1943.

The Man Born to Be King. 1943.

Lord, I Thank Thee. 1943.

Even the Parrot: Exemplary Conversations for Enlightened Children. 1944.

Unpopular Opinions. 1946.

The Heart of Stone by Dante (translator). 1946.

The Just Vengeance. 1946.

Making Sense of the Universe. c. 1946.

Creed or Chaos? and Other Essays in Popular Theology. 1947.

Four Sacred Plays (The Zeal of Thy House; The Devil to Pay; He That Should Come; The Just Vengeance). 1948.

The Lost Tools of Learning. 1948.

The Comedy of Dante Alighieri (translator; with Barbara Reynolds). 1949–62. 3 vols.

The Emperor Constantine: A Chronicle. 1951.

The Days of Christ's Coming. 1953.

The Story of Adam and Christ. 1953.

Introductory Papers on Dante. 1954.

The Story of Noah's Ark. 1956.

Further Papers on Dante. 1957.

The Song of Roland (translator). 1957.

A Treasury of Sayers Stories. 1958.

The Poetry of Search and the Poetry of Statement and Other Posthumous Essays on Literature, Religion, and Language. 1963.

Christian Letters to a Post-Christian World: A Selection of Essays. Ed. Roderick Jellema. 1969.

Striding Folly. 1972.

Lord Peter: A Collection of All the Lord Peter Wimsey Stories. Ed. James Sandoe. 1972.

A Matter of Eternity: Selections from the Writings of Dorothy L. Sayers. Ed. Rosamond Kent Sprague. 1973.

Wilkie Collins: A Critical and Biographical Study. Ed. E. R. Gregory. 1977.

Love All: A Comedy of Manners; Together with Busman's Honeymoon: A Detective Comedy (with Muriel St. Clare Byrne). Ed. Alzina Stone Dale. 1984.

S. S. Van Dine
1887–1939

S. S. VAN DINE was the pseudonym of Willard Huntington Wright, who was born in Charlottesville, Virginia, on October 15, 1887 (although 1888 is frequently given as the year of his birth). Wright, always a precocious child, graduated from Pomona College at the age of sixteen. He then attended Harvard for graduate work and later studied art in Munich and Paris. Wright began preparing for a career in music but soon found work as a journalist. In 1907—the year he married Katharine Belle Boynton, with whom he had one daughter—he became the literary editor of the *Los Angeles Times,* and in 1912 he became the literary and dramatic editor for the *Smart Set.* This fashionable highbrow magazine gave Wright an outlet for his strong opinions on art; his influence did much to improve its intellectual quality, but it alienated many of its former subscribers, reducing the magazine to near-bankruptcy. H. L. Mencken and George Jean Nathan replaced Wright as coeditors in 1914, while Wright went on to act as dramatic and art critic for *Town Topics,* the *Forum,* and other magazines.

From 1914 to 1923 Wright published a number of books on aesthetics and philosophy, including *Modern Painting* (1915), *What Nietzsche Taught* (1915), *The Creative Will* (1916), and *The Future of Painting* (1923). Wright also published his only mainstream novel, *The Man of Promise,* in 1916. Most of these works were commercially unsuccessful.

In 1923 Wright suffered a breakdown from overwork, alcoholism, and drug use. While convalescing he was forbidden by his doctor to strain himself with serious intellectual pursuits. Wright subsequently threw himself into an exhaustive study of the genre of mystery fiction, reading thousands of novels and tales in the genre and later compiling an anthology, *The Great Detective Stories* (1927). He became convinced that he could write his own detective novels, make a fortune, and return to more serious work. The Philo Vance stories proved him right, although he never returned to more serious intellectual matters. He proposed to write six of these novels under the pseudonym S. S. Van Dine (Van Dine is taken from an old family name of Wright's, and S. S. are the initials for "steam ship"), but completed twelve by 1939. They all feature the eccentric and erudite dandy, Philo Vance, who, much like Doyle's Sherlock Holmes, is called in to aid the police on particularly puzzling cases. Wright himself was somewhat of a dandy, becoming famous for his trim Van Dyke and monocle. The Philo Vance novels were extremely popular during Wright's lifetime: each one was a best-seller, and several were made into films. Like Poe and Doyle, Wright attempted to do real detective work and was named honorary police chief of Bradley, New Jersey. He divorced his wife in 1930 and married Claire Eleanor Rulapaugh shortly thereafter. Willard Huntington Wright died on April 11, 1939.

Critical Extracts

DASHIELL HAMMETT   ⟨In *The Benson Murder Case*⟩ Alvin Benson is found sitting in a wicker chair in his living room, a book still in his hand, his legs crossed, and his body comfortably relaxed in a lifelike position. He is dead. A bullet from an Army model Colt .45 automatic pistol, held some six feet away when the trigger was pulled, has passed completely through his head. That his position should have been so slightly disturbed by the impact of such a bullet at such a range is preposterous, but the phenomenon hasn't anything to do with the plot, so don't, as I did, waste time trying to figure it out. The murderer's identity becomes obvious quite early in the story. The authorities, no matter how stupid the author chose to make them, would have cleared up the mystery promptly if they had been allowed to follow the most rudimentary police routine. But then what would there have been for the gifted Vance to do?

This Philo Vance is in the Sherlock Holmes tradition and his conversational manner is that of a high-school girl who has been studying the foreign words and phrases in the back of her dictionary. He is a bore when he discusses art and philosophy, but when he switches to criminal psychology he is delightful. There is a theory that anyone who talks enough on any subject must, if only by chance, finally say something not altogether incorrect. Vance disproves this theory: he manages always, and usually ridiculously, to be wrong. His exposition of the technique employed by a gentleman shooting another gentleman who sits six feet in front of him deserves a place in a *How to be a detective by mail* course.

To supply this genius with a field for his operations the author has to treat his policemen abominably. He doesn't let them ask any questions that aren't wholly irrelevant. They can't make inquiries of anyone who might know anything. They aren't permitted to take any steps toward learning whether the dead man was robbed. Their fingerprint experts are excluded from the scene of the crime. When information concerning a mysterious box of jewelry accidentally bobs up everybody resolutely ignores it, since it would have led to a solution before the three-hundredth page.

> Dashiell Hammett, "Poor Scotland Yard!," *Saturday Review of Literature*, 15 January 1927, p. 510

GILBERT SELDES   The singular thing about th⟨e⟩ success ⟨of S. S. Van Dine⟩ is that it was achieved in spite of the author, who created a disagreeable pedant for his detective and treated him as if he were the most admirable and amiable of men. Crotchety detectives are no novelty; Cuff, in *The Moonstone*, anticipates them as he does nearly everything interesting. Van Dine's Philo Vance, with his implausible English accent, his unparalleled erudition, and his swank, would be enough to turn anyone away from the stories after five pages were it not that the stories, by that time, are more interesting than the detective. The first two novels, *The Benson* and *The "Canary"* Murder Cases, were based on incidents not yet gone from the public mind, those of Elwell and Dot King; they were the best of the lot. The third, *The Greene Murder Case*, was a compilation of nearly all the strange murders noted in criminology, and the solution of the mystery was properly found in two or three dozen German textbooks in the library of the half-dozen victims. The basis of the latest in the series, *The Bishop Murder Case*, is a mixture of Mother Goose and higher mathematics, with such an exposition of the theories of Einstein as I have not discovered in the daily press. ⟨. . .⟩

What constitutes fair dealing with the reader in this type of story has never been well defined. It is, however, considered desirable that the actual criminal should be more or less in plain sight while the detection is going on—the fact that in actual murders he usually manages not to be, is put aside—and nothing is more irritating, or bad form, than the introduction of an unknown at the end to shoulder the blame. The excellent *Bellamy Trial* gave each character exactly its due because each appeared before the jury, the criminal included, and each received just the importance the trial would give him. It would also be fair dealing to make the motive adequate. To complicate mysteries, authors have assigned adequate motive to three or four characters, and it is almost obligatory that several of them should have opportunity as well. Van Dine has built up motive for each of a series of characters, killing them off just as the motivation becomes convincing, and then has had nothing left for his murderer.

This is, of course, the pedantry of murder, and it leads to an interesting speculation. People generally assume that bad work in literature comes from being too conscious of one's public; here is a case where bad work is due to contempt of the public. Van Dine knows perfectly that if twelve human beings are capable of understanding the Einstein theory, only two or three thousand times as many can understand his reduction of it. He knows that all of Philo Vance's vaporings will be skipped, by those who are impressed as well as those who want to get on with the story. Yet there they are, with the affectations of the detective which are not part of the character, with a type of lordly writing which actively holds up the narrative. One feels that these things are deliberate, even wilful, that the author, in full conscious ness of his hold over the public, writes badly "and makes them like it." It may not detract from the popularity of the series, for people are impressed by pedantry and false characterization, but the naïve shag tobacco and the love of the violin of Sherlock Holmes strike us as being more honest and in the end contribute to making him a "character" in every sense. The pedantry in Van Dine's character is, as I have suggested, eating its way into the plots. The technical skill of the books is so great that the author may be able to dispense with credulity, especially motive; but here again he is despising his public, to the detriment of his work.

Gilbert Seldes, "Van Dine and His Public," *New Republic*, 19 June 1929, pp. 125–26

ERNEST BOYD   He was the most interesting and attractive *unlikable* man I have ever known. He made no appeal to the affections—save those of certain members of the opposite sex. His appeal was wholly cerebral. I used to come up from Baltimore, go straight to his apartment in Lexington Avenue, and remain closeted with him alone for a day and a night of solid conversation. He was a brilliant talker and a good listener, as only people who really understand the art of conversation are. His agile mind never seemed to tire; he endlessly discussed and projected books which he or I should write. The first edition of *The Man of Promise* characteristically announces two books as forthcoming, which never appeared. Not that he was unproductive—his record is there to prove the contrary—but he had to live, and plans are a luxury when there is no financial anchor astern. It was a strain under which he broke, to emerge as S. S. Van Dine.

As early as 1915 he was composing a personality for himself, and that personality finally became Philo Vance. It is evident in his constant changes of physical appearance: the Kaiser Wilhelm moustache, the Adolphe Menjou moustache, the Van Dyke beard, and finally the truculent beard of S. S. Van Dine. His serious works were the expression of his interests, but he always maintained that he could do anything. I remember when he proved that he could do the work of a housewife in a tenth of the time wasted by women. Either just before or just after he wrote that excellent and very characteristic novel, *The Man of Promise*, which was a commercial failure, he wrote another, under a pseudonym which I have forgotten, which was so bad, such piffle, that he defied the fool public not to like it! He could never understand that a certain sincerity must exist even in writers of the cheapest fictional merchandise. This book, which I could not read and threw away, failed also. But he was not dismayed. He triumphantly proved his theory when he set himself, in the most adverse of circumstances, to project his own personality (as composed artificially) into fiction and conceal his identity behind a pseudonym.

"I had spent fifteen years building up a cultural reputation for myself in American letters"—I can hear his voice and see the twist of contempt on his thin lips—"I was the author of nine serious books into which I put the fruits of all my research and study and labor. And up to the age of thirty-seven I had barely succeeded in keeping my ledger balanced." Now I see the contemptuous glitter in his eyes: "Each one of my Philo Vance stories has made more money than all my nine serious books put together. My literary earnings for any six months during the past two and a half years have been more than my entire literary earnings for the previous fifteen years. I don't know why these things should be."

Ernest Boyd, "Willard Huntington Wright," *Saturday Review of Literature*, 22 April 1939, p. 8

WILLIAM RUEHLMANN   S. S. Van Dine's dilettantish Philo
Vance was an unlikely minister of vengeance, but even in the drawing-
room novels that made him the best-selling favorite of Franklin Roosevelt
rough justice prevailed. Van Dine (the pseudonym of Willard Huntington
Wright) wrote that "all good detective novels have had for their protagonist
a character of attractiveness and interest, of high and fascinating attain-
ments—a man at once human and unusual, colorful and gifted." Philo Vance
was Van Dine's idea of such a character. He bore a disturbing resemblance
to Holmes:

> He was just under six feet, slender, sinewy, and graceful. His
> chiselled regular features gave his face the attraction of strength
> and uniform modelling, but a sardonic coldness of expression
> precluded the designation of handsome. He had aloof grey eyes, a
> straight, slender nose, and a mouth suggesting both cruelty and
> asceticism.

He was bloodless like Holmes—and, like Holmes, a man with a passion for
arcane minutiae:

> He was something of an authority on Japanese and Chinese
> prints; he knew tapestries and ceramics; and once I heard him
> give an impromptu *causerie* to a few guests on Tanagora figurines
> which, had it been transcribed, would have made a most
> delightful and interesting monograph.

Also like Holmes, Vance's exploits are recounted by a biographer, "Van
Dine" himself, who, as the detective's legal and financial adviser, follows
him slavishly about. ⟨. . .⟩

Vance first appears in *The Benson Murder Case* (1926) and is immediately
placed in a position superior to the police. As a friend of District Attorney
Markham, Vance is called in whenever a crime is committed that defeats
the ratiocinative powers of the authorities—that is to say, he is called in
all the time. Vance's opinion of his official rivals is predictably scornful: "I
say, Markham, . . . it has always been a source of amazement to me how
easily you investigators of crime are misled by what you call clues. You find
a footprint, or a parked automobile, or a monogrammed handkerchief, and
then dash off on a wild chase with your eternal *Ecce signum!*" Pontificates
Philo: "The only crimes that are ever solved are those planned by stupid
people." The Law is usually represented by the stolid Sergeant Heath, who

pursues the obvious with the unrelenting assiduousness of a process server in a one-reeler. Heath in moments of indecision is prone to divest himself of outbursts like these: "What's on the cards? Where do we go from here? I need action." Vance is moved at such junctures to grieve: "And it's stubborn, unimaginative chaps like Heath who constitute the human barrage between the criminal and society! . . . Sad, sad."

It is perhaps even sadder that the only intervening supportive bulwark is Vance, for he takes some little time to catch his man—often at the cost of numerous lives in the interim. At the outset of *The Greene Murder Case* (1927), Vance is summoned to investigate a murder and shooting at the home of a decadent upper-class family. By the time he uncovers the killer a further assault has occurred and three more murders, reducing his viable list of suspects to three. These executions proceed as Vance commits himself to musings such as the following: ". . . Some deep, awful motive lies behind that crime. There are depths beneath depths in what happened last night— obscure fetid chambers of the human soul. Black hatreds, unnatural desires, hideous impulses, obscene ambitions are at the bottom of it. . . ." When he does at long last corner the killer he withholds his knowledge that she is in possession of cyanide capsules; this permits her to kill herself in the very presence of the district attorney. The two surviving suspects then embrace and sail for the Riviera.

William Ruehlmann, *Saint with a Gun: The Unlawful American Private Eye* (New York: New York University Press, 1974), pp. 39–42

ROGER ROSENBLATT   Nobody loves a man who wears a monocle. Vance is not despicable; it is merely impossible to like him actively. Unlike Holmes or Nero Wolfe he has no interesting assistant to warm the narrative. Van Dine, the family lawyer, is too pompous and corny to make Vance attractive in any sense deeper than the Abercrombie and Fitch catalogue. Vance's aloneness conveys no feeling of underlying melancholy, precisely because Van Dine is always, and deliberately, pushing the possibility too hard. Vance's elaborate independence from the world is in fact reassuring; we don't worry for his mental health between cases. Even the love touch of *The Garden Murder Case* is just a touch.

His solitariness is essential to these stories, nevertheless, because over half the murders occur in families: brothers knife brothers; children poison parents. Like the Greeks, Van Dine knew that families are dangerous. Vance stands outside both the story and the institution of the family, which he implicitly criticizes. He is the most important person in the story—he puts it in order by solving the crime—but he is also free of the participants, free of connections. By ending the mystery, he restores his bachelorhood.

Like other detectives Vance imposes order on disorganized events. His loneliness is also like a god's, whose sense of order is higher than and hidden from that of ordinary people. Vance is rich but not conservative; he creates his own systems. As the only one on the case with the power to make his system work, he is relied upon by others. Yet he does not give his sense of order to anyone for future use, certainly not to the police who must start from scratch at every murder.

He stands outside the law as well, openly contemptuous and covertly supportive, in the American way. He does not think the law is evil or unnecessary, merely beside most points: "No. Legal technicalities quite useless in such an emergency. Deeper issues involved. Human issues, d'ye see." He is so confident in his knowledge of human issues that he refers to these murders as "unnatural" and "grotesque" because they jostle his theories of behavior. Vance's idea of justice is purely poetic. More often than not he allows the culprit to cheat the State.

Roger Rosenblatt, "S. S. Van Dine," *New Republic*, 26 July 1975, p. 33

JULIAN SYMONS   Philo Vance, who might be called Wimsey's American cousin, was Wright's wish-fulfilment projection. He is 'a young social aristocrat' who spent some time at Oxford and later 'transferred his residence to a villa outside Florence', although all his cases take place in urban America. Just under six feet tall, slender, sinewy and graceful, he has what was even at the time a slightly outdated Byronic charm. 'His chiselled regular features gave his face the attraction of strength and uniform modelling', although 'a sardonic coldness of expression precluded the designation of handsome'. Like Wimsey he wears a monocle and drops the 'g' at the end of words like *amazin'* and *distressin'*, and he has a ludicrous manner of speech, represented by remarks like: "I note that our upliftin' Press bedecked its front pages this morning with headlines about a pogrom at the old Greene mansion last night. Wherefore?" He has an encyclopedic knowledge about absolutely everything, or at least about everything related to the cases in which he is concerned, a knowledge supported by a tremendous apparatus of footnotes. This learning is continually and unnecessarily obtruded, so that he answers a question from the wooden-headed Sergeant Heath about what he has been doing by saying: "I've been immersed in the terra-cotta ornamentation of Renaissance facades, and other such trivialities, since I saw you last." He expresses always a languid world-weary superiority to the crimes he investigates and solves.

All this may sound intolerable, but there is something more to be said. Van Dine's erudition, at least in matters connected with art, painting, music and comparative religion, was real where Sayers's was defective. Partly in consequence of this, and partly because he took such pains with the idealized self-portrait, Vance does come through as a personality of real intellectual attainment in a way that Wimsey does not. In the early books his knowledge is directly related to the cases in which he is involved, and information is given which enables the intelligent reader to follow the deductions. And the best of the Van Dine stories are models of construction. Utterly removed from real life, they remain fascinating by strict adherence to the rules of their own dotty logic, and through their creator's self-absorbed immersion in his own work. There is a sort of grand imaginative folly about the best books, *The Greene Murder Case* (1928) and *The Bishop Murder Case* (1929), which carries us along once the premises of the story are accepted. In the first of these stories a whole series of murders is carried out which prove to have been copied from material in a great crime library. Do the crimes seem possible? Van Dine is able to show that every one of them can be paralleled in Hans Gross's great handbook on criminal investigation. *The Bishop Murder Case* is an even more astonishing performance. Again there is a series of murders, apparently the work of a maniac who bases himself on nursery rhymes, so that Jonny Sprig is shot through the middle of his wig and Cock Robin is killed by an arrow. Are the crimes meaningless? Obscure intellectual clues are remarked by or planted on Vance, connected with chess, Ibsen's plays, mathematical theories. In the end the murderer dies when Vance swaps the drink he has poisoned after distracting attention by exclaiming in admiration at sight of a Cellini plaque, " 'Berenson told me it was destroyed in the seventeenth century.' " When District Attorney Markham says that his death was murder, the detective's reply is characteristic. " 'Oh, doubtless. Yes—of course. Most reprehensible . . . I say, am I by any chance under arrest?' "

Ogden Nash summed up later feelings about Vance in two lines:

> Philo Vance
> Needs a kick in the pance.

No doubt. Yet admiration should not be withheld, from these two books at least. In their outrageous cleverness, their disdainful disregard of everything except the detective and the puzzle, they are among the finest fruits of the Golden Age.

Julian Symons, *Bloody Murder: From the Detective Story to the Crime Novel: A History* (1972; rev. ed. Harmondsworth, UK: Penguin, 1985), pp. 102–3

JOHN LOUGHERY   Embodying so many of his creator's interests, quirks, and frustrations, Philo Vance could only have been a character of Willard Huntington Wright's design. The long dark night of Willard's breakdown years hadn't given way to a benevolent sleuth or a gracious emissary of justice, on the order of Father Brown or Lord Peter Wimsey, but to a strange, cynical aesthete. An art student and connoisseur, Vance is a man with the intellectual skill to solve brilliantly devised crimes and serve the law better than the police but who does so only on his own terms. His terms involve firm control of the interrogations, emotional detachment from the plight of the victims, more-than-occasional bending of the letter of the law, and a healthy skepticism for circumstantial evidence and mere facts. Needless to add, despite the aggressively flippant manner of Willard's character, the murderer never escapes detection, nor are the police ever of the slightest help in solving the case.

Philo Vance leads the intellectual's ultimate fantasy life. A bachelor, untroubled by women, he lives in quiet luxury, impressing everyone with his formidable vocabulary and occupying his time with whatever scholarly pursuits interest him at the moment. Yet the world-at-large needs him. The men of practical affairs come knocking at his door. The expert help he offers the police with their toughest cases is given largely for the satisfaction of his own curiosity, for the joy of wrestling with a complicated challenge, or as a favor to Markham. So divorced is Vance from the ordinary motives of detectives and police officers that, when the criminal is particularly clever, Vance is apt to unmask him with reluctance, regretfully ending a well-suited match. His respect is often with his adversary. Only grudgingly does Vance admit the necessity of serving something as abstract and unpleasant as "the good of society." Were it not for the involvement of the authorities in each case, Vance is perfectly capable of solving the crime as he would a difficult puzzle—and then letting the guilty one go free, if he had reason to believe that the murderer would resist any further temptations to homicide. His highest regard is reserved for the murderer who commits suicide in preference to a trial and imprisonment, an act he will even tacitly assist in.

Between and during cases, Vance buys Cézanne watercolors at preview exhibitions, reads Freud and Spengler, attends afternoon concerts at Carnegie Hall, and works sporadically on his translations (never completed, as far as we know) of Delacroix's journals and lost Menander plays. Attended to by his friend and assistant S. S. Van Dine, the narrator of all the books, and by his butler, Currie, Vance makes his home in Manhattan in a town house between Park and Madison avenues on 38th Street—an address, by the end of the twenties, as recognizable as Holmes' Baker Street flat. The surroundings include Renoir bathers, Picasso still-lifes, Chinese ceramics, and a vast, esoteric library. An inheritance from an "Aunt Agatha" has made this charmed life possible (Agatha Christie paving the way for Willard Wright?), but Philo Vance makes no apologies for his privileged lifestyle. In the Jazz Age none was needed, as Willard had rightly concluded. A man who knew how to spend his money, a know-it-all with style, had automatic appeal.

What had become of Willard Wright the student of the French realists, the partisan of Moore and Dreiser, when he began his detective novels? He was nowhere to be found in these first enjoyable, never-credible, almost antirealistic tales. If anything, Willard had reverted to the still earlier, more deeply felt influence on his intellectual life: to his beloved Oscar Wilde and a concocted world of fable, elegance, and patrician disdain. No doubt Wilde would have recognized a kindred spirit in Philo Vance, and in 1926 a good number of readers were happy to accept the terms of Van Dine's literary game.

John Loughery, *Alias S. S. Van Dine* (New York: Scribner's, 1992), pp. 186–88

▨ *Bibliography*

Europe After 8:15 (with H. L. Mencken and George Jean Nathan). 1914.
Modern Painting, Its Tendency and Meaning. 1915.
What Nietzsche Taught by Friedrich Nietzsche (editor). 1915.

The Creative Will: Studies in the Philosophy and the Syntax of Aesthetics. 1916.
The Forum Exhibition of Modern American Painters, March Thirteenth to March
        Twenty-fifth, 1916. 1916.
The Man of Promise. 1916.
Informing a Nation. 1917.
Misinforming a Nation. 1917.
The Great Modern French Stories: A Chronological Anthology (editor). 1917.
The Future of Painting. 1923.
The Benson Murder Case: A Philo Vance Story. 1926.
The "Canary" Murder Case: A Philo Vance Story. 1927.
The Great Detective Stories: A Chronological Anthology (editor). 1927.
The Greene Murder Case: A Philo Vance Story. 1928.
The Bishop Murder Case: A Philo Vance Story. 1929.
I Used to Be a Highbrow, But Look at Me Now. 1929.
The Scarab Murder Case: A Philo Vance Story. 1930.
The Kennel Murder Case: A Philo Vance Story. 1933.
The Dragon Murder Case: A Philo Vance Story. 1933.
The Casino Murder Case: A Philo Vance Story. 1934.
The Garden Murder Case: A Philo Vance Story. 1935.
The Kidnap Murder Case: A Philo Vance Story. 1936.
Philo Vance Murder Cases ⟨*The Scarab Murder Case, The Kennel Murder Case,*
        The Dragon Murder Case⟩. 1936.
A Philo Vance Week-End ⟨*The "Canary" Murder Case, The Greene Murder*
        Case, The Bishop Murder Case⟩. 1937.
The Gracie Allen Murder Case: A Philo Vance Story ⟨*The Smell of Murder*⟩.
        1938.
The Winter Murder Case: A Philo Vance Story. 1939.

Edgar Wallace
1875–1932

RICHARD HORATIO EDGAR WALLACE was born in Greenwich, England, on April 1, 1875, the illegitimate child of actor Richard Horatio Edgar and actress Mary Jane Richards. As a boy he went by the name Dick Freeman, after his adoptive father, fish porter George Freeman. He taught himself to read and write and held a variety of jobs before enlisting in the army at the age of eighteen.

While stationed in South Africa, Wallace wrote verse and newspaper articles, many of which were later collected into books. He bought his discharge after six years but stayed in Africa to become a distinguished correspondent for the *Daily Mail* during the Boer War. He married a minister's daughter, Ivy Maud Caldecott, in 1901, shortly before returning to England. The couple had three children before the marriage ended in divorce in 1918.

Wallace traveled around the world as a newspaper correspondent and tried unsuccessfully to become a playwright. In 1905 he wrote his first novel, *The Four Just Men*, a thriller about an anarchist plot against the English foreign secretary. Unable to find a publisher for it, he created his own Tallis Press and launched an advertising campaign offering a reward to the reader who could solve its mystery. The book sold well, but the expense of its promotion put Wallace in debt. Nevertheless, it established his reputation as a mystery writer and went on to spawn five sequels between 1908 and 1928.

Fired from the *Daily Mail* after libel suits were threatened for his reporting, Wallace became a freelance writer for racing papers. At the urging of an editor friend he turned his experiences in the Congo into a series of adventure stories beginning with *Sanders of the River* (1911). Their popularity brought him additional work as a journalist and writer of newspaper serials.

In the early 1920s Wallace entered into a contract with publishers Hodder & Stoughton to produce novels at a predetermined price on a regular basis. Writing with legendary speed, he soon saturated the market with scores of bestselling thrillers that caught the public fancy with their improbable plots and subplots, complex mysteries, stereotypical characters, simple language, and blends of sensationalism and adventure. A tireless self-promoter, Wallace fanned the flames of his notoriety by living an extravagant lifestyle and publicly challenging critics to prove that his prodigious output was partly ghostwritten. At the height of his phenomenal success it was estimated that one out of four books sold in England was an Edgar Wallace novel.

Wallace married his secretary Ethel Violet King in 1921 and had a daughter, Penelope, with her two years later. In 1925 he created the character J. G. Reeder, a traditional detective with an astute grasp of the criminal mind, who became the hero of four novels and story collections. The following year his play *The Ringer* was successfully produced in London. Lured to Hollywood in 1931 by a lucrative offer to write screenplays for RKO Studios, he fell into a diabetic coma while developing the idea for what would later be filmed as *King Kong*. He died of pneumonia on February 10, 1932.

◈ *Critical Extracts*

UNSIGNED   Thoughtless people often confuse the detective story with the dime novel. As a matter of fact, most dime novels are not stories of crime and bewilderment, but tales of adventure, in which the interest is sustained by nothing but the sheer swing of the action from page to page. The publishers of *Angel Esquire* are in error, therefore, when they describe the book as a "rattling good detective story." It is not a detective story, but that much rarer thing, a dime novel as well written as detective stories have been since Poe and Conan Doyle showed us how. There is in the book but one attempt at employing the machinery of mystification and prolonged suspense, and that is quite unsuccessful. On the contrary, we have from chapter to chapter a succession of conflicts and heroics which are of the very essence of the dime novel. There is a brilliant outlaw who is good at heart and holds a roomful of cutthroats at bay until some one puts out the lamp; there is a detective who pulls the good outlaw through a secret door just as he is about to be bludgeoned to death; there is a wicked lawyer who has turned his house into a labyrinth of secret closets, traps, and sealed steel chambers in which he does away with his enemies by flooding the room with the fumes of hydrocyanic acid. To tell of such things with really exceptional literary grace, as the author has done in the present instance, is even harder, we imagine, than to raise the detective story to the level of literature.

Unsigned, [Review of *Angel Esquire*], *Nation*, 12 November 1908, p. 466

ISABEL PATERSON   So Edgar Wallace knows how to dress the skeleton of his extremely ingenious story with fancy and humor. His characters might appear in any kind of fiction and still be plausible; his method of writing is so easy and natural that he must have striven hard for it. He has a strict eye for the minor probabilities, thus diverting attention from the major impossibilities. And since the latter must be granted to any writer of mystery tales, it is a proof of his skills that one can find but one fault. Sometimes the hero is rather incurious, not to say too credulous; is too readily content to wait for explanations concerning the very suspicious conduct and utterances of the heroine.

Isabel Paterson, [Review of *The Clew of the New Pin*], *New York Tribune*, 15 April 1923, p. 21

EDGAR WALLACE   There isn't one of us who is not a story-writer and who has not woven tales in which we figure usually as hero and heroine. This capacity for dreaming is our salvation in a world of ugly realities. Usually we are quite capable of taking ourselves out of ourselves; we dream solutions to monetary difficulties, happy endings to unhappy situations, rewards for toilings, holiday for labour. But sometimes the stark facts are so menacing that we are incapable of making the effort to move the dream-tale into action. We are hypnotized by failure, by foreboding, by the panic of disaster. It is then that the writer of tales becomes the excellent doctor. It is he who starts the right train of thought moving to the desirable destination—which is forgetfulness of all real and ugly things.

The mystery story is just a little different because, if it is written in a workmanlike manner and it doesn't stop to psychologize or enter into laborious details, it doesn't give the official train of thought, which the author's whistle has started on its journey, the least chance of switching itself into a siding or encouraging the passenger to take little walks on his own.

People talk glibly about formula: they say that this author or that writes to a pattern. But a story is just what it makes itself, and how far from formula my own are I know for an extraordinary reason. I very often write short stories of about 23,000 words. It would seem the easiest thing in the world, by a little judicious manipulation, to put two short stories together and make them into one book-length volume. But though I have tried several times to earn a nefarious penny by this practice, I have never succeeded in dovetailing two stories together, and I have had dismal reminders that my unhappy knack of trying something fresh in the way of situation and plot with every story precludes so blending.

The mystery novel, to be successful, should be reducible to a simple problem: did A wrong B, and is C all that he seems? And the art of writing the mystery story is to put this problem into 70,000 or 80,000 words so that the reader does not get bored or tired following clues, or lose his interest altogether in the chase. And that, to my mind, is where the mystery story scores over its more pretentious and ambitious friend, the novel.

Edgar Wallace, "Reflections on the Writing of Mystery Stories" (1927), *Crimson Circle: Magazine of the Edgar Wallace Society* No. 90 (May 1991): 9–10

G. K. CHESTERTON   God forbid that I or anybody else should speak ungratefully or ungraciously of Mr. Edgar Wallace. I have enjoyed hundreds of his stories and hope to enjoy hundreds more; and it seems likely that I shall continue to have the chance of such enjoyment. To despise such stories is of all things the most despicable. It is like despising pantomimes or public-houses or comic songs or common enjoyments of every kind that bind us to the brotherhood of man. And when we are dealing with popular literature of this sound and lively sort it is very ungracious to complain of the amazing multiplicity of the output which a man like Mr. Wallace manages to achieve. It is like complaining that a really good alehouse provides too much ale; which would seem not only a blasphemy but almost a contradiction in terms. It is like complaining that a really good popular singer can sing too many different songs; a complaint that is entirely a compliment. It is unreasonable to abuse Mr. Wallace for having entertained and excited us too much. It is ungenerous to resent generosity. It may well be a pleasure to have given pleasure to so many; and it ought to be a pleasure for them to acknowledge it.

G. K. Chesterton, "On Detective Story Writers" (1929), *Come to Think of It . . .: A Book of Essays* (London: Methuen, 1930), pp. 30–31

H. DOUGLAS THOMSON   Mr. Wallace's work is curiously varied, both in theme and in style. He is a most unusual writer. "When he is good, he is very very good, but when he is bad he is horrid." On the credit side he has these virtues:

(1) His narrative is straightforward, and there is no padding, and no nonsense.

(2) He is genuinely exciting, and relies on no artifices for his creation of atmosphere. He follows the old saw, *Ars est celare artem.*

(3) His humour is never strained. "The Sparrow" and "J. G. Reeder" are inimitable characters, naturally humorous.

(4) He has an inside knowledge of Scotland Yard and police methods.

(5) He is familiar with the lingo of crooks.

On the other hand:

(1) He is too fond of "the most-unlikely-person" theme.

(2) Impossibilities and improbabilities occur too frequently.

(3) He is by no means word-perfect. He calls a napkin a serviette, and is guilty of a phrase like "she shrugged milky shoulders." His grammar, also, is not unimpeachable.

(4) His sensationalism is often extremely crude, and not in perfect taste.

H. Douglas Thomson, "The Wallace Collection," *Masters of Mystery: A Study of the Detective Story* (London: William Collins Sons & Co., 1931), pp. 224–25

ROBERT G. CURTIS   He loved to discuss his plots beforehand, or, rather, the situation from which his plot was to emerge. He would break off in the middle of a conversation, as though the idea had just occurred to him, to outline a story, and seemed to find, in talking about it, considerable aid in building it up.

I remember the first time, many years ago, that he so confided in me. I listened and was duly thrilled.

"But what's the *dénouement?*" I asked finally.

Wallace fixed me with his clear, grey eyes.

"If you mean how does it end," he said sternly, "that is the only thing that doesn't matter. There are a dozen ways of ending a story like that. The important thing is the situation."

This dictum did not, however, apply to all his stories. In the case of many of his best thrillers he thought out the last chapter first, and then proceeded to mystify the public throughout the whole of the rest of the book. Nearly always, when he was halfway through, he would stroll into my room.

"Have you guessed yet who did the murder, Bob?"

If I had not, or if I guessed incorrectly, Wallace would chuckle.

"If you haven't, no one else will," he would say, and go back to his desk with an intensified zest which was almost childlike.

Now and again I deduced accurately. He was almost annoyed.

"I don't think anyone but you would guess that," he said, "but perhaps I'll strengthen it a bit."

He did. When I came to the final chapter I found that he had altered the whole plot, making an entirely different character the villain, but so ingeniously that none of the earlier chapters had to be rewritten.

Robert G. Curtis, *Edgar Wallace—Each Way* (London: John Long, 1932), p. 63

MARGARET LANE   The characters in a typical Wallace thriller run invariably to type. The cast is nearly always the same and may be simplified as follows:

The hero: Usually a detective, occasionally a newspaper reporter. If a detective, he is no ordinary one but an expert sleuth employed by Scotland Yard (Larry Holt in *The Dark Eyes of London*), the Foreign Office (Selby Lowe in *A King by Night*), the Public Prosecutor's Office (Mr J. G. Reeder), the river police (John Wade in *The India Rubber Men*), or some other special branch.

The heroine: A beautiful girl, sometimes of independent means, more usually a secretary, who always in the course of the story turns out to be deeply though innocently involved in a financial plot and therefore the object of the villain's machinations. She is always partly responsible for the solving of the mystery and rarely escapes being locked in an attic or a dungeon with a homicidal monster.

1st villain: The master mind of a criminal gang; his identity is rarely revealed until just before the end of the book, when the plot is narrowed down to a pursuit sequence which ends in his capture or death. Until this point he usually appears to be a sympathetic and blameless character and often pretends to assist the police.

2nd villain: His identity is generally revealed fairly early in the book, and the reader's suspicions are deliberately concentrated on him. He is, however, only the figurehead of the gang, and the tool of No. 1, whom he sometimes betrays.

3rd villain: A monster of some kind, possessed of superhuman strength and savage cunning, employed by villains 1 and 2 in the accomplishment of their crimes. He is usually murdered by them before the end, and commands at least a vestige of the reader's sympathy. He is a frequent though not an inevitable member of the cast.

Minor characters, who are always numerous, usually include a comic petty thief or other criminal, unless, as in the case of Mr Reeder, the humour is supplied by the hero himself.

The main scene of his stories is usually London, sometimes with subsidiary mysteries staged abroad, and the Thames often plays an important part. The police, though continuously baffled (the mystery would soon collapse if they were not), are never held up to ridicule. The love interest is perfunctory and the sexual morality of the characters above reproach. The female associates of even the worst villains turn out to be their wives or daughters, and the heroine, for all her deplorable experiences, is never called upon to endure anything which might bring a blush to the most sensitive cheek. "There is so much nastiness in modern literature which makes me feel physically sick," Edgar once told the Worshipful Company of Stationers, "that I like to write stories which contain nothing more than a little innocent murdering."

Margaret Lane, *Edgar Wallace: The Biography of a Phenomenon* (Garden City, NY: Doubleday, Doran, 1938), pp. 293–94

HOWARD HAYCRAFT   Of Edgar Wallace's countless thrillers, few but his tales of J. G. Reeder qualify as bona-fide detection, and even

the latter require some leniency to come under the rule. Mr. Reeder—
with his square derby, mutton-chop whiskers, umbrella, and apologetic air,
masking relentless courage—is a sure-fire piece of popular character drawing;
but his detective triumphs are likely to depend more upon chance than
upon deduction. The stories are marred, too, by the haste and carelessness
found in most of Wallace's writing. Nevertheless, for entertainment in its
broadest sense, they are unsurpassed. Mr. Reeder's adventures are found in
several books; among the best known in the United States are *Terror Keep*
(1927), *The Murder Book of J. G. Reeder* (1929), *Red Aces* (1930), and *Mr.
Reeder Returns* (1932).

Edgar Wallace's influence in the popularization of the detective story
was immense and immeasurable—even though it came largely from "the
outside."

> Howard Haycraft, *Murder for Pleasure: The Life and Times of the Detective Story* (New
> York: D. Appleton-Century, 1941), pp. 153–54

GRAHAM GREENE   I read *The Four Just Men* for the first time
when I was about ten years old, with enormous excitement, and when I
reread it the other day it was with almost the same emotion. The plain
style sometimes falls into clichés, but not often; the melodrama grips in the
same way as *The New Arabian Nights* (Stevenson, too, had a family history
from which he tried to escape through fantasy); Wallace tells an almost
incredible story with very precise realistic details. The Foreign Secretary
pursued by the four anarchists doesn't dress up as an old Jew, like the
detective in *The Flying Squad*, nor as a toothless Arab beggar, like the
American diplomat in *The Man from Morocco*, and there is no, thank God,
love interest at all. The story moves at a deeper level of invention than he
ever tapped again.

> Graham Greene, "Edgar Wallace" (1964), *Collected Essays* (New York: Viking Press,
> 1969), pp. 228–29

NIGEL MORLAND   The secret of his writing was that he so
absorbed himself in what he was doing. That popular entertainment was
not literature did not bother him; he had no pretensions about his work

being art. ("If a man puts down a book of mine and says, 'That was a damned good story', I ask for no higher praise.") When he was working he was *in* what he was doing, thrilled with the thrills and vastly amused by the comic touches. And he wrote instinctively. I was once shown the first chapters of a thriller and said admiringly: "Uncle Edgar, it must be marvellous to begin a book like that and know all the time what we don't know, till we get to the end, who the villain is." His answer was very abrupt: "Don't be a fool, boy; of course I don't know who it is until I get near the end myself."

He explained to me, no doubt to improve my own writing powers, various points of technique.

One was to the effect that he began a book cold but with a title or an opening paragraph to fire him. From the beginning he worked, as I have said, by blind instinct, letting his storyteller's powers guide him in what he was writing. For example: "If something happens, say, in the fifth chapter which seems all wrong to me, I leave it alone because somehow it gets tied up later on." It was as if he wrote with a part of his mind which thought, planned, reasoned and foresaw; stories poured out of him without anything at all to deter him, a vast power of pure inventiveness that never seemed to slacken. And he could do it in serial form. He once entertained me for days with a story which he told me in snatches when he had time, acting each part with melodramatic richness. It was all about a man whose soul was exchanged for another's and, later, EW turned it into what I consider to be his most ingenious book, *Captains of Souls*.

He was no great stylist. There were plenty of faults in his work but most of them were faults of speed, of pressure to supply a demanding market. The entertainment value, the warmth, the sense of wonder, excitement, humor, made even his indifferent yarns into something very readable, as any Wallace fan will tell you today . . . and he had that unique quality of currency. His books, even those of 60 years ago, have never dated in any real sense.

Nigel Morland, "The Edgar Wallace I Knew," *Armchair Detective* 1, No. 3 (April 1968): 69

COLIN WATSON   A Wallace book, like any other piece of escapist literature, was bought or borrowed as a means of temporary withdrawal from the demanding, worrying, disappointing world in which the reader normally lived. In that world, there were as many three-dimensional characters as he could cope with; it was a welcome change to be among the two-dimensional variety that required no effort to understand. All the cardboard figures were labelled—hero, heroine, villain, comic manservant, policeman—and so sympathy could be simply and accurately apportioned until the time came at the book's end for it to be collected up again like so much play money.

As for silliness of plot: its heavy reliance on coincidence, pseudo-scientific devices, unidentified foreign powers, miraculous survival, intuition, and all other intelligence-defying tricks of the pot-boiling trade—here again, it may be that Wallace offered not an affront but a solace of a kind. People were aware in their hearts that the 1914–18 war had solved nothing and that the public optimism of the politicians masked their impotence and perplexity. There was as yet no question of impending catastrophe, but something seemed to have gone sadly wrong with the process of perpetual improvement that had been assumed to be natural law not only by the Victorians but by many of their successors. To read of events reaching a happy conclusion by manifestly unnatural and illogical means provided relief from the unpleasant feelings of having been let down.

> Colin Watson, "King Edgar, and How He Got His Crown," *Snobbery with Violence: Crime Stories and Their Audience* (New York: St. Martin's Press, 1971), p. 84

ROBERT JACKSON   Before the celebrated Edgar Wallace became a household name, he kept the pot boiling by writing thrillers in serial form. A typical situation would arise when the hero had been trapped in a snake-pit twenty feet deep which men armed with rifles were guarding. 'The snakes were moving in, their forked tongues darting malevolently, their sinuous bodies approaching the victim when . . .' A journalist in Wallace's favourite haunt, the London Press Club, read this mind-chilling sentence at the end of an episode and asked how on earth Wallace would extricate his hero. Wallace advised his colleague to watch how easy it would be the following week. The journalist opened the magazine to see the solution. 'With one bound, our hero was free . . .' Wallace had written.

> Robert Jackson, "The Dilemma," *Francis Camps: Famous Case Histories of the Celebrated Pathologist* (London: Hart-Davis, MacGibbon, 1975), p. 109

JACK ADRIAN   The concept of the outlaw-hero was nothing new and the late nineteenth century in particular saw a proliferation of the breed, especially in the world of the penny blood—sparked off by Harrison Ainsworth's clever sanctification of Dick Turpin in *Rookwood*. But in reality Turpin, Claude Duval, Robin Hood and the rest were at best scallywags, at worst gross thugs. Wallace, single-handed, created what the critic and authority on American pulp fiction Robert Sampson calls the Justice Figure—the 'incorruptible agent for justice' who deals death to evil-doers and is, because of this, pursued by the very law he seeks to uphold. Ironically, in novels such as *The Four Just Men* and *The Council of Justice* Wallace, who always yearned for American acceptance but only got it in the last decade of his life, was writing purely American-style pulp-magazine stories a quarter of a century before the genre existed.

But perhaps it is the style and tone of *The Four Just Men* which more than anything else makes it so singular a thriller when compared to the circulating library sultans of the time. Try Headon Hill, try William LeQueux; dip into, if you can, Fergus Hume or any of the six-bob shockers by the enormously prolific Guy Boothby (fifty-odd books in ten years). Grapple with the sensational novels of Dick Donovan, or Richard Marsh, or Hugh Conway, B. L. Farjeon, Hume Nisbet, even Phillips Oppenheim (at least from this period). All are more or less leaden in style and content.

By comparison *The Four Just Men*—originally published 80 years ago, almost to the month—is immensely, astonishingly readable. There is not a chapter, not a paragraph, not a sentence that bears even the slightest whiff of that late nineteenth-century mustiness that characterises even the best of its contemporaries. It is thumpingly twentieth century.

Jack Adrian, "Introduction," *The Four Just Men* by Edgar Wallace (London: J. M. Dent & Sons, 1985), pp. xiii–xiv

◈ *Bibliography*

The Mission That Failed! A Tale of the Raid and Other Poems. 1898.

Nicholson's Nek. 1900.

War! and Other Poems. 1900.

Writ in Barracks. 1900.

Unofficial Despatches. 1901.

The Four Just Men. 1905.

Smithy. 1905, 1914 (as *Smithy; Not to Mention Nobby Clark and Spud Murphy*).

Angel Esquire. 1908.

The Council of Justice. 1908.

Captain Tatham of Tatham Island. 1909, 1916 (as *The Island of Galloping Gold*),
    1926 (as *Eve's Island*).

Smithy Abroad: Barrack Room Sketches. 1909.

The Duke in the Suburbs. 1909.

The Nine Bears. 1910, 1911 (as *The Other Man*), 1930 (as *Silinski, Master
    Criminal*).

Sanders of the River. 1911.

The People of the River. 1912.

Private Selby. 1912.

The Fourth Plague. 1913.

Grey Timothy ⟨Pallard the Punter⟩. 1913.

The River of Stars. 1913.

The Admirable Carfew. 1914.

Bosambo of the River. 1914.

Famous Scottish Regiments. 1914.

My Life by Evelyn Thaw (ghostwriter). 1914.

Smithy's Friend Nobby. 1914.

Fieldmarshall Sir John French and His Campaigns. 1914.

Heroes All: Gallant Deeds of the War. 1914.

The Standard History of the War. 1914–16. 4 vols.

War of the Nations. 1914–19. 11 vols. (vols. 2–11 by Wallace).

Bones: Being Further Adventures in Mr. Commissioner Sanders' Country. 1915.

*Kitchener's Army and the Territorial Forces: The Full Story of a Great Achieve-
    ment.* 1915. 6 vols.

The Man Who Bought London. 1915.

The Melody of Death. 1915.

1925: The Story of a Fatal Peace. 1915.

Smithy and the Hun. 1915.

The Clue of the Twisted Candle. 1916.

A Debt Discharged. 1916.

The Tomb of Ts'in. 1916.

The Just Men of Cordova. 1917.

The Keepers of the King's Peace. 1917.

Kate Plus Ten. 1917.

The Secret House. 1917.

Down Under Donovan. 1918.

The Man Who Knew. 1918.

Lieutenant Bones. 1918.

Tam o' the Scouts. 1918.

Those Folk of Bulboro. 1918.

The Adventures of Heine. 1919.

The Fighting Scouts. 1919.

The Green Rust. 1919.

The Real Shell-Man. 1919.

The Daffodil Mystery. 1920.

Jack o' Judgement. 1920.

Bones in London. 1921.

The Book of All Power. 1921.

The Law of the Four Just Men. 1921.

The Angel of Terror. 1922.

Captains of Souls. 1922.

The Crimson Circle. 1922.

The Flying Fifty-five. 1922.

Mr. Justice Maxell. 1922.

Sandi, the King-Maker. 1922.

The Valley of Ghosts. 1922.

Bones of the River. 1923.

The Books of Bart. 1923.

Chick. 1923.

The Clue of the New Pin. 1923.

The Green Archer. 1923.

The Missing Million. 1923.

The Dark Eyes of London. 1924.

Double Dan ⟨Diana of Kara-Kara⟩. 1924.

Educated Evans. 1924.

The Face in the Night. 1924.

Room 13. 1924.

Flat 2. 1924.

The Sinister Man. 1924.

The Three Oak Mystery. 1924.

The Black Avons. 1925.

The Blue Hand. 1925.

The Daughters of the Night. 1925.

The Fellowship of the Frog. 1925.

The Gaunt Stranger ⟨*The Ringer*⟩. 1925.

The Hairy Arm ⟨*The Avenger*⟩. 1925.

A King by Night. 1925.

The Mind of Mr. J. G. Reeder ⟨*The Murder Book of Mr. J. G. Reeder*⟩. 1925.

The Strange Countess. 1925.

Barbara on Her Own. 1926.

The Black Abbot. 1926.

The Day of Uniting. 1926.

The Door with Seven Locks. 1926.

The Joker ⟨*The Colossus*⟩. 1926.

The Man from Morocco ⟨*The Black*⟩. 1926.

The Million Dollar Story. 1926.

More Educated Evans. 1926.

The Northing Tramp. 1926.

Penelope of the Polyantha. 1926.

People: A Short Autobiography. 1926.

Sanders ⟨*Mr. Commissioner Sanders*⟩. 1926.

The Square Emerald ⟨*The Girl from Scotland Yard*⟩. 1926.

The Terrible People. 1926.

The Three Just Men. 1926.

We Shall See! ⟨*The Gaol Breaker*⟩. 1926.

The Yellow Snake. 1926.

The Ringer. 1926.

Big Foot. 1927.

The Brigand. 1927.

The Feathered Serpent. 1927.

The Forger ⟨*The Clever One*⟩. 1927.

Good Evans! 1927.

The Hand of Power. 1927.

The Man Who Was Nobody. 1927.

The Mixer. 1927.

Number Six. 1927.

The Squeaker ⟨*The Squealer*⟩. 1927.

Terror Keep. 1927.

This England. 1927.

The Traitor's Gate. 1927.

Again Sanders. 1928.

The Double. 1928.

Elegant Edward. 1928.

The Flying Squad. 1928.

The Gunner ⟨*Gunman's Bluff*⟩. 1928.

The Orator. 1928.

The Thief in the Night. 1928.

The Twister. 1928.

Again the Ringer ⟨*The Ringer Returns*⟩. 1929.

Again the Three Just Men. 1929.

The Big Four. 1929.

The Black. 1929.

The Cat Burglar. 1929.

Circumstantial Evidence. 1929.

Fighting Snub Reilly. 1929.

The Ringer (drama). 1929.

The Terror (drama). 1929.

The Flying Squad (drama). 1929.

For Information Received. 1929.

Forty-eight Short Stories. 1929.

Four Square Jane. 1929.

The Ghost of Down Hill ⟨with *The Queen of Sheba's Belt*⟩. 1929.

The Golden Hades. 1929.

The Governor of Chi-Foo. 1929.

The Green Ribbon. 1929.

The India-Rubber Men. 1929.

The Iron Grip. 1929.

The Lady of Little Hell. 1929.

The Little Green Man. 1929.

The Lone House Mystery. 1929.

The Man Who Changed His Name. 1929.

Planetoid 127 ⟨with *The Sweizer Pump*⟩. 1929.

The Prison-Breakers. 1929.

The Squeaker (drama). 1929.

Red Aces. 1929.

The Reporter. 1929.

The Terror. 1929.

The Calendar. 1930.

The Clue of the Silver Key. 1930.

Killer Kay. 1930.

The Lady Called Nita. 1930.

The Lady of Ascot. 1930.

The Stretelli Case and Other Mystery Stories. 1930.

Mrs. William Jones and Bill. 1930.

White Face. 1930.

The Coat of Arms ⟨*The Arranways Mystery*⟩. 1931.

The Devil Man ⟨*The Life and Death of Charles Peace*⟩. 1931.

The Man at the Carlton. 1931.

On the Spot. 1931.

The Frightened Lady. 1932.

The Guv'nor and Other Stories ⟨*Mr. Reeder Returns*⟩. 1932.

My Hollywood Diary. 1932.

Sergeant Sir Peter ⟨*Sergeant Dunn C.I.D.*⟩. 1932.

The Steward. 1932.

When the Gangs Came to London. 1932.

The Calendar (drama). 1932.

The Green Pack (with Robert Curtis). 1933.

The Last Adventure. 1934.

The Woman from the East and Other Stories. 1934.

The Case of the Frightened Lady. 1934.

The Mouthpiece (with Robert Curtis). 1935.

The Undisclosed Client. 1963.

An African Millionaire. 1972.

The Man Who Married His Cook and Other Stories. 1976.

Two Stories and The Seventh Man. 1981.

The Sooper and Others. Ed. Jack Adrian. 1984.

The Road to London. Ed. Jack Adrian. 1986.